P9-DHN-193

EXPERIENCING GOD

EXPERIENCING GOD

How to Live the Full Adventure of Knowing and Doing the Will of God

Henry T. Blackaby
& Claude V. King

Nashville, Tennessee

© 1994 by Broadman & Holman Publishers
All rights reserved
Study questions © 1998 by Broadman & Holman Publishers

Printed in the United States of America

Published by:
Broadman & Holman Publishers
Nashville, Tennessee

Acquisitions and Development Editor: Vicki Crumpton
Design: Anderson Thomas, Nashville, Tennessee
Typesetting: Desktop Miracles, Dallas, Texas

0–8054–0197–0

Dewey Decimal Classification: 231
Subject Heading: GOD—WILL \ CHRISTIAN LIFE
Library of Congress Card Catalog Number: 94–17651

Art on page 52 is used with permission from *Experiencing God: Knowing and Doing the Will of God* by Henry T. Blackaby and Claude V. King, published by LifeWay Press, 1990.
Unless otherwise noted, Scripture quotations are from the Holy Bible, New King James Version, copyright © 1982 by Thomas Nelson, Inc. Other passages marked NIV, the Holy Bible, New International Version, © 1973, 1978, 1984 by International Bible Society.

Library of Congress Cataloging-in-Publication Data

Blackaby, Henry T., 1935-
Experiencing God : how to live the full adventure of knowing and doing the will of God / Henry T. Blackaby and Claude V. King.
p. cm.
ISBN 0–8054–0197–0 (pbk)
ISBN 0–8054–0196–2 (hc)
1. Christian life—1960- . 2. God—Will. I. King, Claude V., 1954- . II. Title.
BV4501.2.B537 1994
248.4—dc20 94–17651
CIP

10 9 8 7 6 99 00 01 02

To my parents, Mr. and Mrs. G. R. S. Blackaby,

and parents-in-law, Mr. and Mrs. M. A. Wells, Sr.,

for their faithful example before me;

and to my wife Marilynn,

for her faithful companionship,

and my children, Richard, Thomas,

Melvin, Norman, and Carrie,

as we have been experiencing God together.

HENRY T. BLACKABY

CONTENTS

PREFACE

A DEMONSTRATION OF GOD'S POWER

When I first met and heard Henry Blackaby teach in 1986, I had no idea how God was going to use him to reorient my life and ministry. Yet, in the past seven years, I have experienced some of the most radical changes of my life. Henry directed me to the Scriptures. He pointed me to biblical examples of people who experienced a powerful, loving, and personal God at work through them. He showed me how they came to know and do God's will. I felt as though scales fell from my eyes. God's plan to work through His people was so clear and simple. Why had I not seen it so clearly before?

Often I had tried a method or formula for knowing God's will. I tried to follow a set of steps to find God's will. My success record indicated something was wrong. I felt empty, confused, frustrated, and unfulfilled in my ministry.

Henry's teaching caught my attention. He said that we do not find God's will—it is revealed. God always takes the initiative. He gave contemporary illustrations of how ordinary people and churches have experienced God's work in personal, dramatic, and even miraculous ways. I thought about Paul's statement: "My speech and my preaching were not with persuasive words of human wisdom, but in demonstration of the Spirit and of power, that your faith should not be in the wisdom of men but in the power of God" (1 Cor. 2:4–5). That is what I saw in Henry's teaching—a simple, biblical message coupled with a life through which God demonstrated His power. Henry always pointed me to my relationship to God. That was the key to my experience of God's power at work through me.

I studied the Scriptures. I prayed that God would teach me about Himself and His ways through experience, not just theory. My life turned into an exciting adventure. My path of ministry has not always been so thrilling.

MY UTTER FAILURE

Following seminary in 1984, my wife and I resigned our jobs and moved to Gwinnett County, Georgia (near Atlanta). I sensed very strongly that God had called me to be a "tentmaking" church planter—one who provides his own financial support through a secular job and helps start new churches "free of charge." I had studied all the "right" books on church planting and church growth. I dreamed great dreams of what I was going to do for God. I spent eighteen months developing my plans. Step-by-step I began to carry them out.

Six months later our furniture was still in storage. In the middle of a 2 percent unemployment rate, we had no jobs. Our savings were depleted, our checking account empty, and debts were mounting. There was not even the nucleus of a new church. Devastated, we moved back home to live with parents. Until recently, I did not know what was wrong.

STILL CALLED TO BE A TENTMAKING CHURCH PLANTER

I was still confident of my call to be a tentmaking church planter. The only job that I was offered was at the Baptist Sunday School Board as an editor. I could not imagine why God put me behind a desk when so many new churches are needed.

Then I met Henry. He led me to a fresh understanding of knowing God and following Him. My local church association got a new director, James Powers. He had a burden for starting eight new churches by the year 2000. After prayer, I realized this was my opportunity to volunteer as a tentmaking church planter. The association extended a call for me to serve in that way as a volunteer. This time I would not try to work my own plans. I refused to dream my own dreams of what I would do for God.

We decided simply to share with churches the need to reach all people in our county with the gospel. We shared how new churches could be used of God to reach groups and areas that existing churches were not reaching. We talked about the wide variety of ways God might work to start a new church. Then we watched to see where God was at work so we could join Him.

GOD DID IT!

After three months, I had a list of fourteen places or groups that might need a new church. Where did the list come from? A person would stop me after a meeting or church service and say, "God has given me a burden for a new church in . . . ." or "Several people in our area feel like we need a new church for . . . ." After two years, we had six new churches with full-time pastors and another group meeting in a home Bible study with plans to start the seventh new church. Our churches found out that God had far greater plans for us than we could dream.

God called people to serve and gave them a burden. God called churches to be the sponsors of the new missions. We did not have to find ways to motivate them. They were calling on us to equip them to do what God had called them to do. No individual was the key to the growth. No one church was the key. God did it through His people!

A LESSON LEARNED

God allowed me to follow my *own* plans in Georgia, and I failed miserably. He had an important lesson to teach me, and I chose to learn the hard way. I found that I could not plan or even dream how God might want to do His work. I found that my relationship to God was of supreme importance. I learned to love Him more dearly, to pray more faithfully, to trust Him fully, and to wait on Him with anticipation. When He was ready to use me, He would let me know. Then I would have to make the necessary adjustments and obey Him. Until then, I would watch and pray. His timing and His ways always would be best and right.

EXPERIENCING GOD
KNOWING AND DOING THE WILL OF GOD

I had the privilege of working with Henry on an interactive learning course entitled *Experiencing God: Knowing and Doing the Will of God,* which was released in 1990. Henry and I wanted the study to help people *experience* God, not just learn about Him. That was the reason for the course title. We enlisted prayer warriors and prayer ministries across the country to pray for God to guide the development of the course.

We could not have anticipated what God was planning to do through that work. We began to hear of people from nearly every Christian denomination who were using the course in small-group studies. Some whole churches, both small and large, were using the study with their entire congregations. People were sending copies to friends and family all over the world. Groups of missionaries studied the course together and wrote to describe the spirit of revival and renewed sense of call to missions that they experienced. Churches began using the course for training new Christians and even for church planting.

Perhaps the most exciting testimonies we began to hear were from longtime Christians who said things like:

- "I wish I had known these truths forty years ago. My life and ministry would have been totally different."
- "This is the most wonderful time in my Christian life. I never knew I could have an intimate and personal relationship with my heavenly Father."
- "My whole life and attitudes have changed since I began this study."
- "I sensed God's call to missions [or the ministry] while I was studying *Experiencing God*. That is how God got me to the mission field."
- "Our church is not the same church. It has come alive again. We have started eleven new ministries in the past year."

This book you are reading is an outgrowth of that course. Because we saw God working so deeply in people's lives and churches, we wanted to share this message in a different format to make it available to as many people as possible. We have reorganized some of the content for this format, and we have attempted to answer questions and give further explanation and illustrations to help your understanding of the message. After reading this book, you may want to consider going through the interactive study course in a small group as a tool to help you make practical application to your life and your church.

A NEW WALK OF FAITH REQUIRED

In the summer of 1992, Henry asked me to work with him and the Office of Prayer and Spiritual Awakening on a new course entitled *Fresh Encounter: God's Pattern for Revival and Spiritual Awakening.* I prayed and sensed that God wanted me to work with Henry, so I agreed. When I heard the message, however, I began to sense a great urgency from God that the work needed to be completed quickly. With my heavy workload at the Baptist Sunday School Board, I could not see how I could complete the project in my spare time.

Two years before, God had spoken to me through His Word that a time would come when I would need to be free of those job responsibilities to be more fully available to Him. I began to pray and ask Him if this was the time I needed to leave my job and walk by faith. I rehearsed my spiritual markers (see pp. 196–200) and sought the counsel of other believers. By Labor Day weekend, God had convinced me that I must resign my job and walk with Him by faith as I completed this new project. With no source for income in sight, my family joined me on this adventure with God. At Henry's recommendation, I became a Mission Service Corps volunteer and was assigned to his office as a volunteer writer and consultant.

After I announced my resignation and began wrapping up my job assignments, I received a call from Laity Renewal Ministries.

This was a group of men who had formed a nonprofit group in Texas. They had been involved in lay renewal and had supported a Mission Service Corps volunteer in the past. Each of the directors had studied the course *Experiencing God* and saw the renewal God was bringing through that tool. They said, "We heard about your decision to leave the Sunday School Board in order to write *Fresh Encounter*. We have prayed and believe God wants us to take you on as a project."

They hired me to be their executive director and serve as a catalyst for spiritual renewal through Henry's office. They agreed to a salary package and said, "We will take care of securing the finances. You do what God tells you to do." God has provided for our every need!

The whole process of developing the *Fresh Encounter* resources would normally have been placed on a five-year planning cycle in our denominational agencies. But God gave others the same sense of urgency we had, and He worked through many people to accomplish the production of the *Fresh Encounter* resources in an eight-month period of time. We began to realize God was up to something far bigger than any of us would have planned.

During that year, we heard an intensifying cry from God's people for revival unlike anything we had heard before. Even now God is using those tools to guide pastors and churches to return to Him and experience revival. Henry and I stand in awe of what God has done and is doing to accomplish His purposes in our world.

MY PRAYER

God is working more mightily in our world today than ever in history to draw people to Himself. He is working to purify His people in order to exalt His Son Jesus Christ. He is breaking down barriers to the gospel message and is calling people to missions service like never before in history. He is raising up godly leaders and ministries to speak to His people and to a lost world. God is marshaling His forces for a tremendous work of grace in our lifetime!

I pray that God will use this book radically to touch your life for the kingdom's sake. His work in your life will far surpass all your plans and dreams. He will bring purpose and fulfillment to your life and ministry with overflowing joy. He will be calling you to join Him in His mission to reach our world. I pray that you will be very responsive to Him in the coming days.

May the grace, joy, and peace of God be yours through Jesus Christ our living Lord. To Him be glory, now and forever.

Claude V. King
Murfreesboro, Tennessee
July, 1994

Editor's Note: Claude King and Henry Blackaby have worked closely together in writing and developing books and resources. Because the biblical understandings and illustrations in *Experiencing God* come primarily from Henry's personal experience, the following text is written as though Henry were your personal counselor. This first-person approach was selected as a means of making this book a warm and personal message just for you.

INTRODUCTION

Have you ever wanted to know and do God's will? Those who come to Jesus as Savior and Lord join in His mission to reconcile a lost world. God Himself causes you to desire to be a faithful servant. Yet God has far more in store for your life than just to do something for Him. He wants you to experience an intimate love relationship with Him that is real and personal. Jesus said: "This is eternal life, that they may know You, the only true God, and Jesus Christ whom You have sent" (John 17:3).

The heart of eternal life and the heart of this study is for you to *know God* and to *know*

Jesus Christ whom He has sent. Knowing God does not come through a program, a study, or a method. Knowing God comes through a relationship with a Person. This is an intimate love relationship with God. Through this relationship, God reveals Himself, His purposes, and His ways; and He invites you to join Him where He is already at work. When you obey, God accomplishes through you something only He can do. Then you come to *know God* in a more intimate way by *experiencing God* at work through you.

I want to help you move into the kind of relationship to God through which you will truly experience eternal life to the fullest degree possible. Jesus said, "I have come that they may have life, and that they may have it more abundantly" (John 10:10). Would you like to experience life to the full? You may, if you are willing to respond to God's invitation to an intimate love relationship with Him.

RELATIONSHIP TO JESUS CHRIST— A PREREQUISITE

In writing this book I have assumed that you have already trusted Jesus Christ as Savior and you acknowledge Him to be Lord of your life. If you have not made this most important decision in your life, the rest of this book will have little meaning for you because spiritual matters can only be understood by those who have the indwelling Spirit of Christ. "The natural man does not receive the things of the Spirit of God, for they are foolishness to him; nor can he know them, because they are spiritually discerned" (1 Cor. 2:14).

If you sense a need to accept Jesus as your Savior and Lord, now is a good time to settle this matter with God. Ask God to speak to you as you read the following Scriptures:

- Romans 3:23—All have sinned.
- Romans 6:23—Eternal life is a free gift of God.
- Romans 5:8—Because of love, Jesus paid the death penalty for your sins.
- Romans 10:9–10—Confess Jesus as Lord and believe God raised Him from the dead.
- Romans 10:13—Ask God to save you and He will.

To place your faith in Jesus and receive His gift of eternal life you must:

- Recognize that God created you for a love relationship with Him. He wants you to love Him with all your being.
- Recognize that you are a sinner and you cannot save yourself.
- Believe that Jesus paid a death penalty for your sin by His death on the cross and rose from the dead in victory over death.
- Confess (agree with God about) your sins that separate you from Him.
- Repent of your sins (turn from sin to God).
- Ask Jesus to save you by His grace (undeserved favor).
- Turn over the rule in your life to Jesus. Let Him be your Lord.

MY DECISION FOR JESUS

❑ *I have trusted Jesus as my Savior and Lord on ________________. (Date)*

❑ *I have not trusted Jesus as Savior and Lord because ______*

____

❑ *I will trust Jesus Christ as my Savior and Lord right now. Jesus, I am a sinner. Please forgive me of my sins. I trust you as my Lord and Savior. Come live in my heart today.*

If you need help, call on your pastor, a deacon, an elder, or other Christian friend for help. If you have just made this important decision, call someone and share the good news of what God has done in your life. Then share your decision with your church.

LOOKING FOR MORE IN YOUR EXPERIENCE OF GOD?

You may have been frustrated in your Christian experience because you know God has a more abundant life for you than you have experienced. Or you may be earnestly desiring God's directions for your life and ministry. You may have experienced tragedy in your life. Standing bewildered in the middle of a broken life, you don't know what to do. Whatever your present circumstances may be, my earnest prayer is that somehow as you read these pages you will be able to:

- Hear when God is speaking to you.
- Clearly identify the activity of God in your life.
- Believe Him to be and do everything He promises.
- Adjust your beliefs, character, and behavior to Him and His ways.
- See a direction that He is taking in your life and what He wants to do through your life.
- Clearly know what you need to do in response to His activity in your life.
- Experience God doing through you what only God can do!

These are not things that I can do or that this book can do for you. These are things only God can do in your life. I will try to serve as your guide, encourager, and catalyst (one who assists in bringing about an action or reaction) for your deeper walk with God. I will share with you the biblical principles by which God has been guiding my life and ministry. I will be sharing with you some of the "wonderful works" the Lord has done as God's people have applied biblical principles to following Him. I invite you to interact with God throughout the reading of this book so He can reveal to you the ways He wants you to apply these principles in your own life, ministry, and church. To interact with God, take time as you read to pause and pray, asking God to speak to you, to guide you, or to reveal to you His desires for your response.

MY EXPERIENCE WITH GOD

I would describe my present experience with God as:

- ❏ *Frustrated*
- ❏ *Earnestly desiring direction*
- ❏ *Bewildered in the face of tragedy*

I want this study to . . .

YOUR TEACHER

Jesus said, "The Helper, the Holy Spirit, whom the Father will send in My name, He will teach you all things" (John 14:26). The Holy Spirit of God will be your personal Teacher. He is the One who will guide you to apply these principles according to God's will. He will be at work revealing God, His purposes, and His ways to you. Jesus said, "If anyone wills to do His will, he shall know concerning the doctrine, whether it is from God or whether I speak on My own authority" (John 7:17).

This is a fair criteria for this book as well. The Holy Spirit at work in you will confirm in your own heart the truth of Scripture. When I present what I see as a biblical principle, you can depend on the Holy Spirit to confirm whether that teaching comes from God or not. Therefore, your intimate relationship with God in prayer, meditation, and Bible study will be an indispensable part of what God may want to do in your life as you read and seek to apply these truths.

YOUR SOURCE OF AUTHORITY

The Bible is God's Word to you. The Holy Spirit honors and uses God's Word in speaking to you. The Scriptures will be your source of authority for faith and practice. You cannot depend on human traditions, your experience, or the experience of others to be accurate authorities on God's will and ways. Experience and tradition must always be examined against the teaching of Scripture.

Anything significant that happens in your life will be a result of God's activity in your life. He is infinitely more interested in your life than you or I could possibly be. Let the Spirit of God bring you into an intimate relationship with the God of the Universe "who is able to do exceedingly abundantly above all that we ask or think, according to the power that works in us" (Eph. 3:20). Would you pray at the very outset of your reading and surrender your life to God so that He may guide and instruct you in any way He pleases? I pray that the God who has already begun a good work in you will complete it in His time!

As you read this book, you will come across various sections set apart like the one below, including questions to ponder. You might wish to keep a notebook nearby as you consider these questions as they apply the book's message to your own life's circumstances.

MY PRAYER FOR THIS STUDY

God, I pray that in this study You will . . .

I dedicate myself during these weeks to . . .

This is eternal life: that they may know You, the only true God, and Jesus Christ, whom You have sent.

JOHN 17:3

1

KNOWING GOD BY EXPERIENCE

Jesus said that eternal life is knowing God, including God the Son—Jesus Christ. Jesus did not mean that eternal life is "knowing about God." In the Scriptures knowledge of God comes through experience. We come to know God as we experience Him in and around our lives.

You will never be satisfied just to know *about* God. Really knowing God only comes through experience as He reveals Himself to you. Throughout the Bible God took the initiative to reveal Himself to people by experience. Frequently when God revealed Himself to a person, that person gave God a new name or described Him in a new way.

For the Hebrew, a person's name represented his character or described his nature. This is why we frequently see new names or titles used for God following an event where a Bible character experienced God. To know God by name required a personal experience of His presence.

Biblical names, titles, and descriptions of God identify how the men and women of the Bible personally came to know God. The Scripture is a record of God's revelation of Himself to man. Each of the many names for God is a part of that revelation.

THE LORD WILL PROVIDE

For instance, in Genesis 22:1–18 God was in the process of developing Abraham's character to be the father of a nation. God put Abraham's faith and obedience to the test by asking him to sacrifice his son of promise—Isaac. This brought Abraham to a crisis of belief. He had to decide what he really believed about God. Up until this time Abraham had known God by experience as "God Almighty," for God had provided him a son when he and Sarah were in their old age and beyond the human limits of childbearing.

Now God was requiring Abraham to walk with Him by faith. On the way up the mountain to the place of sacrifice, Isaac asked his dad, "Where is the lamb for a burnt offering?" (v. 7). Can you imagine what Abraham might have felt at that moment, knowing that Isaac was the sacrifice?

"Abraham said, 'My, son, God will provide for Himself the lamb for a burnt offering'" (v. 8). Abraham made an adjustment of his life and acted on his belief that God was his Provider. He obeyed God.

When God saw Abraham's faith and obedience, He stopped Abraham from sacrificing Isaac and provided a ram instead. Abraham named that place after the God he had just come to know by experience. He named the place "The-Lord-Will-Provide." In the Bible this is the first time we see the name "The-Lord-Will-Provide." Abraham came to an intimate knowledge of God that day through the experience of God as his Provider.

This is how we also come to know God. We come to know God as we experience Him. God reveals Himself to us through our experience of Him at work in our lives. We can know about God as a Provider as we read this story about Abraham. But we really come to know God as Provider when we experience Him providing something for our lives.

For twelve years I pastored Faith Baptist Church in Saskatoon, Saskatchewan. When we started our first mission church, we called Jack Conner as our mission pastor. But we had no money for moving expenses and no money for a salary. Jack had three children in school, so we felt that we ought to pay him at least $850 a month. We began to pray that God would provide for his move and his needs.

I had never guided a church to do that before. We had now stepped out in faith, believing that God wanted him to pastor our mission in Prince Albert. Except for a few people in California, I didn't know anybody who could help us financially. I began to ask myself, "How in the world will God make this provision?" Then it dawned on me that as long as God knew where I was, He could cause anybody in the world to know where I was. As long as He knew my need, He could place that need on the heart of anybody He chose.

Jack passed immigration and started his move of faith, convinced that God had called him. I then received a letter from First Baptist Church, Fayetteville, Arkansas. They said, "God has laid it on our heart to send one percent of our mission giving to Saskatchewan missions. We are sending a check to use however you choose." I did not know how in the world they got involved with us at that time, but a check came for eleven hundred dollars.

One day I received a phone call at home. The caller made a pledge that completed the $850 a month we needed to provide Jack's salary for one year. Just as I got off the phone, Jack drove into our driveway.

I asked, "Jack, what did it cost to move you?"

He said, "Well, Henry, as best I can tell it cost me eleven hundred dollars."

We began that first step of faith by believing that the God who knows where we are is the God who can touch anybody, anywhere, and cause him or her to know where we are. We made the adjustments and were obedient. We believed that the God who called Jack also said, "I AM Provider." When we were obedient, God demonstrated Himself to be our Provider. That experience led us to a deeper love relationship with an all-sufficient God.

MY EXPERIENCE OF GOD THE PROVIDER

I experienced God as my Provider most meaningfully when God provided . . . for me. As the Lord prompts me I will tell this story to others.

One way I need God to be my provider today is . . .

THE LORD IS MY BANNER

Another experience in the Scriptures reveal God's name as "The-Lord-Is-My-Banner." Joshua and the Israelites were fighting the Amalekites. Moses was overseeing the battle from a nearby mountain. While he held his hands up to God, the Israelites were victorious. When he let his hands down they began to lose. God defeated the Amalekites through Israel that day, and Moses built an altar and gave it the name "The-Lord-Is-My-Banner." A banner is the standard that goes out in front of an army of a tribe or nation to indicate whom it represents. "The-Lord-Is-My-Banner" says we are God's people; He is our God. Moses' uplifted hands gave constant glory to God, indicating that the battle was His and Israel was His. Israel came to know God in a better way that day as they realized anew—We are God's people; the Lord is our Banner. (See Exod. 17:8–15.)

I AM WHO I AM

Moses also had an encounter with God where God revealed a personal name. When Moses was at the burning bush, he asked God, "Indeed, when I come to the children of Israel and say to them, 'The God of your fathers has sent me to you,' and they say to me, 'What is His name?' what shall I say to them?" (Exod. 3:13).

God responded, "I AM WHO I AM." And He said, "Thus you shall say to the children of Israel, 'I AM has sent me to you'" (Exod. 3:14). When God said, "I AM WHO I AM," He was saying, "I am the Eternal One. I will be what I will be." He was saying, "I am everything you will need." During the next forty years, Moses came to know God experientially as Jehovah or Yahweh, the Great I AM. God was everything Moses and Israel needed Him to be.

MY EXPERIENCE OF GOD BEING ALL I NEED

God revealed to me that He was all I needed in 19____ when He . . .

A RELATIONSHIP—NOT JUST A NAME

God reveals Himself with purpose. He created you for a love relationship with Himself. When He reveals Himself to you, He is allowing you to come to know Him by experience. Sometimes that revelation is an expression of God's love for you. Jesus said: "He who has My commandments and keeps them, it is he who loves Me. And he who loves Me will be loved by My Father, and I will love him and manifest Myself to him" (John 14:21).

If you have a love relationship with God, you have come to know God through experience. He has worked in and around your life. For instance, you could not know God as the "Comforter in sorrow" unless you had experienced His comfort during a time of grief or sorrow. You come to know God when He reveals Himself to you. You come to know Him as you experience Him. That is why we have titled this book *Experiencing God.* Our great desire is to assist you in *experiencing* God in greater and more personal dimensions.

Because a Hebrew name described a person's character or nature, the name was closely associated with the person and his presence. Thus, to call on one's name was to seek his presence. God's name is majestic and worthy of our praise. Acknowledging God's name amounts to recognizing God for who He is. Calling on His name indicates you are seeking His presence. Praising His name is praising *Him.* God's names in Scripture can become a call to worship for you. The psalmist said: "Blessed are the people who know the joyful sound! They walk, O LORD, in the light of Your countenance. In Your name they rejoice all day long, and in Your righteousness they are exalted" (Ps. 89:15–16).

Watch for times today to worship God through His names. To focus your attention on His name is to focus attention on the God of the name. His name represents His presence. To worship is to reverence and honor God, to acknowledge Him as worthy of your praise.

SUMMARY

The names of God in Scripture reveal something of His nature, activity, or character. You come to know God by experience at His initiative as He reveals Himself to you. As you experience God, you come to know Him more intimately and personally. As you come to know Him, you will want to express your praise, gratitude, and worship to Him. One of the ways to worship Him is to praise and honor Him by acknowledging His names. Watch for ways in the future that God may bring you to a deeper knowledge of Him through the experiences of your life. Then take time to worship God as you have come to know Him.

EXPERIENCING GOD TODAY

To be reminded of some ways you may have come to know God by experience or by name, read through the following list. See if you can identify names and remember experiences where you have come to know God that way. A more complete list of names from Scripture is included in the appendix. Spend some time worshiping God through His names. Thank Him for revealing Himself to you.

- my witness (Job 16:19)
- bread of life (John 6:35)
- Comforter in sorrow (Jer. 8:18)
- my hope (Ps. 71:5)
- Wonderful Counselor (Isa. 9:6)
- defender of widows (Ps. 68:5)
- the strength of my salvation (Ps. 140:7)
- Faithful and True (Rev. 19:11)
- our Father (Isa. 64:8)
- a sure foundation (Isa. 28:16)
- my friend (Job 16:20)
- Almighty God (Gen. 17:1)
- God of all comfort (2 Cor. 1:3)
- God who avenges me (Ps. 18:47)
- God who saves me (Ps. 51:14)
- our guide (Ps. 48:14)
- our head (2 Chron. 13:12)
- head of the church (Eph. 5:23)

- our help (Ps. 33:20)
- my hiding place (Ps. 32:7)
- a great High Priest (Heb. 4:14)
- Holy One in your midst (Hos. 11:9)
- righteous Judge (2 Tim. 4:8)
- King of kings (1 Tim. 6:15)
- our life (Col. 3:4)
- light of life (John 8:12)
- Lord of lords (1 Tim. 6:15)
- Lord of the harvest (Matt. 9:38)
- mediator (1 Tim. 2:5)
- our peace (Eph. 2:14)
- Prince of Peace (Isa. 9:6)
- my Redeemer (Ps. 19:14)
- refuge and strength (Ps. 46:1)
- my salvation (Exod. 15:2)
- my help (Ps. 42:5)
- the Good Shepherd (John 10:11)
- Lord (Luke 2:29)
- my stronghold (Ps. 18:2)
- my support (2 Sam. 22:19)
- Good Teacher (Mark 10:17)

NAMES GOD HAS REVEALED TO ME

Circle each name of God listed above that has special significance for you. Read the corresponding Scripture passage. Remind yourself of the experience of God that gave this name special meaning.

Beloved, let us love one another, for love is of God; and everyone who loves is born of God and knows God; he who does not love does not know God, for God is love.

1 JOHN 4:7–8

2

KNOWING GOD'S NATURE

When one of my children could not get his own way, he used to say, "You don't love me." Was that true? No, it wasn't true. My love had not changed. At that moment, however, my love was expressing itself differently than he wanted it.

When our only daughter Carrie was sixteen, the doctors told us she had cancer. We had to take her through chemotherapy and radiation. We suffered with Carrie as we watched her experience the sickness that goes along with the treatments. Some people face such an experience by blaming God and questioning why He doesn't love them anymore. Carrie's cancer treatments could have been a very devastating experience for us. Was God loving us still? Yes. Had His love changed? No, His love had not changed.

When you face circumstances like this, you can question and ask God to show you what is going on. We did that. We had to ask Him what we should do. We asked all those questions, but I never said, "Lord, I guess you don't love me."

MY EXPERIENCE WITH GOD'S LOVE

Describe the experience that most dramatically and lastingly defined God's love for you. What questions did you ask during that experience? Did God provide answers for your questions? How? or Why not? Did you ever doubt God's love during this experience? How can you be sure God loves you?

At times I went before the heavenly Father, and I saw behind my daughter the cross of Jesus Christ. I said, "Father, don't ever let me look at circumstances and question Your love for me. Your love for me was settled on the cross. That has never changed and will never change for me." Our love relationship with the heavenly Father sustained us through a very difficult time.[1]

God created you for a love relationship with Himself. He yearns for you to love Him. The call to relationship is also a call to be on mission with Him. If you want to know God's will, you must respond to His invitation to love Him wholeheartedly. God works through those He loves to carry out His kingdom purposes in the world. As you begin to think about knowing and doing God's will, you need to know who God is. Let's look at three aspects of His nature. Each of these characteristics of God has special implications for your doing His will.

GOD'S NATURE AND HIS WILL

1. God is love: His will is always best.
2. God is all-knowing: His directions are always right.
3. God is all-powerful: He can enable you to accomplish His will.

GOD IS LOVE: HIS WILL IS ALWAYS BEST

According to 1 John 4:16, "God is love." This does not say that God loves, though He does love with a perfect and unconditional love. The Scripture says that God's very nature is love. God can never function contrary to His own nature. Never in your life will God ever express His will toward you except that it is an expression of perfect love. He can't! God's kind of love always seeks the very best for a person. Therefore, He can never give you second best. His nature will not let Him.

God does bring discipline, judgment, and wrath on those who continue in sin and rebellion. Even His discipline, however, always is based on love. "For whom the Lord loves He chastens, and scourges every son whom He receives" (Heb. 12:6). Because His nature is love, I am always confident that however He expresses Himself to me is always best. Two other verses describe His love toward us: "For God so loved the world that He gave His only begotten Son" (John 3:16), and "By this we know love, because He laid down His life for us" (1 John 3:16). Your trust in the love nature of God is crucial. This has been a powerful influence in my own life. I never look on circumstances without seeing them on the backdrop of the cross. That is where God clearly demonstrated once and for all time His deep love for me. My love relationship with God determines everything I do.

No matter what the circumstances are, His love never changes. Long before our experience with Carrie's cancer, I had made a determination: No matter what the circumstances, I would never look at those circumstances except against the backdrop of the cross. In the death and resurrection of Jesus Christ, God forever convinced me that He loved me. The cross, the death of Jesus Christ, and His resurrection are God's final, total, and complete expression that He loves us.

Have you ever heard someone say something like this: "I'm afraid to surrender totally to the Lord because He might send me to Africa as a missionary"? Such a statement indicates a lack of trust and understanding of the love of God. He would not call you to Africa unless He knew that such a call would be best for you. Many missionaries in Africa would not want to be anywhere else in the world. They love Africa and they know God gave them His very best when He called them there.

One missionary couple came home with their two children for a year of furlough before returning to their work in Zimbabwe. Their schedule in the States was so full and hurried they said, "We can't wait to get back to Africa. We love African time!" Where they work in Africa there is no electricity. They go to bed when it gets dark, and they sleep until they wake up. When they go to a village for a meeting, no schedule pushes them. When they arrive, they send word throughout the village by children, a crowd gathers, and they meet until they are finished. The pace is very different from the pace in the States.

Never allow your heart to question the love of God. Settle it on the front end of your desiring to know Him and experience Him, that He loves you. He created you for that love relationship. He has been pursuing you in that love relationship. Every dealing He has with you is an expression of His love for you. God would cease to be God if He expressed Himself in any way other than *perfect love!* Your relationship with God right now reveals what you believe about Him. It is spiritually impossible for you to believe one way and practice another. If you really believe that God is *love,* you will also accept the fact that His will is always *best.*

GOD'S PURPOSE WITH ME

God created me for . . .

I show what I believe about God and how I live out the relationship with God by . . .

GOD'S COMMANDS ARE FOR YOUR GOOD

When you hear words like *commands, judgments, statutes,* or *laws,* your first impression may be a negative one. God's commands, however, are expressions of His nature of love. In the following passages He says the commands are for our own good. They are your life.

> What does the LORD your God require of you, but to fear the LORD your God, to walk in all His ways and to love Him, to serve the LORD your God with all your heart and with all your soul, and to keep the commandments of the LORD and His statutes which I command you today for your good? (Deut. 10:12–13).
>
> He said to them, "Set your hearts on all the words which I testify among you today, which you shall command your children to be careful to observe—all the words of this law. For it is not a futile thing for you, because it is your life, and by this word you shall prolong your days in the land which you cross over the Jordan to possess." (Deut. 32:46–47)

The foundation of these passages is God's love relationship with you. When you come to know God by experience, you will be convinced of His love. When you are convinced of His love, you can believe Him and trust Him. When you trust Him, you can obey Him. When you love Him, you have no problem obeying Him. "For this is the love of God, that we keep His commandments. And His commandments are not burdensome" (1 John 5:3).

God loves you deeply and profoundly. Because He loves you, He has given you guidelines for living lest you miss the full dimensions of the love relationship. Life also has some "land mines" that can destroy you or wreck your life. God does not want to see you miss out on His best, and He does not want to see your life wrecked.

Suppose you had to cross a field full of land mines. A person who knows exactly where every one of them is buried offers to take you through it. Would you say to him, "I don't want you to tell me what to do. I don't want you to impose your ways on me"? I don't know about you, but I would stay as close to that person as I could. I certainly would not go wandering off. His directions to me would preserve my life. He would say, "Don't go that way, because that way will kill you. Go this way and you will live."

GOD'S COMMANDS FOR ME

God's command that I need most to listen to says . . .

Why does God give me this command?

THE PURPOSE OF GOD'S COMMANDS

God wants you to have life and have it abundantly. When God gives you a command, He is trying to protect and preserve the best He has for you. He does not want you to lose it. When God gives a command, He is not restricting you. He is freeing you. God's purpose is that you might prosper and live:

> When your son asks you in time to come, saying, "What is the meaning of the testimonies, the statutes, and the judgments which the LORD our God has commanded you?" then you shall say to your son: ". . . The LORD commanded us to observe all these statutes, to fear the LORD our God, for our good always, that He might preserve us alive, as it is this day. Then it will be righteousness for us, if we are careful to observe all these commandments before the LORD our God, as He has commanded us." (Deut. 6:20–21, 24–25)

God has given His commands so you may prosper and live life to its fullest measure. Let me give you an example. Suppose the Lord says, "I have a gift for you—a beautiful, wonderful expression of what love is. I will provide you with a spouse—a husband or a wife. Your relationship with this person will bring out the very best in you. It will give you an opportunity to experience some of the deepest and most meaningful expressions of human love. That individual will release in you some wonderful things, affirm some things in you, and be there to strengthen you when you lose heart. Within that relationship, your mate will love you, believe in you, and trust you. Out of that relationship I will bless the two of you with children, and those children will sit on your knee and say, 'Daddy, I love you.'"

But then He says, "You shall not commit adultery" (Matt. 5:27). Is that command to limit or restrict you? No! It is to protect and free you to experience love at its human best. What happens if you break the command and commit adultery? The love relationship is ruptured between husband and wife. Trust is gone. Hurt sets in. Guilt and bitterness creep in. Even the children begin to respond differently. Scars may severely limit the future dimensions of love you could have experienced together.

God's commands are designed to guide you to life's very best. You will not obey Him, however, if you do not believe Him and trust Him. You cannot believe Him if you do not love Him. You cannot love Him unless you know Him. If, however, you really come to know Him as He reveals Himself to you, you will love Him. If you love Him, you will believe and trust Him. If you believe and trust Him, you will obey Him. God has given His commands so you may prosper and live life to its fullest measure. If you love Him, you will obey Him! If you do not obey Him, you do not really love Him (see John 14:24). God is love. Because of His love, His will for you is always best. God also is all-knowing, so His directions are always right.

GOD IS ALL-KNOWING: HIS DIRECTIONS ARE ALWAYS RIGHT

By nature God is omniscient—that is, He is all-knowing. He possesses all knowledge—past, present, and future. Nothing is outside the knowledge of God. Whenever God expresses Himself to you, therefore, His directions are always right. When God gives you a directive, you can count on the fact that God has already considered every factor that must be considered. You will never follow a directive that God has given and find out later that God must have been mistaken. His directions are always right.

GOD'S KNOWLEDGE AND ME

Since God knows everything, what does He know about me? Why are His directions always right and never wrong?

Have you ever asked God to give you several alternatives so you can choose the one that is best for you? How many options does

God have to give you so you will have the right one? God always gets it right the first time!

As you seek to know and do God's will, you will want to wait before Him until you clearly know His will and His directions for carrying it out. Human wisdom and knowledge will not be adequate, but God's wisdom and knowledge are always adequate. You will not have to argue with God about whether His will is the right course of action. Even when His will doesn't make sense from your human perspective, your obedience will reveal that His will was right.

One of our churches in Vancouver believed that God was calling them to begin three new mission churches with different language groups. The church had only seventeen members itself. All human reason would rule out such a big assignment for such a small church. They were counting on money from our Home Mission Board to pay the pastors' salaries. One pastor was already in the process of relocating when we received word that the Board would not be able to fund any new work in our area for the next three years.

The church didn't have the funds to do what God had called them to do. They sought my counsel. I suggested that they first go back to the Lord and clarify their call. When they did, they returned and said, "We still believe God has called us to start all three new churches." Now they had to walk by faith and trust God to be their provider.

During this time, I changed jobs and moved to Atlanta. A few months later I spoke by phone with the secretary of the association in Vancouver. She had some exciting news. Six years earlier, I led a series of meetings in a church in California. An elderly woman came to me and said she wanted to leave part of her estate for use in Vancouver missions. The secretary reported that they had just received a letter from an attorney in California. This woman had died. The attorney informed them that they would be receiving a check for over $150,000. That amount was sufficient to pay for every new mission church that Vancouver church had begun.

Did God know what He was doing when He told a seventeen-member church to begin three new churches? Yes. Did He know that the funds would not be available from the Home Mission Board? Yes. Did God know that the funds would be available from another source exactly when they were needed? Yes. None of these details caught God by surprise. He is all-knowing. This small church in Vancouver knew that, and they believed God was right when He called them to a huge assignment. When God provided, everyone developed a greater trust in their all-knowing God.

Whenever God gives you a directive, it is always right. God's will is always best. You never have to question whether His will is best or right. It always is best and right. This is true because He loves you and knows all. Because He loves you perfectly, you can trust Him and obey Him completely. Not only is God loving and all-knowing, but He also is all-powerful. No matter how big the assignment He gives you, He is able to accomplish His purposes through you.

GOD'S DIRECTIONS FOR MY LIFE

God most recently showed me His directions for my life when He asked me to . . .

How did His directions test my faith? As I follow God's directions, what do I learn about my relationship to Him?

GOD IS ALL-POWERFUL: HE CAN ENABLE YOU TO ACCOMPLISH HIS WILL

God is omnipotent—that is, He is all-powerful. He was able to create the world out of nothing. He can accomplish anything He purposes to do. In fact He says that He will: "My counsel shall stand, and I will do all My pleasure. . . . Indeed I have spoken it; I will also bring it to pass. I have purposed it; I will also do it" (Isa. 46:10–11). If He ever asks you to do something, He Himself will enable you to do it. For instance:

- God enabled Noah and his sons to build a huge boat that spared the lives of every animal species during the great flood (Gen. 6–9).
- God enabled Gideon and 300 men to defeat an army of 120,000 (Judg. 7–8).
- Christ Jesus enabled His twelve disciples to heal people and to cast out demons (Matt. 10).
- God enabled Paul to carry the gospel to the Gentiles and establish churches throughout Asia Minor and all the way to Rome (his calling: Acts 9; his missionary journeys: Acts 13–28).

When your life is in the middle of God's activity, He will start rearranging a lot of your thinking. God's ways and thoughts are so different from yours and mine that they will often sound wrong, crazy, or impossible. Often, you will realize that the task is far beyond your power or resources to accomplish. When you recognize that the task is humanly impossible, you need to be ready to believe God and trust Him completely.

You need to believe that He will enable and equip you to do everything He asks of you. Don't try to second-guess Him. Just let Him be God. Turn to Him for the needed power, insight, skill, and resources. He will provide you with all you need.

God will begin to make Himself known to you very simply, as He would to a child. As you respond to Him in a simple childlike trust, you will find a whole new way of looking at life begin to unfold for you. Your life will be fulfilling. You will never have to sense an emptiness or lack of purpose. He always fills your life with

Himself. When you have Him, you have everything there is. As He was to Moses, He will be to you, the "I Am that I Am."

SUMMARY

Three characteristics of God's nature have a significant influence on your knowing and doing His will. Because God is love, His will is always best. As you follow and obey Him, He will always direct you in ways that are best for you and for the world into which He calls you. Because God is all-knowing, you will never have to question the rightness of His directions—even when they don't make sense. His directions are always right. Because God is all-powerful, you do not have to doubt your ability, strength, or resources to complete His assignments for you. He will enable you to accomplish all that He calls you to do.

EXPERIENCING GOD TODAY

Meditate on the truths in this chapter, and ask God to love you and reveal Himself to you in these ways. Ask Him to develop in you a confidence to trust Him anytime He has an assignment for you.

- God is love. His will is always best.
- God is all-knowing. His directions are always right.
- God is all-powerful. He can enable you to accomplish His will.

Now answer the following questions.

- If God were to give you a clear assignment that you knew came from Him, what reason could you give for choosing to obey Him?
- Why does God give you commands about how to live your life?

- When God gives you a directive, how much should you trust your human knowledge, common sense, and wisdom to guide your actions?
- How should you respond to an assignment from God when you know you don't have the power, skills, or resources to accomplish what He is asking you to do?

ENDNOTES

1. In chapter 14, "God Speaks through Circumstances," I will tell you how God used the circumstance of Carrie's cancer to bring glory to Himself and renew prayer ministries all over the world. By the way, Carrie now has graduated from college, is preparing for a career related to missions, and is doing fine.

Jesus said to them, "My food is to do the will of Him who sent me, and to finish His work."

JOHN 4:34

3

DOING GOD'S WILL

For Jesus, doing God's will was more important than food. Doing God's will is important for you too. When people seek to know and do the will of God, many ask the question, "What is God's will for my life?" Perhaps unconsciously, they focus on themselves, their lives, and what they are to do. A seminary professor of mine, Gaines S. Dobbins, used to say, "If you ask the wrong question, you are going to get the wrong answer." Sometimes we assume that every question is a legitimate question. When we pursue an answer and always come up wrong, we cannot figure out what is happening. When you begin asking questions, always check to see if you have asked the right question before you pursue the answer.

"What is God's will for my life?" is not the best question to ask. I think the right question is simply, "What is God's will?" Once I know God's will, then I can adjust my life to Him and His purposes. In other words, what is it that God is purposing where I am? Once I know what God is doing, then I know what I need to do. The focus needs to be on God and His purposes, not my life!

Now, that does not mean that God has no will concerning your life. He certainly does. He has a purpose and plan for your life. But the plan He has for your life is based on what He is doing in His world. He has a great purpose in mind for all humankind throughout all time. His desire is for you to become involved in what He is doing. Finding out what He is doing helps you know what He will want to do through you.

GOD'S WORK IN HIS WORLD

To seek God's will for my life, what must I first find out about God?

When I am involved in God's work, what can I know about what He wants to do through me?

DON'T JUST DO SOMETHING

We are a "doing" people. We always want to be doing something. The idea of doing God's will sounds fairly exciting. Once in a while someone will say, "Don't just stand there; do something."

Sometimes individuals and churches are so busy doing things they think will help God accomplish His purpose that He can't get their attention long enough to use them as servants to accomplish what He wants. We often wear ourselves out and accomplish very little of value to the kingdom.

I think God is crying out and shouting to us, "Don't just do something. Stand there! Enter into a love relationship with Me. Get to know Me. Adjust your life to Me. Let Me love you and reveal Myself to you as I work through you." A time will come when the doing will be called for, but we cannot skip the relationship. The relationship with God must come first.

Jesus said, "I am the vine, you are the branches. He who abides in Me, and I in him, bears much fruit; for without Me you can do nothing" (John 15:5). Do you believe Him? Without Him you can do nothing. He means that. Believe Him and trust what He says to be true. If you are experiencing a time of fruitlessness right now, you may be trying to do things on your own that God has not initiated.

God wants you to come to a greater knowledge of Him by experience. He wants to establish a love relationship with you. He wants to involve you in His kingdom purposes. But He alone has the right to initiate what you are to be involved in. When you allow Him to guide you and work through you, then He will accomplish His work through you.

Notice what Jesus had to say concerning those who have wearied themselves by trying to do things in their own strength: "Come to Me, all you who labor and are heavy laden, and I will give you rest. Take My yoke upon you and learn from Me, for I am gentle and lowly in heart, and you will find rest for your souls. For My yoke is easy and My burden is light" (Matt. 11:28–30).

A yoke is an instrument built for two oxen to work together. Jesus' invitation is for you to get into His yoke with Him—to get involved in His work (God's work). When you work where He is already working, He accomplishes His work with and through you in such a way that the yoke is easy and the burden is light.

GOD'S FIRST CALL TO ME

If I am weary from "doing good for God," what should I do differently?

GOD IS INTERESTED IN A LOVE RELATIONSHIP

I have been asked, "Does God plan your life for eternity and then turn you loose to work out His plan?" God's plan is for a love relationship with you. We get in trouble when we try to get God to tell us if He wants us to be a Christian businessperson, a music director, an education director, a preacher, or a missionary. We want to know if He wants us to serve in our home country or go to Japan or Canada. God doesn't usually give you a one-time assignment and leave you there forever. Yes, you may be placed in one job at one place for a long time; but God's assignments come to you on a daily basis.

He calls you to a relationship where He is Lord—where you are willing to do and be anything He chooses. If you will respond to Him as Lord, He may lead you to do and be things you would have never dreamed of. If you don't follow Him as Lord, you may lock yourself into a job or an assignment and miss something God wants to do through you. I've heard people say things like: "God called me to be a . . . , so this other thing couldn't possibly be His will." Or "My spiritual gift is . . . , so this ministry couldn't be God's will for me."

God will never give you an assignment that He will not, at the same time, enable you to complete. That is what a spiritual gift is—a supernatural empowering to accomplish the assignment God gives you.

Don't, however, focus on your talents, abilities, and interests in determining God's will. I have heard so many people say, "I would really like to do that; therefore, it must be God's will." That kind of response is self-centered. We need to become God-centered instead.

When He is Lord, your response should be something like this: "Lord, I will do anything that Your kingdom requires of me. Wherever You want me to be, I'll go. Whatever the circumstances, I'm willing to follow. If You want to meet a need through my life, I am Your servant; and I will do whatever is required."

GOD'S ASSIGNMENT FOR ME

Will God ever give me an assignment that He will not enable me to complete? Which is more important: my relationship with God or my assignment? Why?

THE FARMER WAS MY MAP

For twelve years I pastored in Saskatoon, Saskatchewan, Canada. One day a farmer said to me, "Henry, come out and visit with me at my farm." His directions went something like this: "Go a quarter mile past the edge of the city, and you will see a big red barn on your left. Go to the next road and turn to your left. Take that road for three-quarters of a mile. You'll see a tree. Go right for about four miles, and then you will see a big rock. . . ." I wrote all of this down, and one day I got there!

The next time I went to the farmer's house, the farmer was with me. Since there was more than one way to get to his house, he could have taken me any way he wanted to. This time I didn't need the instructions I had written down. You see, he was my "map."

What did I have to do? I simply had to listen to him. Every time he said "Turn," I did just what he said. He took me a way I had never been. I probably couldn't retrace that route on my own. The farmer was my "map." He knew the way.

JESUS IS YOUR WAY

Often people approach knowing and doing God's will this way: They ask, "Lord, what do You want me to do? When do You want me to do it? How shall I do it? Where shall I do it? What will the outcome be?"

Isn't this response most typical of us? We are always asking God for a detailed "road map." We say, "Lord, if You could just tell me where I am heading, then I will be able to set my course and go."

He says, "You don't need to. What you need to do is follow Me one day at a time." We need to come to the place where our response to God will be: "Lord, just tell me what to do one step at a time, and I will do it."

Who is the one who really knows the way for you to fulfill God's purpose for your life? God is! Jesus said, "I am the way, the truth, and the life" (John 14:6).

- He did not say, "I will show you the way."
- He did not say, "I will give you a road map."
- He did not say, "I will tell you which direction to head."
- He said, "I am *the* way." Jesus knows the way; He is your way.

If you were to do everything that Jesus tells you one day at a time, you always would be right in the center of where God wants you to be. Can you trust God to guide you that way? You might say, "No, Jesus does not really know God's will for my life." But He does! Jesus is God. You might say, "No, Jesus might mislead me and take me the wrong way." But He won't. You might think that Jesus would rather you wait until He tells you all the details before you start to follow Him. But that is not the pattern we see in His life or in the Scriptures.

God would be more interested in your responding to Him this way: "Yes, if I follow Jesus one day at a time, I will be right in the center of Your will for my life." When you get to the place where you trust Jesus to guide you one step at a time, you experience a new freedom. If you don't trust Jesus to guide you this way, what happens if you don't know the way you are to go? You worry every time you must make a turn. You often freeze up and cannot make a decision. This is not the way God intends for you to live your life.

I have found in my own life that I can release the way to Him. Then I take care of everything He tells me one day at a time. He gives me plenty to do to fill each day with meaning and purpose. If I do everything He says, I will be in the center of His will when He wants to use me for a special assignment.

GOD'S WAY FOR ME

Why is my daily relationship *with Jesus so important to knowing God's will?*

ABRAM FOLLOWED ONE DAY AT A TIME

Abram (God later changed his name to Abraham) is a good example of this principle at work in a Bible character. He walked by faith and not by sight. In the following Scripture, read about the call of Abram to do God's will. Watch to see how much detail he was given before he was asked to follow.

> Now the LORD had said to Abram, "Get out of your country, from your family and from your father's house, to a land that I will show you. I will make you into a great nation; I will bless you and make your name great; and

> you shall be a blessing. I will bless those who bless you, and I will curse him who curses you; and in you all the families of the earth shall be blessed."
>
> So Abram departed as the LORD had spoken to him, and Lot went with him. And Abram was seventy-five years old when he departed from Haran. Then Abram took Sarai his wife and Lot his brother's son, and all their possessions that they had gathered, and the people whom they had acquired in Haran, and they departed to go to the land of Canaan. So they came to the land of Canaan. (Gen. 12:1–5)

God said, "Get out of your country." How specific was God? He gave Abram this much detail: "to the land I will show you." That is all God asked Abram to do. God promised to do the rest. Would you be willing to follow God's directions for your life with that little detail?

GOD SELDOM GAVE EXTENSIVE DETAILS ON THE FRONT END

Does God call people to follow Him without giving them all the details up front? Many times, as with Abram, God called people just to follow Him. He is more likely to call you to follow one day at a time than He is to spell out all the details before you begin to obey Him.

In some cases God gave more details than in others. We will look at Moses' call and discover that God gave him a bigger picture of the assignment than He usually gave. In every case, however, the individuals had to stay close to God for daily guidance. For Moses and the children of Israel, God provided daily guidance through the cloud by day and the fire by night.

For Peter, Andrew, James, John (Matt. 4:18–20, 21–22), Matthew (Matt. 9:9), and Paul (Acts 9:1–20), God gave very little detail about their assignment. He basically said, "Just follow me, and I will show you." What He wants of you is this: "But seek first the kingdom of God and His righteousness, and all these things shall be added to you. Therefore do not worry about tomorrow, for tomorrow will worry about its own things. Sufficient for the day is its own trouble" (Matt. 6:33–34).

GOD'S WAY OF MAKING ASSIGNMENTS

Based on Biblical examples, is God in the habit of giving long-range details when He gives an assignment in kingdom work? Does He ever call me to follow even when I do not know much about His assignment?

SUMMARY

God is far more interested in a love relationship with you than He is in what you can do for Him. His desire is for you to love Him. As He fills you with His presence, He will guide you to do things. But even as you do those things, He will be the One at work through you to accomplish His purposes. He is all you need. The Christ in you is your way. He is your "map." When you follow His leadership one day at a time, you will always be right in the middle of God's will for your life.

EXPERIENCING GOD TODAY

God is absolutely trustworthy. You can trust Him to guide you and provide for you. Remember: "It is God who works in you both to will and to do for His good pleasure" (Phil. 2:13). Would you carefully consider doing the following?

- Agree with God that you will follow Him one day at a time.
- Agree to follow Him even when He does not spell out all the details.

- Agree that you will let Him be your Way.

MY SURRENDER TO GOD'S WAY

Lord, I will do anything that Your kingdom requires of me. Wherever You want me to be, I'll go. Whatever the circumstances, I'm willing to follow. If You want to meet a need through my life, I am Your servant; and I will do whatever is required.

If anyone serves Me, let him follow Me; and where I am, there My servant will be also. If anyone serves Me, him My father will honor.

JOHN 12:26

4

BEING GOD'S SERVANT

To be involved in God's work, you must be a servant. Many Scripture passages describe Jesus as God's Servant. He came as a servant to accomplish God's will in the redemption of humanity. Paul described Jesus' servant attitude and commended it to us in this way:

> Let this mind be in you which was also in Christ Jesus, who, being in the form of God, did not consider it robbery to be equal with God, but made Himself of no reputation, taking the form of a bondservant, and coming in the likeness of men. And being found in appearance as a man, He humbled Himself and became obedient to the point of death, even the death of the cross. (Phil. 2:5–8)

We are to develop the servant attitude of Christ which calls for humility and obedience. In His instructions to His disciples about servanthood, Jesus (the Son of Man) described His own role of service: "And whoever desires to be first among you, let him be your slave—just as the Son of Man did not come to be served, but to serve, and to give His life a ransom for many" (Matt. 20:27–28).

Jesus also told us about our relationship to Him, "As the Father has sent Me, I also send you" (John 20:21). When you respond to God's call to salvation, you join Him in His mission of world redemption. The call to salvation is a call to be on mission with Him. In this new relationship you move into a servant role with God as your Lord and Master.

Some would define a servant like this: "A servant is one who finds out what his master wants him to do, and then he does it." The human concept of a servant is that a servant goes to the master and says, "Master, what do you want me to do?" The master tells him, and the servant goes off *by himself* and does it. That is not the biblical concept of a servant of God. Being a servant of God is different from being a servant of a human master. A servant of a human master works *for* his master. God, however, works *through* His servants.

My understanding of a servant of God is more like the potter and the clay. God described His relationship to Israel as being like a potter with his clay:

> The word which came to Jeremiah from the LORD, saying, "Arise and go down to the potter's house, and there I will cause you to hear My words." Then I went down to the potter's house, and there he was, making something at the wheel. And the vessel that he made of clay was marred in the hand of the potter; so he made it again into another vessel, as it seemed good to the potter to make.
> Then the word of the LORD came to me, saying: "O house of Israel, can I not do with you as this potter?" says the LORD. "Look, as the clay is in the potter's hand, so are you in My hand, O house of Israel!" (Jer. 18:1–6)

To be useful, the clay has to be moldable; and once made into a vessel, it has to remain in the hand of the potter to be used. Clay that is not moldable is not useful. The clay has to be responsive to the potter so the potter can make any vessel of his choosing. Then the clay vessel has to remain in the potter's hand. When the potter has finished making the vessel of his choosing, that vessel has no ability to do anything whatsoever. It now has to remain in the potter's hand. Suppose the potter molds the clay into a cup. The cup has to remain in the potter's hands so the potter can use that cup in any way he chooses.

GOD'S PREPARATION FOR ME TO BE A SERVANT

What are some ways God has been molding my life for service? Have I been moldable? Why is it important for me to remain in close relationship with God?

HUMAN SERVANT AND DIVINE MASTER

That is very different from the way a servant works for a human master. When you come to God as His servant, He first wants you to allow Him to mold and shape you into the instrument of His choosing. Then He can take your life and put it where He wills and work through it to accomplish His purposes. Just as a cup cannot do anything on its own, you do not have any ability to do the command of the Lord except to be where He wants you to be. As you obey, He does His work through you. This concept will become even more clear to you as we look at Jesus' example in chapter 6.

A servant of God's has to do two things: (1) be moldable and (2) remain available for the Master's (Potter's) use. Then the Master can use that instrument as He chooses. The servant can do nothing of kingdom value by himself or herself. As Jesus said, "The Son can do nothing of Himself" (John 5:19) and "Without Me you can do nothing" (John 15:5). With God working through His servant, that servant can do anything God can do. Wow! Unlimited potential! Servanthood does require obedience. A servant of God must do what he is instructed, and he must remember who is accomplishing the work—God is.

If you have been working from a human approach to servanthood, this concept should change your approach to serving God. You do not get orders, then go out and carry them out on your own. You relate to God, respond to Him, and adjust your life so that He can do what He wants through you.

EXPO 86

For six years I worked with the Southern Baptist churches in Vancouver, British Columbia. When the World's Fair (Expo 86) was coming to Vancouver, our association of churches was convinced that God wanted us to try to reach the twenty-two million people who would attend the fair. But we only had about two thousand members in our association's churches. How could two thousand people make an impact on such a mass of tourists from all over the world?

Two years before the fair, we sought the Lord's directions and began to set those plans in motion. The total income for our whole association was $9,000. The following year our income was about $16,000. The year of the World's Fair we set a budget for $202,000. We had commitments that would probably provide 35 percent of that budget. Sixty-five percent of that budget was dependent on prayer and God's provision.

Can you operate a budget on prayer? Yes. But when you do that, you are attempting something only God can do. What do most of us do? We set the practical budget, which is the total of what we can do. Then we set a hope or faith budget. The budget we really trust and use, however, is the one we can reach by ourselves. We often don't trust God to do anything.

As an association of churches, we decided that God had definitely led us to the work that would cost $202,000. That became our operating budget. All of our people began praying for God to provide and do everything we believed He had led us to do during the World's Fair. At the end of the year, I asked our treasurer how much money we had received. From Canada, the United States, and other parts of the world we had received $264,000.

People from all over came to assist us. During the course of the fair, we saw almost twenty thousand people come to know and trust Jesus Christ as Savior and Lord. You cannot explain that except in terms of God's intervention. Only God could have done that. God did it with a people who had determined to be servants who were moldable and remained available for the Master's use.

DEPENDENT ON GOD ALONE

What have I seen God do that only He can do? Now what am I praying for God to do? What can I do to make sure He answers this prayer?

ELIJAH WAS A SERVANT

Elijah was one of the great Old Testament prophets of Israel and a servant of God (1 Kings 17:1). Under the leadership of King Ahab and his wife, Jezebel, the people of Israel were being led away to serve Baal, a Canaanite fertility god. In 1 Kings 18:16–39 Elijah challenged the prophets of Baal to a public test to prove once and for all whose God was the true God. Elijah took a big risk in being a servant of God. He was outnumbered 850 to 1.

Elijah proposed that the prophets of Baal prepare a sacrifice and ask their god to send fire to consume it. He would do the same and appeal to the God of Israel for fire. Baal—who was no god—did not answer his prophets' pleas. Elijah repaired the altar of the Lord and prepared his sacrifice. God did answer by fire, consuming the sacrifice (and even the stone altar) as Elijah had proposed. If God had not displayed His own work by coming in fire, Elijah would have utterly failed. That would probably have cost him his life.

Throughout this process, Elijah had to stay with God and do everything God commanded him to do. In his prayer, Elijah said, "Let it be known that I am Your servant, and that I have done all these things at Your word" (1 Kings 18:36). Elijah was acting in obedience to God's command and not based on his own initiative. He went where God told him when God told him and did what God told him. Then God accomplished His own purposes through Elijah. Elijah attributed the work to God when he said, "You have turned their hearts back to You again" (1 Kings 18:37). Elijah wanted the people to identify the Lord as the True God. That is exactly how the people responded!

Did Elijah or God bring down the fire from Heaven? God did. What was Elijah doing? Being obedient. Elijah had no ability to do what God was about to do. When God, however, did something only He could do, all the people knew that He was the True God.

God did this mighty work, but He acted through His obedient servant Elijah.

ORDINARY PEOPLE

When you begin to think about working with God on His mission to redeem a lost world, you may ask, "What can one ordinary person do?" One of the wonderful Scriptures that has helped me at this point describes Elijah: "Elijah was a man with a nature like ours, and he prayed earnestly that it would not rain; and it did not rain on the land for three years and six months. And he prayed again, and the heaven gave rain, and the earth produced its fruit" (James 5:17–18).

In this Scripture you learn that this mighty man of God was one ordinary person just like you and me. Elijah was "ordinary" just as we are ordinary. But when this ordinary man prayed, God responded. Elijah was ordinary, but he humbled himself in the role of a servant. He obeyed everything God instructed him to do, and God was able to work through Elijah to influence powerfully a whole nation to return to God.

PETER AND JOHN WERE ORDINARY MEN

Peter and John were two of the first disciples selected by Jesus. After Jesus' resurrection, God healed a crippled beggar through Peter. Peter and John were called before the Sanhedrin to give an account of their actions. Filled with the Holy Spirit, Peter spoke boldly to the religious leaders. Notice the response of the leaders: "Now when they saw the boldness of Peter and John, and perceived that they were uneducated and untrained men, they marveled. And they realized that they had been with Jesus" (Acts 4:13).

All of the persons that you see in the Scriptures were ordinary people. Their relationship with God and the activity of God made them extraordinary. Did you notice this statement—the leaders recognized that Peter and John "had been with Jesus"? Anyone who will take the time to enter into an intimate relationship with God can see God do extraordinary things through his or her life.

D. L. MOODY WAS AN ORDINARY SHOE SALESMAN

Dwight L. Moody was a poorly educated, unordained shoe salesman who felt the call of God to preach the gospel. Early one morning he and some friends gathered in a hayfield for a season of prayer, confession, and consecration. In that prayer meeting Henry Varley said, "The world has yet to see what God can do with and for and through and in a man who is fully and wholly consecrated to Him."

Moody was deeply moved by those words. Later, he listened to the great preacher Charles H. Spurgeon. Moody's biographer described how he responded:

> "The world had yet to see! With and for and through and in! A man!" Varley meant any man! Varley didn't say he had to be educated, or brilliant, or anything else! Just *a man!* Well, by the Holy Spirit in him, he'd [Moody] be *one* of those men. And then suddenly, in that high gallery, he saw something he'd never realized before,—it was not Mr. Spurgeon, after all, who was doing that work: it was God. And if God could use Mr. Spurgeon, why should He not use the rest of us, and why should we not all just lay ourselves at the Master's feet, and say to Him, "Send me! Use me!"

Dwight L. Moody was an ordinary man who sought to be fully and wholly consecrated to Christ. Through this one ordinary life God began to do the extraordinary. Moody became one of the greatest evangelists of modern times. During much of the nineteenth century he preached in revival services across Britain and America where thousands and thousands came to Christ.

Could God work in extraordinary ways through your life to accomplish significant things for His kingdom? You might say, "Well, I am not a D. L. Moody." You don't have to be a D. L. Moody. God doesn't want you to be a D. L. Moody. God wants you to be you and let Him do through you whatever He chooses. When you believe that nothing significant can happen through you, you have said more about your belief in God than you have said about yourself. You have said that God is not capable of doing anything significant through you. The truth is, He is able to do anything He pleases with one ordinary person fully consecrated to Him.

GOD'S PLAN FOR ME

When I say that I cannot do something significant for God, have I said more about my belief in God or about myself? What is God able to do through me? What must I be to Him?

JOHN THE BAPTIST

Don't be surprised that God's standards of excellence are different from ours. How long was the public ministry of John the Baptist? Perhaps six months. What was Jesus' estimate of John's life? "For I say to you, among those born of women there is not a greater prophet than John" (Luke 7:28). None greater! He had six months wholly yielded to God, and the Son of God put that stamp of approval on his life.

Don't measure your life by the world's standards. Don't do it. Many denominations are doing it. Many pastors and staff leaders are doing it. Many churches are doing it. Think about it. By the world's standards, a person or church may look pretty good, yet in God's sight be utterly detestable. Similarly, a person or church may be wholly yielded to Him and very pleasing to Him and in the world's eyes be insignificant. Could a pastor who faithfully serves where God put him in a small rural community be pleasing to the Lord? Sure, if that is where God put him. God will look for and reward faithfulness, whether the person has been given responsibility for little or much.

An ordinary person is who God most likes to use. Paul said God deliberately seeks out the weak things and the despised things because it is from them that He can receive the greatest glory (see 1 Cor. 1:26–31). Then everyone will know that only God could have done it. If you feel weak, limited, ordinary, you are the best material through which God can work!

GOD'S STANDARDS OF MEASUREMENT

What standard of measurement do I tend to use to measure my work for God? How does God measure my success for Him? If I feel weak, limited, or ordinary, what kind of material am I?

SUMMARY

The call to salvation is a call to be on mission with God as He reconciles a lost world to Himself through Christ. This calling requires that you be a servant of God. Jesus gave you the best model of servanthood, which was both humble and obedient. As a servant you must be moldable and remain available for the Master's use.

Even though you may consider yourself to be an ordinary person, God will prepare you; and then He will do His work through you, revealing Himself to a watching world.

EXPERIENCING GOD TODAY

Do you want to be a servant of God? Do you want to see God accomplishing things through you that only God can do? Do you want to experience the rest and the success Jesus described in Matthew 11:28–30? If so, find out where the Master is—then that is where you need to be. Find out what the Master is doing—then that is what you need to be doing. Jesus said: "If anyone serves Me, let him follow Me; and where I am, there My servant will be also. If anyone serves Me, him My father will honor" (John 12:26).

MY SURRENDER AS GOD'S SERVANT

God, I want to be Your servant. I know that I can do nothing on my own. I know that I cannot achieve the success that You call me to achieve. I depend entirely on You to do Your work through me. I know that You can do anything You choose to do. I give myself completely to You. Work through me any way You want to work. Show me where You are at work and include me in that work. I will not question Your call. I will do any work You show me to do wherever that work is. Lord, accept the worship and dedication of Your servant today.

Surely the Lord GOD does nothing, unless He reveals His secret to His servants the prophets.

AMOS 3:7

5

SEVEN REALITIES OF EXPERIENCING GOD

When God gets ready to do something, He reveals to a person or His people what He is going to do. God accomplishes His work through His people. This is the way God works with you. The Bible is designed to help you understand the ways of God. Then, when God starts to act in your life, you will recognize that it is God.

In studying the way God involved the men and women of the Bible in His work, I recognized three similarities these men and women shared:

- When God spoke, they knew it was God.
- They knew what God was saying.
- They knew what they were to do in response.

GOD REVEALS HIS WORK TO ME

Has God ever spoken to me in a way that I knew it was God? What did God say to me? What did God expect me to do in response?

SEVEN REALITIES OF EXPERIENCING GOD

1. God is always at work around you.
2. God pursues a continuing love relationship with you that is real and personal.
3. God invites you to become involved with Him in His work.
4. God speaks by the Holy Spirit through the Bible, prayer, circumstances, and the church to reveal Himself, His purposes, and His ways.
5. God's invitation for you to work with Him always leads you to a crisis of belief that requires faith and action.
6. You must make major adjustments in your life to join God in what He is doing.
7. You come to know God by experience as you obey Him and He accomplishes His work through you.

I also see common experiences that I call the seven realities of experiencing God. These are not steps to knowing and doing the will of God. They do, however, identify ways God works with a person or group to involve them in His work.

The remainder of this book will focus on these realities to help you understand how God works in and through your life. In this chapter I will give an overview. You will probably notice that I frequently repeat different aspects of this cycle. Many of the personal experiences I will share with you cannot be neatly fitted into any one category. At times various aspects of the realities will be more prominent than others. I will use the repetition in different situations to help you learn how you can respond to God's activity in your own life.

After reading through the seven realities you may have questions like:

- What is involved in a love relationship with God?
- How can I know when God is speaking?
- How do I know where God is at work?
- What kinds of adjustments does God require me to make?
- What is the difference between adjustment and obedience?

As I have worked with groups and individuals in many settings, I have been asked questions like these. I will try to answer many of your questions during the remaining chapters of this book.

MOSES' EXAMPLE

Moses' call and ministry are good examples of how God worked with Bible characters. His early life and call to ministry are described in chapters 2, 3, and 4 of Exodus. You may want to read those chapters as a background for the following discussion. Other passages help us see how Moses came to know and follow God's

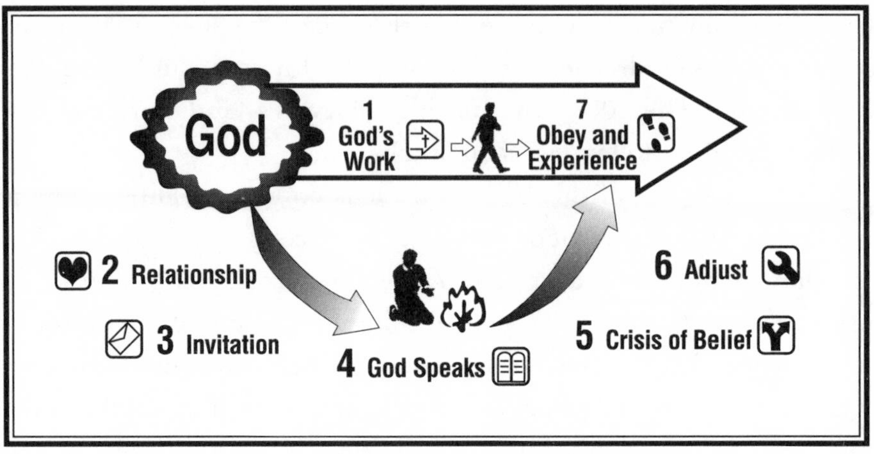

will. The experience of Moses at the burning bush seems to illustrate these realities. I have chosen to use his experience to illustrate for you the way I see God working in the Scriptures to accomplish His purposes through people. The illustration of The Seven Realities of Experiencing God below describes the way God worked with Moses. Notice that key words for each of the seven realities are on the diagram. Let's take a look at each of the realities and see how Moses experienced that reality.

REALITY 1:

God is always at work around you.

God did not create the world and then leave it to function on its own. He has been actively involved throughout history. In fact, He is orchestrating history. Because of sin, humanity has been separated from a right relationship with God. God Himself is working in His world to bring about redemption of those who are lost and dying without Him. The Father is working through Christ to reconcile the world to Himself. For some reason, God has chosen to do His work through His people. As He works to carry out His mission, He seeks to move a person into the mainstream of His activity.

GOD IS ALWAYS AT WORK

When did God begin to work in our world? What is His will in working through Christ? Through whom has He chosen to do His work? As God works, where does He prepare to bring me?

God already was at work around Moses when He came to Moses at the burning bush. God had a purpose that He was working out in Moses' world. Even though Moses was an exile in the desert, he was right on God's schedule, right in the fullness of God's timing, right in the middle of God's will.

Years earlier, God told Abraham that his descendants would be in bondage; but He would deliver them and give to them the Promised Land. God was watching and waiting for the right time to carry out His purposes for Israel. The time came when: "The children of Israel groaned because of the bondage and they cried out; and their cry came up to God because of the bondage. So God heard their groaning, and God remembered His covenant with Abraham, with Isaac, and with Jacob. And God looked upon the children of Israel, and God acknowledged them" (Exod. 2:23–25).

At the time God was about to deliver the children of Israel, the important factor was not what the will of God was for Moses. The important factor was what the will of God was for Israel. God was at work with Israel, and He was preparing to bring Moses into the mainstream of His activity.

REALITY 2:

God pursues a continuing love relationship with you that is real and personal.

God created humanity for a love relationship with Him. More than anything else, God wants us to love Him with our total being. He is the One who initiates the love relationship. In fact, He began with the sending of His Son Jesus. He clearly demonstrated how important the love relationship was to Him when He permitted Jesus to die in order to make it possible.

This love relationship with God is both real and personal. It is an intimate love relationship. This is probably the most important aspect of knowing and doing the will of God. If your love relationship with God is not right, nothing else will be right.

GOD PURSUES A LOVE RELATIONSHIP WITH ME

For what did God create me? How did He show me how important that love relationship with Him is? What is the most important aspect of knowing and doing the will of God?

God took the initiative to come to Moses and initiate a love relationship with him that was real and personal. Moses had led the sheep he was tending to "Horeb, the mountain of God" (Exod. 3:1). Very likely Moses had come to the mountain for a time of worship, but God interrupted Moses' plans by revealing Himself at the burning bush. God told Moses that He would go with Moses into Egypt. Many texts throughout Exodus, Leviticus, Numbers, and Deuteronomy illustrate how God pursued a continuing love relationship with Moses. Here is one example:

> Then the LORD said to Moses, "Come up to Me on the mountain and be there; and I will give you the tablets of stone, and the law and commandments which I have written, that you may teach them." . . . Then Moses went up into the mountain, and a cloud covered the mountain. Now the glory of the LORD rested on Mount Sinai. . . .

> Moses went into the midst of the cloud and went up into the mountain. And Moses was on the mountain forty days and forty nights. (Exod. 24:12, 15–16, 18)

Time and time again God invited Moses to talk with Him and to be with Him. God initiated and maintained a continuing relationship with Moses. This relationship was based on love, and daily God fulfilled His purposes through His "friend" Moses. The relationship with God was very practical as God guided and provided for His people under Moses' leadership. (For other examples of the love relationship, you may want to read Exod. 33:7–34:10 or Num. 12:6–8.)

REALITY 3:
God invites you to become involved with Him in His work.

God is a sovereign Ruler of the universe. He is the One who is at work, and He alone has the right to take the initiative to begin a work. He does not ask us to dream our dreams for Him and then ask Him to bless our plans. He is already at work when He comes to us. His desire is to get us from where we are to where He is working. When God reveals to you where He is working, that becomes His invitation to join Him. When God reveals His work to you, that is His timing for you to begin to respond to Him.

GOD'S INVITATION FOR ME TO BE INVOLVED IN HIS WORK

What right do I have to initiate a work for God? When God reveals where He is working, what does that become for me?

God's purpose was to deliver the children of Israel and establish them as a nation. Moses was the one through whom God wanted to work to accomplish that. God invited Moses to become involved with Him in His work. He said: "I have come down to deliver them [the Israelites] out of the hand of the Egyptians, and to bring them up from that land to a good and large land. . . . Come now, therefore, and I will send you to Pharaoh that you may bring My people, the children of Israel, out of Egypt" (Exod. 3:8, 10).

REALITY 4:

God speaks by the Holy Spirit through the Bible, prayer, circumstances, and the church to reveal Himself, His purposes, and His ways.

The testimony of the Bible from Genesis to Revelation is that God speaks to His people. In our day, God speaks to us through the Holy Spirit. He uses the Bible, prayer, circumstances, and the church (other believers). No one of these methods of God's speaking is, by itself, a clear indicator of God's directions. But when God says the same thing through each of these ways, you can have confidence to proceed.

God is going to be revealing Himself so you can trust Him and have faith in Him. He is going to reveal His purposes so you will be involved in His work rather than some other work. He reveals His ways so you can accomplish His purposes in a way that will glorify Him. God's ways are not our ways. You cannot discover these truths about God on your own. Truth is revealed.

GOD SPEAKS TO ME

Through what four ways does God speak? What does He seek to reveal when He speaks to me? When can I be confident to proceed?

God spoke to Moses through a unique experience at a burning bush to reveal Himself, His purposes, and His ways to Moses.

> And the Angel of the LORD appeared to him in a flame of fire from the midst of a bush. . . . God called to him from the midst of the bush and said, "Moses! Moses!" And he said, "Here I am."
>
> Then He said, "Do not draw near this place. Take your sandals off your feet, for the place where you stand is holy ground." Moreover He said, "I am the God of your father—the God of Abraham, the God of Isaac, and the God of Jacob."
>
> And the LORD said, "I have surely seen the oppression of My people who are in Egypt, and have heard their cry because of their taskmasters, for I know their sorrows. So I have come down to deliver them out of the hand of the Egyptians, and to bring them up from that land to a good and large land." (Exod. 3:2–8)
>
> "If there is a prophet among you, I, the LORD, make Myself known to him in a vision; I speak to him in a dream. Not so with My servant Moses; he is faithful in all My house. I speak with him face to face." (Num. 12:6–8)

God came and talked to Moses about His will. God wanted Moses to go to Egypt so He could deliver the Israelites through him. God revealed to Moses His holiness, His mercy, His power, His name, His purpose to keep His promise to Abraham and give Israel the Promised Land, and many other things not described in the Scriptures above. When God spoke through this burning bush, Moses knew it was God. He knew what God said, and he knew what he had to do to respond to the Lord.

REALITY 5:
God's invitation for you to work with Him always leads you to a crisis of belief that requires faith and action.

God is wanting to reveal Himself to a watching world. He does not call you to get involved just so people can see what you can do. He calls you to an assignment that you cannot do without Him. The assignment will have God-sized dimensions.

When God asks you to do something that you cannot do, you will face a crisis of belief. You will have to decide what you really believe about God. Can He and will He do what He has said He wants to do through you? What you do in response to His invitation reveals what you believe about God regardless of what you say.

This major turning point is where many people miss out on experiencing God's mighty power working through them. If they cannot see exactly how everything can be done, they will not proceed. They want to walk with God by sight. To follow God, you will have to walk by faith, and faith always requires action.

GOD'S INVITATION LEADS TO CRISIS OF BELIEF

What does God's invitation to me to work with Him always lead me to? What two things will this require from me? To follow God, what must I always walk by?

God's invitation for Moses to work with Him led to a crisis of belief that required faith and action. Moses expressed this crisis of belief when he made the following statements to God:

- "Who am I, that I should go to Pharaoh, and that I should bring the children of Israel out of Egypt?" (Exod. 3:11)
- "Indeed, when I come to the children of Israel and say to them, 'The God of your fathers has sent me to you,' and they

say to me, 'What is His name?' what shall I say to them?" (Exod. 3:13)

- "But suppose they will not believe me or listen to my voice; suppose they say, 'The LORD has not appeared to you?'" (Exod. 4:1)
- "O my Lord, I am not eloquent, neither before nor since You have spoken to Your servant; but I am slow of speech and slow of tongue." (Exod. 4:10)
- "O my Lord, please send by the hand of whomever else You may send." (Exod. 4:13)

Moses offered many objections. He questioned whether God could do it through him (Exod. 3:11), whether the Israelites would believe God had appeared to him (Exod. 4:1), and whether he was capable of speaking eloquently enough to get the job done (Exod. 4:10).

In each case Moses was really doubting God more than himself. He faced the crisis of belief—Is God really able to do what He says? God finally convinced Moses that he was to be involved in God's deliverance of Israel. Moses' faith is described in Hebrews, however, as a model of self-sacrifice and trust in an Almighty God. Once God let Moses know what He was about to do, that revelation became Moses' invitation to join Him. The writer of Hebrews describes Moses' faith and action:

> By faith Moses, when he became of age, refused to be called the son of Pharaoh's daughter, choosing rather to suffer affliction with the people of God than to enjoy the passing pleasures of sin, . . . By faith he forsook Egypt, not fearing the wrath of the king; for he endured as seeing Him who is invisible. By faith he kept the Passover and the sprinkling of blood, lest he who destroyed the firstborn should touch them. By faith they passed through the Red

> Sea as by dry land, whereas the Egyptians, attempting to do so, were drowned. (Heb. 11:24–29)

REALITY 6:
You must make major adjustments in your life to join God in what He is doing.

This is a second major turning point at which many miss out on experiencing God. To get from where you are to where God is will require major adjustments. These adjustments may relate to your thinking, circumstances, relationships, commitments, actions, and/or beliefs. Some people think that these adjustments are not major. However, anytime you go from where you are to where God is you will have to make major adjustments. To move from your way of thinking or acting to God's way of thinking or acting will require adjustments. You cannot stay where you are and go with God at the same time.

GOD CALLS FOR ADJUSTMENTS IN MY LIFE

> *To join in what God is doing, what adjustments must I make in my life? From whose way must I move? To whose way must I move? If I make these adjustments, what will God accomplish through me?*

Moses had to make major adjustments in his life to join God in what He was doing. Moses couldn't stay in the desert and stand before Pharaoh at the same time. God said: "'Go, return to Egypt; for all the men who sought your life are dead.' Then Moses took his wife and his sons and set them on a donkey, and he returned to the land of Egypt" (Exod. 4:19–20).

Moses made the necessary adjustments to orient his life to God. Moses had to come to the place where he believed God could do everything He said He would do. Then he had to leave his job and in-laws and move to Egypt. After making these adjustments, he was in a position where he could obey God. That did not mean he was going to do something all by himself for God. It meant he was going to be where God was working so God could do what He had purposed to do in the first place. Moses was a servant who was moldable, and he remained at God's disposal to be used as God chose. God accomplished His purposes through Moses.

REALITY 7:

You come to know God by experience as you obey Him and He accomplishes His work through you.

Once you have determined to follow God by faith and you have made the required adjustments to God, you must obey Him. When you do what He tells you, no matter how insensible it may seem, God accomplishes what He purposed through you. Not only do you experience God's power and presence, but so do those who observe what you are doing.

EXPERIENCE GOD AS I OBEY HIM

What is the connection between my obedience and my experimental knowledge of God?

Moses came to know God by experience as he obeyed God, and God accomplished His work through Moses. Many texts throughout Exodus, Leviticus, Numbers, and Deuteronomy illustrate how God revealed Himself to Moses. As Moses obeyed God, God accomplished through Moses what Moses could not do. Here is one example where Moses and the people came to know God as their Deliverer. The people were on their way out of Egypt when they came to the Red Sea. They couldn't go forward, and the Egyptian army was coming from behind them. The people could see no way out, but then God spoke:

> And the LORD said to Moses, "Why do you cry to me? Tell the children of Israel to go forward. But lift up your rod, and stretch out your hand over the sea and divide it. And the children of Israel shall go on dry ground through the midst of the sea. And I indeed will harden the hearts of the Egyptians, and they shall follow them. So I will gain honor over Pharaoh and over all his army. . . ."
>
> Then Moses stretched out his hand over the sea; and the LORD caused the sea to go back by a strong east wind all that night, and made the sea into dry land, and the waters were divided. So the children of Israel went into the midst of the sea on the dry ground, and the waters were a wall to them on their right hand and on their left. And the Egyptians pursued and went after them. . . .
>
> Then the LORD said to Moses, "Stretch out your hand over the sea, that the waters may come back upon the Egyptians, on their chariots, and on their horsemen." And Moses stretched out his hand over the sea; and when the morning appeared, the sea returned to its full depth. . . . But the children of Israel had walked on dry land in the midst of the sea, and the waters were a wall to them on their right hand and on their left.
>
> So the LORD saved Israel that day out of the hands of the Egyptians, and Israel saw the Egyptians dead on the seashore. Thus Israel saw the great work which the LORD had done in Egypt; so the people feared the LORD, and believed the LORD and His servant Moses. (Exod. 14:15–17, 21–23, 26–27, 29–31)

Moses must have felt humility and unworthiness to be used in such a significant way. Moses obeyed and did everything God told him. Then God accomplished through Moses all He intended. Every step of obedience brought Moses (and Israel) to a greater knowledge of God (see Exod. 6:1–8).

SUMMARY

God is at work reconciling a world to Himself. Because He loves you, He wants to involve you in His work. He begins by pursuing a love relationship that is both real and personal. He then invites you to be involved with Him. He reveals Himself, His purposes, and His ways. If you want to experience God's mighty power at work in and through you, you must walk by faith, make major adjustments, and obey whatever God tells you to do.

EXPERIENCING GOD TODAY

Spend some time in prayer with your heavenly Father. Pray through the Seven Realities of Experiencing God, and ask the Father to help you understand how He works with His people.

1. God is always at work around you.
2. God pursues a continuing love relationship with you that is real and personal.
3. God invites you to become involved with Him in His work.
4. God speaks by the Holy Spirit through the Bible, prayer, circumstances, and the church to reveal Himself, His purposes, and His ways.
5. God's invitation for you to work with Him always leads you to a crisis of belief that requires faith and action.
6. You must make major adjustments in your life to join God in what He is doing.

7. You come to know God by experience as you obey Him and He accomplishes His work through you.

MY SURRENDER TO GOD'S REALITIES

God, thank You for revealing Your ways to me. Help me understand each one of these realities. Show me how each of the realities relates to my life right now. Do I need to focus on one of these realities? Show me how. I want You to work through me. I am ready to make the major adjustments in my life that You require. I am ready to believe You and everything You ask me to do. I am ready to obey You and see You accomplish Your work through me. Thank You that I may experience Your presence and Your power. Work through me today, O Lord.

My Father has been working until now, and I have been working. . . . Most assuredly, I say to you, the Son can do nothing of Himself; but what He sees the Father do; for whatever He does, the Son also does in like manner. For the Father loves the Son, and shows Him all things that He Himself does.

JOHN 5:17, 19–20

GOD IS AT WORK AROUND YOU

When I want to learn how to know and do the will of God, I always look to Jesus. I can find no better model than Him. Although Jesus was God, He was also completely human. During His thirty-three years on earth, Jesus perfectly fulfilled every assignment God gave Him. He never failed to do His Father's will. He never sinned.

Would you like to understand how Jesus came to know and do the will of God? Jesus described His process in John 5 above. This is one of the clearest statements of how Jesus knew what to do. Before looking at Jesus' approach to knowing and doing His Father's will, however, let's review Jesus' relationship to the Father.

GOD'S MODEL FOR MY EXPERIENCE OF HIM

Who is the model God has given me to understand how to experience Him through obeying Him? While on earth, what did Jesus do with every assignment God gave Him?

THE TRINITY

Jesus was and still is God. Although we may have difficulty understanding it, God the Father, Jesus the Son, and God the Holy Spirit are all three Persons of the Godhead. They are not three separate gods. They are all one God. God is so great and majestic, our human minds cannot fully understand His nature.

Throughout the Scriptures, we can see that when God chose to reveal Himself to humanity, He did it in one of three ways: in the Person of the Father, the Son, or the Spirit. Whenever God is working, all three Persons of the Trinity are working.

The disciples had trouble understanding this truth also. Even after three years with Jesus, Philip asked, "Lord, show us the Father," and Jesus responded, "Have I been with you so long, and yet you have not known Me, Philip? He who has seen me has seen the Father. . . . Do you not believe that I am in the Father, and the Father in Me? The words that I speak to you I do not speak on My own authority; but the Father who dwells in Me does the works" (John 14:9–10).

As we look together at the ministry of Jesus, we need to keep in mind that He was fully human. Therefore, He is an example of what perfect humanity would look like. He is the best possible model for us to follow. But, at the same time, Jesus was also fully God. Jesus described the way His Father guided His own work, but He also said that He and His Father are one. Don't let the majesty of this truth distract you from the wonderful example Jesus has given us to follow.

GOD INVOLVES US

The first thing Jesus recognized is that His Father was always at His work. God did not create the world and then just leave it to run all by itself. He is not just sitting in some heavenly place passively observing all the activity on earth. God is orchestrating history. He is present and in the middle of all history. God is the One who is at work redeeming a lost world. His desire is to involve His people and His servants. Paul described this relationship to the church at Corinth:

> Therefore, if anyone is in Christ, he is a new creation; old things have passed away; behold, all things have become new! Now all things are of God, who has reconciled us to Himself through Jesus Christ, and has given us the ministry of reconciliation, that is, that God was in Christ reconciling the world to Himself, not imputing their trespasses to them, and has committed to us the word of reconciliation. Now then, we are ambassadors for Christ, as though God were pleading through us. (2 Cor. 5:17–20)

God has been at work in our world. He is presently at work in our world. Because of His love He wants us to have the privilege of working with Him as His ambassadors. God, however, is the One who is present to do His work through us.

Not only did Jesus acknowledge that His Father was working, but He also said that His Father now had Him [Jesus] working. Then Jesus described His approach to knowing and doing God's will. I would outline it like this:

JESUS' EXAMPLE

The Father has been working right up until now.
Now the Father has Me working.
I do nothing on My own initiative.
I watch to see what the Father is doing.
I do what I see the Father already is doing.
You see, the Father loves Me.
He shows Me everything that He, Himself, is doing.

THE FATHER'S WORK THROUGH JESUS

This description of Jesus' reveals several of the key elements in the Seven Realities of Experiencing God. God is at work. He pursues a love relationship and invites Jesus to be involved with Him by revealing what He is doing. Jesus then makes the adjustment to do what His Father is doing. Jesus spoke several times about this relationship:

- "My doctrine is not Mine, but His who sent Me." (John 7:16)
- "When you lift up the Son of Man, then you will know that I am He, and that I do nothing of Myself; but as My Father taught Me, I speak these things." (John 8:28)
- "If I do not do the works of My Father, do not believe Me; but if I do, though you do not believe Me, believe the works, that you may know and believe that the Father is in Me, and I in Him." (John 10:37–38)

- "For I have not spoken on My own authority; but the Father who sent Me gave Me a command, what I should say and what I should speak." (John 12:49)
- "The words that I speak to you I do not speak on My own authority; but the Father who dwells in Me does the works." (John 14:10)
- "For I have given to them the words which You [the Father] have given Me." (John 17:8)

Later, Peter recognized that this was the relationship Jesus had with His Father. He explained, "Jesus of Nazareth, a Man attested by God to you by miracles, wonders and signs *which God did through Him in your midst*" (Acts 2:22, italics added). God the Father did His work through Jesus the Son.

Jesus realized that He could do nothing by Himself. Yet with the Father at work in Him, He could do anything. If Jesus was that dependent on the Father, then you and I should realize we are even more dependent on God the Father to be working in and through us.

This is not just a step-by-step approach for knowing and doing the will of God. It describes a love relationship through which God accomplishes His purposes. Once you have an intimate love relationship with God, He will show you what He is doing. Your job as a servant is to follow Jesus' example: Do what the Father is already doing—*watch to see where God is at work and join Him!*

JOINING GOD'S WORK

If I am to join God in His work, what must I watch for?

WATCHING FOR GOD AT WORK ON THE CAMPUS

While I pastored Faith Baptist Church in Saskatoon, we began to sense God leading us to an outreach ministry to the college campus. I had never done student work. Our church had never done student work. Our denominational student ministries department recommended we begin with a Bible study in the dorms. For almost two years we tried to start a Bible study in the dorms, and it did not work.

One Sunday I pulled our students together and said, "This week I want you to go to the campus and watch to see where God is working and join Him." They asked me to explain. God had impressed on my heart these two Scriptures: "There is none righteous, no, not one; there is none who understands; there is none who seeks after God" (Rom. 3:10–11) and "No one can come to Me [Jesus] unless the Father who sent Me draws him" (John 6:44).

I went on to explain, "According to these passages, no one is going to seek God on his own initiative. No one will ask after spiritual matters unless God is at work in his life. When you see someone seeking God or asking about spiritual matters, you are seeing God at work. That is something only God does in a life."

For example, when Jesus passed through a crowd, He always looked for where the Father was at work. The crowd was not the harvest field. The harvest field was within the crowd. In Jericho, Jesus saw Zacchaeus in a tree. Jesus may have said to Himself, "Nobody can seek after Me with that kind of earnestness unless My Father is at work in his heart." So Jesus pulled away from the crowd and said, "Zacchaeus, make haste and come down, for today I must stay at your house" (Luke 19:5). What happened? Salvation came to that household that night. Jesus always looked for the activity of the Father and joined Him. Salvation came as a result of Jesus' joining His life to the activity of His Father.

I told our students, "If someone starts asking you spiritual questions, whatever else you have planned, don't do it. Cancel what you are doing. Go with that individual and look to see what God is doing there." That week our students went out to see where God was at work on the campus and to join Him.

On Wednesday one of the girls reported, "Oh Pastor, a girl who has been in classes with me for two years came to me after class today. She said, 'I think you might be a Christian. I need to talk to you.' I remembered what you said. I had a class, but I missed it. We went to the cafeteria to talk. She said, 'Eleven of us girls in the dorm have been studying the Bible, and none of us are Christians. Do you know somebody who can lead us in a Bible study?'"

As a result of that contact, we started three Bible study groups in the women's dorms and two in the men's dorm. For almost two years we tried to do something for God and failed. For three days we looked to see where God was working and joined Him. What a difference that made! Over the following years many students trusted Christ as Savior and Lord. Many of those surrendered to full-time ministry and are now serving as pastors and missionaries all over the world.

WATCHING FOR GOD AT WORK AROUND ME

In the past, have I been watching for the Father's work around me or planning and doing my own work for the Father?

GOD IS ALWAYS ACTIVE

Right now God is working all around you and in your life. One of the greatest tragedies among God's people is that while they have a deep longing to experience Him, they are experiencing God day after day but do not know how to recognize Him. If this has been true of your own Christian experience, I pray that this book will help you learn ways to recognize clearly the activity of God in and around your life. I pray that God will open your spiritual eyes to see what He is doing. The Holy Spirit and the Word of God will instruct you and help you know when and where God is working.

Once you know where He is working, you can adjust your life to join Him where He is working.

Once you join God in what He is doing, you will experience Him accomplishing His activity through your life. When you enter this kind of intimate love relationship with God, you will know and do the will of God and experience Him in ways you have never known Him before. Only God can bring you into that kind of relationship, but He stands ready to do so.

GOD WORKING AROUND ME

Once I know where God is working, what can I do? What will happen to me once I enter a love relationship with Him?

DON'T BYPASS THE LOVE RELATIONSHIP

Many people want God to call them to a big assignment. However, they try to bypass the love relationship. As we will see later, the love relationship is why God created you. That is far more important to Him than what you do. So anticipate that God will start working with you and drawing you to an intimate love relationship that is real and personal. When the love relationship is right, God will be free to begin giving you assignments at His initiative. Whenever you do not seem to be receiving assignments from God, focus on the love relationship and stay there until the assignment comes.

WHAT GOD WILL NOT LET ME BYPASS

What should I do if I have not received an assignment from the Lord?

FOCUS ON THE CALL TO AN ASSIGNMENT

I believe many people today are seeking God's call to ministry or an assignment backwards. We teach people to discover their spiritual gifts and then look for an assignment in which they can use their gifts. That can be a frustrating experience for a person looking for their first assignment from God. You see, a spiritual gift is a manifestation of the Holy Spirit at work through a person in carrying out a God-given assignment. Normally, a person will not know his or her spiritual giftedness without first receiving an assignment. When God gives an assignment, a person obeys and God accomplishes what He intended through the person. The evidence of God's supernatural activity is what we usually identify as spiritual gifts. A person who has never accepted an assignment will not likely know or see his or her spiritual gifts.

Seeking to identify gifts instead of the assignment also can be severely limiting for a believer who only bases his or her future usefulness to God on his or her past usefulness. The way many people teach about spiritual gifts, God can only use you in assignments that require gifts you have seen evidenced in the past. Consequently many people get an assignment from God and say, "That couldn't possibly be from God. That is not the area of my gifts." If it is an assignment from God, you obey Him and you will see the manifestation of the Holy Spirit in new ways you may never have experienced before.

The common approach to spiritual gifts also can become very self-centered, rather than God-centered, if you take the initiative to decide on an assignment that you think fits you. Truth is not discovered; it is revealed. Only God can tell you what He is doing or is wanting to do through your life. You will not be able to figure that out on your own.

Wait just a moment! This may cause you to disagree violently with me. Before you shut this book, let me share with you what I see as spiritual giftedness in the Scriptures. If you are having trouble at this point, pause and pray right now that the Holy Spirit will be your Teacher. Don't accept what I have to say unless the Holy

Spirit confirms it and it is in keeping with the teaching of Scripture. Ask God to help you understand the relationship between a God-given assignment and a spiritual gift.

GOD'S ASSIGNMENT FOR ME

Will every assignment from God be in the area of spiritual gifts I know I have? What will I see when I carry out God's assignment? If God calls me to an assignment for which I have never experienced a spiritual giftedness, how should I respond?

THE OLD TESTAMENT PATTERN

The Old Testament is the kindergarten for understanding the Holy Spirit's work in the New Testament. In the Old Testament the Holy Spirit came upon individuals to help them achieve an assignment God had given them. Moses had an assignment as an administrator and national religious leader. Moses, however, didn't think he was gifted for this assignment, so he argued with God.

God knew exactly what He was doing when He called Moses. Moses' success was not dependent on Moses' skills, abilities, likes, preferences, or past successes. God first gave Moses an assignment, and then God equipped him with His Holy Spirit to administrate and lead. When Moses obeyed God, he used his "spiritual giftedness." The results revealed that God was at work through Moses doing things Moses could not do on his own.

David was called to be king when he was a shepherd. How could he possibly be king when he had never been king? Even David's father thought David was the least likely of his sons to be king of the nation. The Spirit of God came upon David, however, and equipped him to be king.

God gave each of the judges an assignment. Then the Spirit of God came upon each one and equipped him or her to complete the assignment given. Ezekiel was called to be a prophet. How could he possibly be a prophet? The Scripture says the Spirit of God came upon him and caused him to do everything God asked of him (Ezek. 2–3). Here is the pattern we see in the Old Testament:

- God gave an assignment to a person.
- The Holy Spirit was given to that person to equip him or her for the assignment.
- The proof of the Spirit's presence was that the person was able to complete the assignment effectively through the supernatural enabling of the Holy Spirit.

The workmen of the Tabernacle are a clear example. God gave Moses specific details about how to build the Tabernacle (Exod. 25–30). He wanted it done exactly as He had instructed Moses. Then God said, "See, I have called by name Bezalel the son of Uri, the son of Hur, of the tribe of Judah. And I have filled him with the Spirit of God, in wisdom, in understanding, in knowledge, and in all manner of workmanship. . . . And I, indeed I, have appointed with him Aholiab . . . and I have put wisdom in the hearts of all the gifted artisans, that they may make all that I have commanded you" (Exod. 31:2–3, 6).

How would Moses have known if the Spirit of God was upon those men? He would have watched them at work. If they were enabled to carry out the assignment God had given, Moses would have known the Spirit of God was upon them.

Throughout the Old Testament, the Spirit of God always was present to equip an individual to carry out a divine assignment. God didn't give a person some *thing*. God *Himself* was the *Gift*. The Spirit manifested His presence by equipping each individual to function where God had assigned him. The results reflected God's activity.

LEARNING FROM THE BIBLE

What gift did God give people in the Old Testament? When people functioned where God assigned them, what did the results always reflect?

THE HOLY SPIRIT EQUIPS EACH MEMBER TO FUNCTION IN THE BODY

The first part of 1 Corinthians 12 talks about the Holy Spirit enabling each member. Verse 7 says, "But the manifestation of the Spirit is given to each one for the profit of all." The Holy Spirit is the Gift (Acts 2:38). The Holy Spirit manifests (makes visible, clear, known; reveals) Himself to each member of the body for the common good of the body.

All members of the church—Christ's body—are gifted by the Holy Spirit's presence. Each person's experience of the Holy Spirit is for the good of the body, not for himself or herself. That is why we need each other. Without a healthy and functioning body, a church will miss much of the good God provides for it.

When members of a church begin considering spiritual gifts, they sometimes run into difficulty by thinking that God gives them some *thing*—like an ingredient called administration. No, He doesn't give some *thing;* He gives *Himself.* The Gift is a Person. The Holy Spirit equips you with His administrative ability. So His administration begins to become your administration. What you observe when you see a spiritual gift exercised is a manifestation of the Holy Spirit—you see the Holy Spirit equipping and enabling an individual with His abilities and capabilities to accomplish God's work.

Jesus said: "The Father who dwells in Me does the works" (John 14:10). Even in Jesus' miraculous works, the Father was manifesting Himself. The Father was in Jesus, and He worked through Jesus to accomplish His purposes. Then Jesus said about you: "Without Me you can do nothing" (John 15:5).

A spiritual gift is a manifestation of God at work through you. God works in and through you to bear fruit. The focus is on God and what He does through you. When you focus on some *thing* you receive to do something good for God, the focus is usually on self rather than God.

Now, you may have been through a study on spiritual gifts that seemed to prove very helpful to you. Often when people have a positive experience with a spiritual gifts inventory, it is because the person has been involved with assignments from God before. What he or she sees of God manifested in those experiences is described as a spiritual gift. This is the pattern I see in the Scriptures: God gives an assignment and the Holy Spirit manifests Himself through a person in accomplishing the assignment through him or her.

Focus your attention on hearing God's call to an assignment, His invitation for you to join Him. When you adjust your life to Him and obey Him, the Holy Spirit will be at work in you enabling you to accomplish all that God desires.

THE HOLY SPIRIT EQUIPS ME

To whom does the Holy Spirit reveal Himself? Why? Which members of the church are gifted by the Spirit? What is a spiritual gift? Should I place a greater focus on the gift or the assignment?

SUMMARY

God is always at work in His world. He is working to bring about world redemption through His Son Jesus Christ. Jesus described the way He knew and did the will of His Father. Because the

Father loved His Son, He showed the Son what He was doing. Jesus watched to see where the Father was working and joined Him. You can follow that same pattern by watching to see where God is at work. When He shows you, join Him in His work. Focus your attention on God's call to an assignment rather than on your spiritual gifts, personal desires, personal skills, abilities, or resources. Once you understand God's call to an assignment, obey Him and He will work through you to accomplish His purposes.

EXPERIENCING GOD TODAY

Reflect about your own experiences with God. Can you identify times when God was at work around you—and you knew it? Do you now realize God was working around you in past situations and you did not recognize it as God's work at the time?

MY SURRENDER TO GOD'S WORK

Dear God, I know You are always at work around me. Thank You that You are redeeming this lost world through Jesus. I want to be a participant in that work. Thank You that You have chosen to work through ordinary people like me. I am ready to work. Let me see where You are working. I seek Your invitation to join You in Your work. I wait for You to take the initiative. I want to work with You because I love You and I want to continue in this wonderful love relationship You have started with me. Make me attentive to Your Holy Spirit. Show me Your assignment for me. I am reporting for duty when You are ready. I know You will work through me to accomplish Your perfect will.

Jesus said to him, "You shall love the Lord your God with all your heart, with all your soul, and with all your mind. This is the first and great commandment."

MATTHEW 22:37–38

GOD PURSUES A LOVE RELATIONSHIP WITH YOU

God Himself pursues a love relationship with you. He is the One who takes the initiative to bring you into this kind of relationship. He created you for a love relationship with Himself. That is the very purpose of your life. This love relationship can and should be real and personal to you.

This love relationship, however, is not a one-sided affair. He wants you to know Him and worship Him. Most of all, He wants you to love Him. Jesus said, "He who has My commandments and keeps them, it is he who loves Me. And he who loves Me will be loved by My Father, and I will love him and manifest Myself to him"(John 14:21). If you want God to reveal Himself to you, you must love Him and obey Him.

GOD'S PURPOSE FOR MY LIFE

God's purpose for me is a . . .

What two characteristics should this relationship have to me?

What three ways do I respond in this relationship? If I want God to reveal Himself to me, what must I do?

OBEDIENCE AND LOVE

Jesus said, "If you love Me, keep My commandments" (John 14:15). When you obey Jesus, you show that you love and trust Him. The Father loves those who love His Son. For those who love Him, Jesus said He would love them and show Himself to them. Obedience is the outward expression of your love of God.

The reward for obedience and love is that He will show Himself to you. Jesus set an example for you in His life. He said, "But that the world may know that I love the Father, and as the Father gave Me commandment, so I do" (John 14:31). Jesus was obedient to every command of the Father. He demonstrated His love for the Father by obedience.

A love relationship with God requires that you demonstrate your love by obedience. This is not just a following of the "letter" of the law, but it is a following of the "spirit" of the command as well. If you have an obedience problem, you have a love problem. Focus your attention on God's love. If you were standing before God, could you describe your relationship to Him by saying, "I love You with all my heart and all my soul and all my mind and all my strength"?

DIFFICULTY WITH THE RELATIONSHIP

One of our church members always was having difficulty in his personal life, in his family, at work, and in the church. One day I went to him and asked, "Can you describe your relationship with God by sincerely saying, 'I love You with all of my heart'?"

The strangest look came over his face. He said, "Nobody has ever asked me that. No, I could not describe my relationship with God that way. I could say I obey Him, I serve Him, I worship Him, and I fear Him. But I cannot say that I love Him."

I realized that everything in his life was out of order because God's basic purpose for his life was out of order. God created us for a love relationship with Him. If you cannot describe your relationship with God by saying that you love Him with all your being, then you need to ask the Holy Spirit to bring you into that kind of a relationship.

If I were to try to summarize the entire Old Testament, it would be expressed in this verse: "Hear, O Israel: The LORD our God, the LORD is one! You shall love the LORD your God with all your heart, with all your soul, and with all your strength" (Deut. 6:4–5).

THE GREATEST COMMANDMENT

This heart-cry of God is expressed throughout the Old Testament. The essence of the New Testament is the same. Quoting from Deuteronomy, Jesus said the greatest commandment in the law is: "And you shall love the Lord your God with all your heart, with all your soul, with all your mind, and with all your strength" (Mark 12:30). Everything depends on this! Everything in your Christian life, everything about knowing Him and experiencing Him, everything about knowing His will depends on the quality of your love relationship to God. If that is not right, nothing in your life will be right. Notice what God has to say about a love relationship:

> I call heaven and earth as witnesses today against you, that I have set before you life and death, blessing and cursing; therefore choose life, that both you and your descendants may live; that you may love the LORD your God, that you may obey His voice, and that you may cling to Him, for He is your life. (Deut. 30:19–20)
>
> For God so loved the world that He gave His only begotten Son, that whosoever believes in Him should not perish but have everlasting life. (John 3:16)
>
> He who has My commandments and keeps them, it is he who loves me. And he who loves Me will be loved by My Father, and I will love him and manifest Myself to him. (John 14:21)
>
> Who shall separate us from the love of Christ? Shall tribulation, or distress, or persecution, or famine, or nakedness, or peril, or sword? . . . No, in all these things we are more than conquerors through Him who loved us. . . . [Nothing] shall be able to separate us from the love of God which is in Christ Jesus our Lord. (Rom. 8:35, 37, 39)
>
> By this we know love, because He laid down His life for us. And we also ought to lay down our lives for the brethren. (1 John 3:16)
>
> In this the love of God was manifested toward us, that God has sent His only begotten Son into the world, that we might live through Him. In this is love, not that we loved God, but that He loved us and sent His Son to be the propitiation for our sins. . . . We love Him because He first loved us. (1 John 4:9–10, 19)

Do you realize that the Lord does not just give you life—He *is* your life? He has drawn you to Himself. He sent His only Son to provide eternal life for you. Jesus laid down His life for you. You did not initiate a love relationship with God. He initiated a love relationship with you. In fact, God loved you before you came into the world. He began to demonstrate His love for you on the cross of Jesus.

Because God has loved you, He wants you to love Him as well. The Scriptures above indicate some of the ways you can express your love for Him. You can choose life, listen to His voice, hold fast to Him, believe in His only Son, obey His commands and teachings, and be willing to lay down your life for your Christian brothers and sisters.

When you do love God, He promises to respond with His blessings. You and your children will live under His blessings. By trusting in Jesus, you have eternal life. The Father will love you. God will come to make His home with you. He will make you more than a conqueror over all difficulties. You never will be separated from His love.

What is the one thing God wants from you? He wants you to love Him with all your being. That is the greatest commandment. Your experiencing God depends on your having this relationship of love. A love relationship with God is more important than any other single factor in your life.

WHAT EVERYTHING DEPENDS ON

Everything in my experience with God depends on the quality of my . . .

If that is not right, what in my life will be right? Why does God want me to love Him?

YOUR FIRST LOVE

Picture in your mind a tall ladder leaning against a wall. Now think about your life as a process of climbing that ladder. Wouldn't it be a tragedy to get to the top of the ladder and find you placed it against the wrong wall? One life to live and you missed it!

Your relationship to God (Father, Son, and Spirit) is the single most important aspect of your life. If it is not right, nothing else is important.

If you knew that all you had was a relationship with Him, would you be totally and completely satisfied? Many people would say, "Well, I would like to have that relationship, but I sure would like to do something" or "I sure would like for Him to give me a ministry or give me something to do."

We are a "doing" people. We feel worthless or useless if we are not busy doing something. The Scripture leads us to understand that God is saying, "I want you to love me above everything else. When you are in a relationship of love with Me, you have everything there is." To be loved by God is the highest relationship, the highest achievement, and the highest position in life.

That does not mean you will never do anything as an expression of your love for Him. God will call you to obey Him and do whatever He asks of you. However, you do not need to be doing something to feel fulfilled. You are fulfilled completely in a relationship with God. When you are filled with Him, what else do you need?

NO COMPETITORS

Do you really want to love the Lord your God with all of your heart? He will allow no competitors. He says:

> No one can serve two masters; for either he will hate the one and love the other, or else he will be loyal to the one

> and despise the other. You cannot serve God and mammon. (Matt. 6:24)
>
> When you have eaten and are full—then beware, lest you forget the LORD. . . . (for the LORD your God is a jealous God among you). (Deut. 6:11, 12, 15)
>
> So it shall be, when the LORD your God brings you into the land of which He swore to your fathers, to Abraham, Isaac and Jacob, to give you large and beautiful cities which you did not build, houses full of all good things, which you did not fill, hewn-out wells which you did not dig, vineyards and olive trees which you did not plant—when you have eaten and are full—then beware, lest you forget the LORD who brought you out of the land of Egypt, from the house of bondage. You shall fear the LORD your God and serve Him, and shall take oaths in His name. You shall not go after other gods, the gods of the peoples who are all around you (for the LORD your God is a jealous God among you). (Deut. 6:10–15)
>
> Therefore do not worry, saying, "What shall we eat?" or "What shall we drink?" or "What shall we wear?" For after all these things the Gentiles seek. For your heavenly Father knows that you need all these things. But seek first the kingdom of God and His righteousness, and all these things will be added to you. (Matt. 6:31–33)

Out of His love for you, He will provide all else that you need—when you love Him and Him alone.

THE PURSUIT

God always takes the initiative in this love relationship. God must take the initiative and come to us if we are to experience Him. This is the witness of the entire Bible. He came to Adam and Eve in the

Garden of Eden. In love He fellowshipped with them, and they with Him. He came to Noah, Abraham, Moses, and the prophets. God took the initiative for each person in the Old Testament to experience Him in a personal fellowship of love. This is true of the New Testament as well. Jesus came to the disciples and chose them to be with Him and experience His love. He came to Paul on the Damascus Road. In our natural human state, we do not seek God on our own initiative. "There is none righteous, no, not one; there is none who understands; there is none who seeks after God. They have all turned aside; they have together become unprofitable; there is none who does good, no, not one" (Rom. 3:10–12).

Sin has affected us so deeply that no one seeks after God on his own initiative. Therefore, if we are to have any relationship with Him or His Son, God will have to take the initiative. This is exactly what He does. God draws us to Himself. The Scriptures testify to the drawing activity of God:

> No one can come to Me unless the Father who sent Me draws him. . . . Everyone who has heard and learned from the Father comes to Me. . . . Therefore I have said to you that no one can come to Me unless it has been granted to him by My Father. (John 6:44–45, 65)
>
> The LORD has appeared to me of old saying: "Yes, I have loved you with an everlasting love; Therefore with lovingkindness I have drawn you. (Jer. 31:3)
>
> I drew them with gentle cords, with bands of love, and I was to them as those who take the yoke from their neck. (Hos. 11:4)

The love that God focuses on your life is an everlasting love. Because of that love, He has drawn you to Himself. He has drawn you with cords of love when you were not His friend, when you were His enemy. He gave His own Son to die for you. To firmly anchor the experiencing of God and the knowing of His will, you must be absolutely convinced of God's love for you.

Paul. God came to Saul, known later as Paul (Acts 9:1–19). Saul was actually opposing God and His activities and fighting against God's Son Jesus. Jesus came to Paul and revealed the Father's purposes of love for him. This also is true in our lives. We do not choose Him. He chooses us, loves us, and reveals His eternal purposes for our lives.

The Disciples. Jesus said to those who were His disciples: "You did not choose Me, but I chose you. . . . You are not of the world, but I chose you out of the world" (John 15:16, 19). Didn't Peter choose to follow Jesus? No. Jesus chose Peter. Peter responded to the invitation of God. God took the initiative.

Jesus and Peter.

> When Jesus came to the region of Caesarea Philippi, He asked His disciples, saying, "Who do men say that I, the Son of Man, am?"
>
> So they said, "Some say John the Baptist, some Elijah, and others Jeremiah or one of the prophets."
>
> He said to them, "But who do you say that I am?"
>
> Simon Peter answered and said, "You are the Christ, the Son of the living God."
>
> Jesus answered and said unto him, "Blessed are you, Simon Bar-Jonah, for flesh and blood has not revealed this to you, but My Father who is in heaven." (Matt. 16:13–17)

Jesus said that Peter was responding to God's initiative in his life. Jesus asked the disciples who men said He was. Then He asked them who they said He was. Peter answered correctly, "You are the Christ." Then Jesus made a very significant statement to Peter, "This was not revealed to you by man, but by my Father in heaven."

In essence Jesus was saying, "Peter, you could never have known and confessed that I am the Christ unless My Father had been at work in you. He caused you to know who I am. You are responding to the Father's activity in your life. Good!"

Do you realize that God determined to love you? Apart from that, you never would have become a Christian. He had something in mind when He called you. He began to work in your life. You began to experience a love relationship with God where He took the initiative. He began to open your understanding. He drew you to Himself. What did you do?

When you responded to His invitation, He brought you into a love relationship with Himself. But you would never know that love, be in the presence of that love, or be aware of that love if God had not taken the initiative. The following Scriptures describe the initiatives God takes to have a love relationship with you.

> And the LORD your God will circumcise your heart and the heart of your descendants, to love the LORD your God with all your heart and with all your soul, that you may live. (Deut. 30:6)
>
> All things have been delivered to me by my Father, and no one knows who the Son is except the Father, and who the Father is except the Son, and the one to whom the Son wills to reveal Him. (Luke 10:22)
>
> You did not choose Me, but I chose you and appointed you to go and bear fruit, and that your fruit should remain. (John 15:16)
>
> For it is God who works in you both to will and to do for His good pleasure. (Phil. 2:13)

> By this we know love, because He laid down His life for us. (1 John 3:16)
>
> Behold, I stand at the door and knock. If anyone hears My voice and opens the door, I will come in to him and dine with him, and he with Me. (Rev. 3:20)

God always takes the initiative to establish a love relationship with you.

SEEKING GOD

Why do I not seek after God on my own initiative? If I am to have a relationship with God, who must take the initiative? What is required for me to anchor firmly the experiencing of God and to know His will for certain?

CREATED NOT FOR TIME, BUT ETERNITY

God did not create you for time; He created you for eternity. Time (your lifetime on earth) provides the opportunity to get acquainted with Him. It is an opportunity for Him to develop your character in His likeness. Then eternity will have its fullest dimensions for you.

If you just live for time (the here and now), you will miss the ultimate purpose of creation. If you live for time, you will allow your past to mold and shape your life today. Your life as a child of God ought to be shaped by the future (what you will be one day). God uses your present time to mold and shape your future usefulness here on earth and in eternity.

You may have some things in your past that are having a strong limiting influence on your life today. These may include handicaps, a troubled family background, failures, shame over some personal or family "secret," or such things as pride, success, fame, recognition, excessive wealth, and so forth. You may realize that you are primarily being shaped by your past rather than your future.

Paul struggled with this problem. Here was his approach to dealing with his past and present:

> If anyone else thinks he may have confidence in the flesh, I more so: circumcised the eighth day, of the stock of Israel, of the tribe of Benjamin, a Hebrew of the Hebrews; concerning the law, a Pharisee; concerning zeal, persecuting the church; concerning the righteousness which is the law, blameless.
>
> But what things were gain to me, these I have counted loss for Christ. Yet indeed I also count all things loss for the excellence of the knowledge of Christ Jesus my Lord, for whom I have suffered the loss of all things, and count them as rubbish, that I may gain Christ and be found in Him, not having my own righteousness, which is from the law, but that which is through faith in Christ, the righteousness which is from God by faith; that I may know Him and the power of His resurrection, and the fellowship of His sufferings, being conformed to His death, if, by any means, I may attain to the resurrection from the dead.
>
> Not that I have already attained, or am already perfected; but I press on, that I may lay hold of that for which Christ Jesus has also laid hold of me. Brethren, I do not count myself to have apprehended; but one thing I do, forgetting those things which are behind and reaching forward to those things which are ahead, I press toward the goal for the prize of the upward call of God in Christ Jesus. (Phil. 3:4–14)

Paul was a true and faithful Jew from the royal tribe of Benjamin. He was faultless in keeping the laws of the Pharisees. He was zealous for God. But he considered all these things as rubbish and loss. More than anything else Paul wanted to know, Christ, be found in Him, and become like Him to attain a *future* blessing (resurrection from the dead). In order to focus on the future, he forgot the past. He strained toward the future. He pressed toward the future goal of a heavenly prize.

Paul's real desire was to know Christ and become like Him. You, too, can so order your life under God's direction that you come to know Him, love Him only, and become like Christ. Let your present be molded and shaped by what you are to become in Christ. You were created for eternity!

You need to begin orienting your life to the purposes of God. His purposes go far beyond time and into eternity. Make sure you are investing your life, time, and resources in things that are lasting and not things that will pass away. If you don't recognize that God created you for eternity, you will invest in the wrong direction. You need to store up treasures in heaven.

> Do not lay up for yourselves treasures on earth, where moth and rust destroy and where thieves break in and steal; but lay up for yourselves treasures in heaven, where neither moth nor rust destroys and where thieves do not break in and steal. For where your treasure is, there your heart will be also. . . . But seek first the kingdom of God and His righteousness, and all these things shall be added to you. (Matt. 6:19–21, 33)

This is why a love relationship with God is so important. He loves you. He knows what is best for you. Only He can guide you to invest your life in worthwhile ways. This guidance will come as you "walk" with Him and listen to Him.

WALKING WITH GOD

God created the first man and woman, Adam and Eve, for a love relationship with Himself. After Adam and Eve had sinned, they heard God walking in the garden in the cool of the day. They hid from Him because of their fear and shame. Try to sense the heart of a loving Father when He asked that wonderful love question, "Where are you?" (Gen. 3:9). God knew that something had happened to the love relationship.

When your relationship is as it ought to be, you will always be in fellowship with the Father. You will be there in His presence expecting and anticipating the relationship of love. When Adam and Eve were not there, something had gone wrong.

Early each day, I have an appointment with God. I often wonder what happens when the God who loves me comes to meet me there. How does He feel when He asks, "Henry, where are you?" and I am just not there. I have found this to be true in my own walk with the Lord: I keep that time alone with God, not in order to have a relationship, but because I have a relationship. Because I have that love relationship with the Lord, I want to meet with Him in my quiet time. I want to spend the time there. Time with Him enriches and deepens the relationship I have with Him.

I hear many persons say, "I really struggle trying to have that time alone with God." If that is a problem you face, let me suggest something to you. Make the priority in your life to come to love Him with all your heart. That will solve most of your problem with your quiet time. Your quiet time is because you know Him and, therefore, love Him, not only in order to learn about Him. The apostle Paul said it was "the love of Christ" that compelled or constrained him (2 Cor. 5:14).

Suppose you were dating a person you loved and intended to marry. What is the primary reason you date (spend time with) that person? Is it because you want to find out about his likes and dislikes or family background? Is it because you want to find out about her knowledge and education? Or is it because you love him and enjoy being with him?

When two people love each other and plan to marry, they are concerned about finding out information about each other. That is not, however, the primary reason why they date. They spend time together because they love each other and enjoy being together.

Similarly, you will learn much about God, His Word, His purposes, and His ways as you spend time with Him. You will come to know Him during the day as you experience Him working in and through your life. Learning about Him is not, however, why you should want to have a quiet time with Him. The more you know Him and experience His love, the more you will love Him. Then you will want that time alone with Him because you do love Him and enjoy His fellowship.

GOD'S FELLOWSHIP WITH ME

How can I always be in fellowship with the Father? My love relationship with God makes me want to do what each day? What does time with God do for my relationship with Him? Why do I spend time with God?

REAL, PERSONAL, AND PRACTICAL

The relationship God wants to have with you will be real and personal. Some ask the question, "Can a person actually have a real, personal, and practical relationship with God?" They seem to think that God is far off and unconcerned about their day-to-day living. That is not the God we see in the Scriptures. From Genesis to Revelation we see God relating to people in real, personal, intimate, and practical ways. Use your Bible to read the stories described below. Watch to see how the person's relationship with the Lord was very real, practical, and personal.

Adam and Eve. God had intimate fellowship with Adam and Eve, walking in the garden with them in the cool of the day. When they sinned, God came after them to restore the love relationship. He met a very practical need by providing clothing to cover their nakedness (Gen. 3:20–21).

Hagar. Hagar had been used, mistreated, and abused by Sarai. She fled for her life. When she reached the end of her own resources, when she had nowhere else to turn, when all hope was gone, God came to her. In her relationship to God, she learned that God saw her, knew her needs, and would lovingly provide for her. God is very personal (Gen. 16:1–13).

Solomon. Solomon's father, David, had been a man who sought the Lord with his whole heart. Solomon had a heritage of faith and obedience to follow. He had the opportunity to ask and receive anything he wanted from God. Solomon demonstrated his love for God's people by asking for a discerning heart. God granted his request and gave him wealth and fame as well. Solomon found his relationship with God to be very practical (1 Kings 3:5–13).

The Twelve Disciples. The disciples also had a real, personal, and practical relationship with Jesus, the Son of God. Jesus had chosen them to be with Him. What a pleasure it must have been to have such an intimate relationship with Jesus! When they were given a very difficult assignment, Jesus did not send them out helpless. He gave them authority they had never known before over evil spirits (Mark 6:7–13).

Peter in Prison Awaiting Execution. In some places of the world obedience to the Lord results in imprisonment. This was Peter's experience (Acts 12:1–17). In answer to prayer, the Lord miraculously delivered him. This was so dramatic and practical, Peter first thought it was a dream. The praying Christians thought he was an angel. Soon they all discovered that the Lord's deliverance was real. That deliverance probably saved Peter's life.

John. In exile on the island of Patmos, John was spending the Lord's Day in fellowship with God (Rev. 1:9–20). During this time of fellowship in the Spirit, the revelation of Jesus Christ came to John to "show His servants—things which must shortly take place" (Rev. 1:1). This message has been a genuine challenge and encouragement to the churches from John's day to this.

Do you sense, as you read the Scripture, that God became real and personal to people? Do you sense that their relationship with God was practical? Was He also real and personal to Noah? to Abraham? to Moses? to Isaiah? Yes! Yes! Yes! Has God changed? No! This was true in the Old Testament. It was true during the time of Jesus' life and ministry. It was true after the coming of the Holy Spirit at Pentecost. Your life also can reflect that kind of real, personal, and practical relationship as you respond to God's working in your life.

Love must be real and personal. A person cannot love without another "someone" to love. A love relationship with God takes place between two real beings. A relationship with God is real and personal. This has always been His desire. All His efforts are expended to bring this desire to reality. God is a Person pouring His life into yours.

If, for some reason, you cannot think of a time when your relationship to God has been real, personal, and practical, you need to spend some time evaluating your relationship to Him. Go before the Lord in prayer and ask Him to reveal the true nature of your relationship to Him. Ask Him to bring you into that kind of relationship. If you come to the realization that you have never entered a saving relationship with God, return to the introduction on page 2 for help in settling that most important issue now.

Some people say to me, "Henry, what you are suggesting about doing God's will is not practical in our day." I always have to differ with them. God is a very practical God. He was in Scripture. He is the same today. When He provided manna, quail, and water for the children of Israel, He was being practical. When Jesus fed five thousand, He was being practical. The God I see revealed in biblical times is real, personal, and practical. I just trust God to be practical and real to me too.

The constant presence of God is the most practical part of your life and ministry. Unfortunately we often assign God to a limited place in our lives. Then we call on Him whenever we need help. That is the exact opposite of what we find in the Word of God. He is the One who is working in our world. He invites you to relate to Him so He can accomplish His work through you. His whole plan for the advance of the kingdom depends on His working in real and practical ways through His relationship to His people.

Knowing and experiencing God through a real and personal relationship was practical in the Scriptures. I believe you will find that this kind of walk with God will be exceedingly practical. God can make a practical difference in your relationships in your family, in your church, and with other people. You can encounter God in such a way that you know you are experiencing Him.

SUMMARY

No one seeks after God on his or her own initiative. God takes the initiative to pursue a continuing love relationship with you. That love relationship is very real, personal, and practical. More than anything else that you might do, God wants you to love Him with your total being. He created you for that very purpose. If your love relationship with Him is out of line, everything else related to knowing, doing, and experiencing God's will will be messed up.

When you find you are not receiving assignments from the Lord, focus your attention on the love relationship. God may be waiting until you respond to His loving invitation to a relationship before entrusting an assignment to you.

EXPERIENCING GOD TODAY

Adam and Eve walked with God in the cool of the day. Take some time to "walk with God" and cultivate a more intimate relationship with Him today or this week. If your location, physical condition, and weather permit, find a place outside to walk. Use this time to get out of your routine. You may even want to plan a special trip for part of a day just to be alone with God. The place could be:

- your neighborhood
- a city park
- a garden
- a wooded area in the country
- a lakeshore
- a sandy beach
- a mountain road
- anywhere

Spend the time walking and talking with God. If the location permits, you may even want to talk out loud. Focus your thoughts on your love of your heavenly Father. Praise Him for His love and mercy. Thank Him for expressions of His love to you. Be specific. Express to God your love for Him. Take time to worship Him and adore Him. Then just spend time with Him. Talk to Him about your concerns, and listen to what He may want to say to you.

After your walk, reflect on your feelings. Consider some of the following questions:

- How did you feel as you walked and talked with God?
- What aspect of your love relationship with God did you become aware of?

- If this was a difficult or an emotionally uneasy time, why do you think it was?
- What happened that was especially meaningful or joyful?
- Would this be the kind of experience you might want to repeat on a fairly regular basis? If so, how regular?

MY SURRENDER TO GOD'S LOVE RELATIONSHIP

God, You have shown me again the deep meaning and total necessity of a continuing love relationship with You. Thank You that You love me so much. Forgive me when I fail to spend time with You each day. I commit myself right now to spending time every morning with You before I start my day in other pursuits. Continue to pursue me Father, and show me how to express my love to You in real, personal, and practical ways. Let me be fully aware of the real, personal, and practical ways You are expressing Your love for me. I love You. I worship You. I will serve You in time and for all eternity.

*It is God who works in you both to will
and to do for His good pleasure.*

PHILIPPIANS 2:13

GOD TAKES THE INITIATIVE

Not only does God take the initiative by pursuing a love relationship with you, but He also initiates the invitation for you to be involved with Him in His work. God doesn't consult the servant before He begins His work. In order to be rightly oriented to God and His work, you need a God-centered life.

Part of the Book of Genesis is the record of God accomplishing His purposes through

Abraham. It is not the record of Abraham's walk with God. Can you see the difference of focus? The focus of the Bible is God.

The essence of sin is a shift from a God-centered to a self-centered life. The essence of salvation is a denial of self. We must come to a denial of self and a return to God-centeredness. When this happens, God can accomplish through us the purposes He had before He created the world.

GOD-CENTERED OR SELF-CENTERED LIVING

What do I need to be rightly oriented to God? What is the focus of the Bible? What should the focus of my life be? Sin is a shift from . . . to . . . living. What is the essence of salvation? When I become God-centered, what can God do?

GOD-CENTERED LIVING

God-centered living is characterized by:

- confidence in God
- dependence on God and His ability and provision
- life focused on God and His activity
- humbleness before God
- denying self
- seeking first the kingdom of God and His righteousness
- seeking God's perspective in every circumstance
- holy and godly living

The following are biblical examples of God-centered living:

Joseph. Potiphar's wife daily begged Joseph to come to bed with her. He told her he could not do such a wicked thing and sin against God. When she tried to force him, he fled the room and went to prison rather than yield to temptation (Gen. 39). Joseph kept his focus on God rather than his fleshly appetites.

Joshua and Caleb. When God was ready for Israel to enter the Promised Land, Moses sent spies to survey the land. Unlike ten of the spies (described below), Joshua and Caleb said, "If the Lord delights in us, then He will bring us into this land . . . [do not] fear the people of the land" (Num. 14:8–9). They were willing to trust the word from God and proceed with confidence in the God who called them rather than in their own strength and abilities.

King Asa. In his earlier years King Asa was God-centered. Facing Zerah the Cushite's army in battle, Asa said, "LORD, it is nothing for You to help, whether with many or with those who have no power; help us, O LORD our God, for we rest on You, and in Your name we go against this multitude. O LORD, you are our God; do not let man prevail against you" (2 Chron. 14:11). God delivered the enemy into his hand; and the nation was at peace.

SELF-CENTERED LIVING

In contrast to God-centered living, self-centered living is characterized by:

- life focused on self
- pride in self and self's accomplishments
- self-confidence
- depending on self and self's own abilities
- affirming self
- seeking to be acceptable to the world and its ways
- looking at circumstances from a human perspective
- selfish and ordinary living

The following are some biblical examples of self-centered living:

Adam and Eve. God placed Adam and Eve in a beautiful and bountiful garden. He told them not to eat from the tree of the knowledge of good and evil. Eve saw that the fruit of that tree was pleasing to the eye and desirable for gaining wisdom, so she ate it (Gen. 2:16–17; 3:1–7). She shared with Adam, and he also ate the forbidden fruit. They displayed a self-centered lifestyle when they attempted to become like God in violation of His command. Their self-centered living led to a broken love relationship with their creator.

Ten Spies. God had promised and was about to give the land of Canaan to Israel. Moses sent twelve men into the Promised Land to explore it and bring back a report. The land was bountiful, but the people living there were seen as giants (Num. 13–14). Though Joshua and Caleb were ready to trust God, ten of the spies said, "We are not able to go up against the people, for they are stronger than we" (Num. 13:31). Rather than looking to God, they looked at self. They couldn't see how their strength could conquer the enemy. Little did they know what God had done to prepare the way.

Forty years later Rahab, an inhabitant of Jericho, described what God had done. She explained that when the people heard about God's deliverance of Israel from Egypt, "our hearts melted; neither did there remain any more courage in anyone because of you, for the LORD your God, He is God in heaven above and on earth beneath" (Josh. 2:11). The self-centered living of the ten spies cost Israel another forty years of waiting in the wilderness.

King Asa. King Asa and Judah were being threatened by Baasha, king of Israel. Once before, when facing such an army, Asa led the people to trust in the Lord. This time instead of turning to God for help, Asa sent gold and silver from the temple and his own palace to Ben-Hadad king of Aram asking for his help in this conflict (2 Chron. 16:1–3). Though once God-centered and trusting, King Asa became self-centered and dependent on himself. God scolded Asa and said, "You have done foolishly; therefore from now on you shall have wars" (2 Chron. 16:9). Because of his self-centeredness, the one thing Asa feared would plague him the rest of his life.

Self-centeredness is a subtle trap. God-centeredness may make no sense from a human perspective. Like King Asa, you can avoid being self-centered at one time and fall right into the trap at another time. God-centeredness requires a daily death of self and submission to God: "Unless a grain of wheat falls into the ground and dies, it remains alone; but if it dies, it produces much grain. He who loves his life will lose it, and he who hates his life in this world will keep it for eternal life" (John 12:24–25).

BECOMING GOD-CENTERED

To be God-centered, what must I have confidence in? What must I not have confidence in? What must I depend on? What must I not depend on? What must I seek first? What must I seek in every circumstance?

GOD'S PURPOSES, NOT OUR PLANS

To live a God-centered life, you must focus your life on God's purposes, not your own plans. You must seek to see from God's perspective rather than from your own distorted human perspective. When God starts to do something in the world, He takes the initiative to come and talk to somebody. For some divine reason, He has chosen to involve His people in accomplishing His purposes.

God was about to destroy the world with a flood when He came to Noah (Gen. 6:5–14). When God prepared to destroy Sodom and Gomorrah, He came to tell Abraham about it (Gen. 18:16–21; 19:13). God came to Gideon when He was about to deliver the Israelites from the oppression of Midian (Judg. 6:11–16). God came to Saul (later called Paul) on the road to Damascus when He was ready to carry the gospel message to the Gentiles around the known world (Acts 9:1–16). Without doubt, the most important factor in each situation was *not* what the individual wanted to do for God. The most important factor was what God was about to do.

Let's use Noah for an example. What about all the plans he had to serve God? They would not make much sense in light of the coming destruction, would they? Noah was not calling God in to help him accomplish what he was dreaming he was going to do for God. *You never find God asking persons to dream up what they want to do for Him.*

We do not sit down and dream what we want to do for God and then call God in to help us accomplish it. The pattern in the Scripture is that we submit ourselves to God and we wait until God shows us what He is about to do, or we watch to see what God is doing around us and join Him.

Who delivered the children of Israel from Egypt? Moses or God? God did. God chose to bring Moses into a relationship with Himself so that He—God—could deliver Israel. Did Moses ever try to take matters about the children of Israel into his own hands? Yes, he did. Read this account of Moses' attempt to assume a leadership role for God's people:

> Now it came to pass in those days, when Moses was grown, that he went out to his brethren and looked at their burdens. And he saw an Egyptian beating a Hebrew, one of his brethren. So he looked this way and that way, and when he saw no one, he killed the Egyptian and hid him in the sand. And when he went out the second day, behold, two Hebrew men were fighting, and he said to the one who did the wrong, "Why are you striking your companion?"

> Then he said, "Who made you a prince and a judge over us? Do you intend to kill me as you killed the Egyptian?" So Moses feared and said, "Surely this thing is known!"
>
> When Pharaoh heard of this matter, he sought to kill Moses. But Moses fled from the face of Pharaoh and dwelt in the land of Midian. (Exod. 2:11–15)

In Exodus 2:11–15 Moses began to assert himself in behalf of his own people. What might have happened if Moses had tried to deliver the children of Israel through a human approach? Thousands and thousands would have been slain. Moses tried to take Israelite matters into his own hands. That cost him forty years of exile in Midian working as a shepherd (and reorienting his life to God-centered living).

When God delivered the children of Israel, how many were lost? None. In the process God even led the Egyptians to give the Israelites their gold, silver, and clothes. Egypt was plundered, the Egyptian army was destroyed, and the Israelites did not lose a single person!

Why do we not realize that doing things God's way is always best? We cause some of the wreck and ruin in our churches because we have a plan. We implement the plan and get out of it only what we can do. God (Jesus) is the head over the body, the church. Oh, that we would discover the difference when we let God be the Head of that body. He will accomplish more in six months through a people yielded to Him than we could do in sixty years without Him.

GETTING MY LIFE IN FOCUS

To live a God-centered life, what must I focus my life on? What will God never ask me to do for Him?

GOD'S WAYS

God desires that His people follow His ways. He created us. He knows us. He knows our world, and He knows the past, present, and future. God's ways will always be best and right. When God's people do not follow His ways, the consequences can be very damaging. God had offered Israel great fulfillment, but their failure to follow Him was costly. He said to Israel: "I am the LORD your God, who brought you out of the land of Egypt. Open your mouth wide, and I will fill it. But My people would not heed My voice, and Israel would have none of Me. So I gave them over to their own stubborn heart, to walk in their own counsels" (Ps. 81:10–12).

God's ways would have been so much better than the ways Israel chose for herself. God said, "Oh, that My people would listen to Me, that Israel would walk in My ways! I would subdue their enemies, and turn My hand against their adversaries!" (Ps. 81:13–14).

God wants us to adjust our lives to Him so He can do through us what He wants to do. God is not our servant to make adjustment to our plans. We are His servants, and we adjust our lives to what He is about to do and to His ways of doing it. If we will not submit, God *will* let us follow our own devices. In following them, however, we will never experience what God is waiting and wanting to do in our behalf or through us for others.

Israel was brought out of Egypt with many miraculous signs and wonders. They walked through the sea on dry ground and saw the Egyptian army destroyed when the sea returned over it. They saw God provide bread from heaven, flocks of quail to eat, and fresh water from a rock. Wouldn't you think they could trust God to do just about anything? When they got to the Promised Land, they could not trust Him to deliver the Promised Land to them. For that reason, they spent the next forty years wandering in the wilderness.

In Psalm 81, God reminded Israel that He would have conquered their enemies quickly if they had only followed His plans rather than their own devices.

FOLLOWING GOD'S WAYS

> *Why is it more important for me to adjust myself to God's ways than to follow my own plans?*

YOU NEED TO KNOW WHAT GOD IS ABOUT TO DO

One year denominational leaders came to Vancouver to discuss long-range plans for an emphasis which we had scheduled in the metropolitan area. Top people from several agencies were going to work with us to accomplish many wonderful things. Yet in my mind I was asking, "But what if God has called our nation to judgment before that time?" I realized how much I needed to know what God had in mind for Vancouver. Planning what I wanted to do in the future could have been totally irrelevant.

When God called the prophets, He often had a two-fold message. The first desire of God was: "Call the people to return to Me." If the people failed to respond, they needed to hear the second message: "Let them know that they are closer to the moment of judgment than they have ever been." Do you suppose it was important that the prophets understand what God was about to do? When God was prepared to bring a terrible judgment to Jerusalem and destroy the entire city, was it important to know what God was about to do? Certainly! *Understanding what God is about to do where you are is more important than telling God what you want to do for Him.*

What good would Abraham have done by telling God how he was planning to take a survey of Sodom and Gomorrah and go door-to-door witnessing the day before God was going to destroy the cities? What good would you do by making long-range plans in your church if, before you ever get to implement them, God brings judgment on your nation?

You need to know what God has on His agenda for your church, community, and nation at this time in history. Then you and your church can adjust your lives to God, so that He can move you into the mainstream of His activity before it is too late. Though God likely will not give you a detailed schedule, He will let you know one step at a time how you and your church need to respond to what He is doing.

Martin Luther. What was God about to do when He started to tell Martin Luther that "the just shall live by faith"? He was going to bring people all over Europe to an understanding that salvation was a free gift and that each person had direct access to Him. He was bringing about a great Reformation. As you study great movements of God in church history, you will notice in every case that God came to someone and the person released his life to God. Then God began to accomplish His purposes through that individual.

John and Charles Wesley, George Whitefield. When God began to speak to John and Charles Wesley, He was preparing for a sweeping revival in England that saved England from a bloody revolution as France had experienced. There stood a couple of men, along with George Whitefield and some others, through whom God was able to do a mighty work and turn England completely around.

In your community there are some things that are about to happen in the lives of others. God wants to intercept those lives. Suppose He wants to do it through you. He comes to you and talks to you. But you are so self-centered, you respond, "I don't think I am trained. I don't think I am able to do it. And I . . ."

Do you see what happens? The focus is on self. The moment you sense that God is moving in your life, you give Him a whole list of reasons why He has got the wrong person or why the time is not right. That is what Moses did. I wish you would seek God's perspective. God knows that you can't do it! But He wants to do it Himself *through* you.

FINDING WHAT GOD IS ABOUT TO DO

What is more important than making long-range plans for the future? How much of His future plans should I expect God to show me? What does God know about my abilities to do His God-sized work?

GOD TAKES THE INITIATIVE

All the way through the Scripture, God takes the initiative. When He comes to a person, He always reveals Himself and His activity. That revelation is always an invitation for the individual to adjust his life to God. None of the people God ever encountered could remain the same after the encounter. They had to make major adjustments in their lives in order to walk obediently with God.

God is the Sovereign Lord. I try to keep my life God-centered because He is the One who is the Pacesetter. He is always the One to take the initiative to accomplish what He wants to do. When you are God-centered, even the desires to do the things that please God come from God's initiative in your life because "it is God who works in you both to will and to do for His good pleasure" (Phil. 2:13).

What often happens when we see God at work? We immediately get self-centered rather than God-centered. Somehow *we* must reorient our lives to God. We must learn to see things from His perspective. We must allow Him to develop His character in us. We must let Him reveal His thoughts to us. Only then can we get a proper perspective on life.

If you keep your life God-centered, you will immediately put your life alongside His activity. When you see God at work around you, your heart will leap within you and say, "Thank You, Father. Thank You for letting me be involved where You are." When I am in the middle of the activity of God and God opens my eyes to let me see where He is working, I always assume that God wants me to join Him.

God always takes the initiative. He does not wait to see what we want to do for Him. After He has taken the initiative to come to us, He does wait until we respond to Him by adjusting ourselves to Him and making ourselves available to Him.

You must be careful to identify God's initiative and distinguish it from your selfish desires. A self-centered life will have a tendency to confuse its selfish desire with God's will. Circumstances, for instance, cannot always be a clear direction for God's leadership. "Open" and "closed doors" are not always indications of God's directions. In seeking God's direction, check to see that prayer, the Scripture, and circumstances agree in the direction you sense God leading you.

Now, you may still be saying, "That all sounds good, but I need some practical help in learning how to apply these concepts." In every situation God demands that you depend on Him, not on a method. The key is not a method but a relationship to God. Let me see if I can help you by telling you about a man who learned to walk with God by prayer and faith.

George Mueller was a pastor in England during the nineteenth century. He was concerned that God's people had become very discouraged. They no longer looked for God to do anything unusual. They no longer trusted God to answer prayers. They had so little faith. (Doesn't that sound like many of our churches?)

God began to lead George to pray. George's prayers were for God to lead him to a work that could only be explained by the people as an act of God. George wanted the people to learn that their God was a faithful, prayer-answering God. He came upon the verse in Psalm 81:10 that you read earlier: "Open your mouth wide, and I will fill it." George began to seek God's provisions for His work in a way that God would be pleased to provide. God began to lead George in a walk of faith that became an outstanding testimony to all who hear of his story.

When George felt led of God to do some work, he prayed for the resources needed, but told no one of the need. He wanted everyone to know that God had provided for the need only in answer to prayer and faith. During his ministry in Bristol, George started the Scriptural Knowledge Institute for distribution of Scripture and for religious education. He also began an orphanage. By the time of his death, George Mueller had been used by God to build four orphan houses that cared for two thousand children at a time. Over ten thousand children had been provided for through the orphanages. He distributed over eight million dollars that had been given to him in answer to prayer. When he died at ninety-three, his worldly possessions were valued at eight hundred dollars.

How did he know and do the will of God? The following is George Mueller's description of his approach:

> I never remember . . . a period . . . that I ever sincerely and patiently sought to know the will of God by the teaching of the Holy Ghost, through the instrumentality of the Word of God, but I have been always directed rightly. But if honesty of heart and uprightness before God were lacking, or if I did not patiently wait upon God for instruction, or if I preferred the counsel of my fellow men to the declarations of the Word of the living God, I made great mistakes.

What helped George Mueller know God's will? He mentioned these things that helped him:

- He sincerely sought God's direction.
- He waited patiently on God until he had a word from God in the Scriptures.
- He looked to the Holy Spirit (Ghost) to teach him through God's Word.

What led him to make mistakes in knowing God's will? He knew the following things led to his making mistakes:

- Lacking honesty of heart
- Lacking uprightness before God
- Impatience to wait for God
- Preferring the counsel of men over the declarations of Scripture

Here is how he summed up the way he entered into a "heart" relationship with God and learned to discern God's voice:

> 1. I seek at the beginning to get my heart into such a state that it has no will of its own in regard to a given matter. Nine-tenths of the trouble with people generally is just here. Nine-tenths of the difficulties are overcome when our hearts are ready to do the knowledge of what His will is.
> 2. Having done this, I do not leave the result to feeling or simple impression. If so, I make myself liable to great delusions.
> 3. I seek the Will of the Spirit of God through, or in connection with, the Word of God. The Spirit and the Word must be combined. If I look to the Spirit alone without the Word, I lay myself open to great delusions also. If the Holy Ghost guides us at all, He will do it according to the Scriptures and never contrary to them.

4. Next I take into account providential circumstances. These often plainly indicate God's Will in connection with His Word and Spirit.
5. I ask God in prayer to reveal His will to me aright.
6. Thus, (1) through prayer to God, (2) the study of the Word, and (3) reflection, I come to a deliberate judgment according to the best of my ability and knowledge, and if my mind is thus at peace, and continues so after two or three more petitions, I proceed accordingly.[1]

I hope this has helped. Don't get discouraged if it still seems vague. We have much more to cover in the following chapters.

SUMMARY

Your love relationship with God prepares you to be involved in God's work by developing God-centered living. Focusing your attention on God's plans, purposes, and ways rather than your own is essential. Any other focus will misguide your involvement in God's work. Like George Mueller, you need to reach a point where you have no will of your own. Then God can cause you to desire His will above all else.

God Himself is the One who initiates your involvement in His work. He does not ask you to dream up something you can do for Him. You need to know what He is doing or is about to do where you are. That is the most important thing to know. In the next chapter I will help you to understand how God shows you what He is doing.

EXPERIENCING GOD TODAY

Take a few minutes to review George Mueller's approach to knowing and doing God's will. Then pray and ask God to help you come to the place that you have no will of your own. If you have a set of self-made plans for what you want to do for God, surrender them and let God reveal His plans instead. Ask God to begin guiding your praying. Ask Him to begin speaking to you through His Word. Ask God to give you a keen sensitivity to circumstances as you seek His will. Continue seeking, but be patient and wait on His timing for your involvement in His purposes.

MY SURRENDER TO GOD'S INITIATIVE

Dear God, take the initiative in my life. Reveal Yourself and Your activity to me so I may recognize Your invitation and join in. Help me come to the place where I have no will of my own. Take away all my selfish, self-centered plans. Replace all my plans with Your plans and purposes. Show me how to pray. Square up my praying with what You are saying to me through Scripture, through the Holy Spirit, and through circumstances. Give me patience to trust and wait. Your timing is perfect. I will trust You to show me how, when, and where to join in Your wonderful work. Thank You for choosing to work through me. Make me Your obedient servant.

ENDNOTES

1. For further reading on George Mueller, see *Answers to Prayer from George Mueller's Narratives,* compiled by A. E. C. Brooks, Moody Press, and *George Mueller by Faith,* Coxe Bailey, Moody Press.

God was in Christ reconciling the world to Himself . . .
and has committed to us the word of reconciliation.
Now then, we are ambassadors for Christ, as though
God were pleading through us.

2 CORINTHIANS 5:19–20

GOD INVITES YOU TO JOIN HIM

The Bible reveals that God always has been involved in the world to reconcile it to Himself. He has never been absent from it or from what is taking place in history. When we read the Bible, we are reading the redemptive activity of God in our world. We see that He chooses to take the initiative and involve His people with Him. He chooses to work through them to accomplish His purposes.

When God was ready to judge the world, He came to Noah. He was about to do something, and He was going to do it through Noah. When God was ready to build a nation for Himself, He came to Abraham. God was going to accomplish His will through Abraham. When God heard the cry of the children of Israel and decided to deliver them, He appeared to Moses. God came to Moses because of His purpose. He planned to deliver Israel through Moses.

This is true all through the Old Testament and New Testament. When God's fullness of time had come to redeem a lost world through His Son, He gave twelve men to His Son to prepare them to accomplish His purposes.

When He is about to do something, He takes the initiative and comes to one or more of His servants. He lets them know what He is about to do. He invites them to adjust their lives to Him so He can accomplish His work through them. The prophet Amos indicated that, "Surely the Lord GOD does nothing, unless He reveals His secret to His servants the prophets" (Amos 3:7).

GOD'S TIMING

As God's obedient child, you are in a love relationship with Him. He loves you and wants to involve you in His work. When He is ready, He will show you where He is working so you can join Him. Don't get in a hurry. God may spend years preparing your character or developing your love relationship with Him. Don't get discouraged if the assignment or "call" does not come immediately. God knows what He is doing. Until He reveals what He is doing so you can join Him, you don't have to worry about not being about the Father's business.

Jesus, for instance, was twelve when He went about the Father's business in the temple. Yet, He was thirty before He began the ministry God had prepared Him for. The Son of God spent the better part of thirty years as a carpenter, waiting until the Father was ready for Him to begin His public ministry.

In this process of knowing and doing God's will, you may ask the question: Why doesn't God give me a big assignment? God might say to you, "You are asking Me to involve you in my great movements, but I am trying to get you simply to understand how to believe Me. I can't give you that assignment yet." God has to lay some basic foundations in your life before He can prepare you for the larger tasks.

Have you ever said something like, "Lord, if You just give me a great assignment, I will serve You for all I am worth"?

God might respond, "I really want to, but I can't. If I were to put you into that kind of assignment, you would never be able to handle it. You are just not ready."

Then you may argue, "Lord, I am able. I can handle it; just try me." Do you remember any of the disciples who thought they were able to handle a bigger assignment?

On the night before Jesus' crucifixion, Peter said, "Lord, I am ready to go with You, both to prison and to death."

Jesus answered, "I tell you, Peter, the rooster shall not crow this day before you will deny three times that you know Me" (Luke 22:33–34). Is it possible that He also knows exactly what you would do? Trust Him. Do not insist that God give you something that you think you are ready for. That could lead to your ruin.

God is far more interested in accomplishing His kingdom purposes than you are. He will move you into every assignment that He knows you are ready for. Let God orient you to Himself. The servant does not tell the Master what kind of assignment he needs. The servant waits on his Master for the assignment. So be patient and wait. Waiting on the Lord should not be an idle time for you. Let God use times of waiting to mold and shape your character. Let

God use those times to purify your life and make you into a clean vessel for His service.

As you obey Him, God will prepare you for the assignment that is just right for you. Any assignment, however, that comes from the Maker of the universe is an important assignment. Don't use human standards to measure the importance or value of an assignment.

WHEN GOD IS READY FOR ME

What kind of relationship do I have with God? Why should I not get in a hurry to do God's work? What must happen before God sets a big task before me? What is God preparing me for?

REVIEWING JESUS' EXAMPLE

You may be asking, "How does God invite me to be involved with Him?" Let's review Jesus' example from John 5:17, 19–20. (See chap. 6.) "My Father has been working until now, and I have been working. . . . Most assuredly, I say to you, the Son can do nothing of Himself, but what He sees the Father do; for whatever He does, the Son also does in like manner. For the Father loves the Son, and shows Him all the things that He Himself does."

Jesus' Example:

- The Father has been working right up until now.
- Now God has Me working.
- I do nothing on My own initiative.
- I watch to see what the Father is doing.
- I do what I see the Father is already doing.
- You see, the Father loves Me.
- He shows Me everything that He is doing.

God has been at work in our world from the very beginning, and He still is at work. Jesus indicated this in His life. He announced that He had come, not to do His own will, but the will of the Father who had sent Him (John 4:34; 5:30; 6:38; 8:29; 17:4). To know the Father's will, Jesus said He watched to see what the Father was doing. Then Jesus joined Him by doing the same work.

The Father loved the Son and took the initiative to come to Him and reveal what He (the Father) was doing or was about to do. The Son kept on looking for the Father's activity around Him so He could unite His life with the Father's activity.

LEARNING FROM THE BIBLE

What do I learn about the Father from Jesus' example? What should I be watching for? What should I be doing?

GOD'S REVELATION IS YOUR INVITATION

The key way Jesus knew how to do the Father's will was to watch to see what the Father was doing. Jesus watched to see where the Father was at work. When He saw, He did what He saw the Father doing. For Jesus the revelation of where the Father was working was His invitation to join in the work. When you see the Father at work around you, that is your invitation to adjust your life to Him and join Him in that work.

Elisha's Servant. Is it possible for God to be working around you and you not see it? Yes. Elisha and his servant were in the city of Dothan, surrounded by an army. The servant was terrified, but Elisha was calm. "And Elisha prayed, and said, 'LORD, I pray, open his eyes that he may see.' Then the LORD opened the eyes of the young man, and he saw. And behold, the mountain was full of horses and chariots of fire all around Elisha" (2 Kings 6:17). Only when the Lord opened the servant's eyes did he see God's activity all around him.

Jerusalem's Leaders. Jesus wept over Jerusalem and its leaders as He prophesied the destruction that would take place in A.D. 70. He said, "If you had known, even you, especially in this your day, the things that make for your peace! But now they are hidden from your eyes" (Luke 19:42). God was in their midst performing wonderful signs and miracles, and His own people did not even recognize Him. They did not see the Father's work. They had not developed the love relationship with the Father, even though they had been diligent students of the Scriptures.

Jesus condemned the Jews for missing out on the most important part of life—a love relationship with God. He said to them, "You search the Scriptures, for in them you think you have eternal life; and these are they which testify of Me. But you are not willing to come to Me that you may have life" (John 5:39–40).

Two factors are important for you to recognize the activity of God around you: (1) You must be living in an intimate love relationship with God; and (2) God must take the initiative to open your spiritual eyes so you can see what He is doing.

Unless God allows you to see where He is working, you will not see it. When God reveals to you what He is doing around you, that is your invitation to join Him. Recognizing God's activity is dependent on your love relationship with Him and His taking the initiative to open your spiritual eyes to see it.

SEEING GOD'S REVELATION AS MY INVITATION

How am I to respond to God's invitation? How can I recognize God's activity?

WORKING WHERE GOD IS AT WORK

Our church sensed that God wanted us to help start new churches all across Central and Western Canada. We had hundreds of towns and villages that had no evangelical church. To know where to start churches, some churches would start with a population study or survey.

Then they would apply human logic to decide where the most promising and productive places might be. By now you know that I would take a different approach.

We tried to find out what God already was doing around us. We believed that He would show us where He was at work, and that revelation would be our invitation to join Him. We began praying and watching to see what God would do next in answer to our prayers.

Allan was a small town forty miles from Saskatoon. It never had a Protestant church. One of our members felt led to conduct a Vacation Bible School for the children in Allan. We said, "Let's find out if God is at work here."

We conducted the Vacation Bible School. At the end of the week, we had a "parents' night." We said to the group, "We believe God may want us to establish a Baptist church in this town. If any of you would like to begin a regular Bible study group and maybe be a part of a new church, would you just come forward?"

From the back of the hall came a lady. She was weeping. She said, "I have prayed for thirty years that there would be a Baptist church in this town, and you are the first people to respond."

From behind her came an elderly man named "T.V." George. (He repaired televisions.) He too was deeply moved and weeping. He said, "For years I was active in a Baptist church. Then I went into alcohol. Four and a half years ago I came back to the Lord. I promised God then that I would pray four to five hours every day until God brought us a Baptist church in our town. You are the first people to respond."

We didn't have to take a survey. God had just shown us where He was at work! That was our invitation to join Him. We went back and joyfully shared with our church what God was doing. The church immediately voted to start a new church in Allan. As of today, that church in Allan has started one church and two mission churches of their own.

God hasn't told us to go away and do some work for Him. He has told us that He is already at work trying to bring a lost world to Himself. If we will adjust our lives to Him in a love relationship, He will show us where He is at work. That revelation is His invitation to us to get involved in His work. Then, when we join Him, He completes His work through us.

KNOWING WHERE GOD IS AT WORK

God has tried, at times, to get our attention by revealing where He is at work. We see it, but we do not immediately identify it as God's work. We say to ourselves, *Well, I don't know if God wants me to get involved here or not. I had better pray about it.* By the time we leave that situation and pray, the opportunity to join God may pass us by. A tender and sensitive heart will be ready to respond to God at the slightest prompting. God makes your heart tender and sensitive in the love relationship we already have talked about.

If you are going to join God in His work, you need to know where He is working. The Scriptures tell us some things that only God can do. Learn to identify these; and when you see something happen that only God can do, you will know it is God's activity. This does not deny God's initiative because unless God opens your spiritual eyes, you will not know it is Him at work. But when God does invite you, He will be able to convince you that He is the One working.

WORKING WHERE GOD WORKS

Why do I not always immediately identify something as God's work? How can my heart be what God needs it to be for me to recognize and participate in His work?

THINGS ONLY GOD CAN DO

The Scriptures say that no one can come to Christ except the Father draws him (John 6:44). No one will seek God or pursue spiritual things unless the Spirit of God is at work in his life. Suppose a neighbor, a friend, or one of your children begins to inquire after spiritual things. You do not have to question whether that is God drawing him or her. He is the only one who can do that. No one will ever seek after God unless God is at work in his life.

Many people who have begun applying this understanding to their witnessing have found great freedom. They pray and watch to see how God is working in the lives of others. When they see or hear someone seeking after God, that becomes their invitation to bear witness to the God they know and serve.

The following Scriptures describe other things that God does. Read them carefully to identify those things God does.

> "If you love Me, keep My commandments. And I will pray the Father, and He will give you another Helper, that He may abide with you forever—the Spirit of truth. . . . you know Him, for He dwells with you and will be in you." (John 14:15–17)
>
> "But the Helper, the Holy Spirit, whom the Father will send in My name, He will teach you all things, and bring to your remembrance all things that I said to you." (John 14:26)
>
> "And when He has come, He will convict the world of sin, and of righteousness, and of judgment." (John 16:8)

When you are saved, you enter a love relationship with Jesus Christ—God Himself. At that point the Counselor, the Spirit of truth, comes to take up residence in your life. He is ever present to teach you. The Holy Spirit also convicts people of guilt regarding sin. He convicts the world of righteousness and judgment. Here is a summary of some things only God can do:

THINGS ONLY GOD CAN DO

God draws people to Himself.

God causes people to seek after Him.

God reveals spiritual truth.

God convicts the world of guilt regarding sin.

God convicts the world of righteousness.

God convicts the world of judgment.

IDENTIFYING GOD'S ACTIVITY

When you see one of these things happening you can know God is at work. God is at work when you see someone coming to Christ, asking about spiritual matters, coming to understand spiritual truth, experiencing conviction of sin, being convinced of the righteousness of Christ, and being convinced of judgment.

When I was speaking in a series of meetings, Bill, a plant manager, said, "You know, I have not been looking on the job to see the activity of God." He mentioned Christian people in key positions in his plant. He wondered if God had not placed them in those positions for a purpose. He decided to get these coworkers together and say, "Let's see if God wants us to take this entire plant for Jesus Christ."

Does that sound like something God might want to do? Yes! In fact your job is not just a place to earn a paycheck. It is a place God wants to use you to influence people for the kingdom's sake. Suppose you were in Bill's place. You plan to bring these Christians together. How would you find out what to do next?

Pray. You start by praying. Only the Father knows what He has purposed. He knows the best way to get it done. He even knows why He brought these individuals together in this plant and why He gave Bill the burden to bring them together. After you pray, get up off your knees and watch to see what God does next. Watch to see what people are saying when they come to you.

Make the connection. Suppose someone in the plant comes to Bill and says, "My family is really having a tough time financially. I am having an especially tough time with my teenager."

Bill had just prayed, "Oh God, show me where You are at work." He needs to make the connection between his prayers and what happens next. If you do not connect what happens next, you may miss God's answer to your prayer. Always connect what happens next. Then what should Bill do?

Ask probing questions. Ask the kind of questions that will reveal what is happening in that person's life. Learn to ask questions of people who cross your path to find out what God is doing in their lives. For instance, ask probing questions like these:

- How can I pray for you?
- What can I pray for you?
- Do you want to talk?
- What do you see as the greatest challenge in your life?
- What is the most significant thing happening in your life right now?
- Would you tell me what God is doing in your life?
- What is God bringing to the surface in your life?
- What particular burden has God given you?

Listen. Suppose the person responds, "I really don't have a relationship with God. But in the last little while with this problem with my teenager, I sure have been thinking about it." Or "When I was a kid, I used to go to Sunday School. My mother and dad made me go. I got away from it, but the financial problems we are under have really caused me to think about this." Those statements sound like God is at work in the person's life. He may be drawing the person to Himself, causing the person to seek after God or bringing conviction of sin.

When you want to know what God is doing around you, pray. Watch to see what happens next. Make the connection between your prayer and what happens next. Ask probing questions and then listen. Be ready to make whatever adjustments are required to join God in what He is doing.

SEEING GOD AT WORK

What things will I see a person doing that may show me God is at work? When I see God at work, where do I start to understand what to do next?

A VISITOR CAME BY "ACCIDENT"

We had a man visit our church by "accident." (I actually don't believe there are any "accidents" or mere coincidences in the life of a believer.) He saw on the bottom of our bulletin, "Pray for our mission in Kyle; pray for our mission in Prince Albert; pray for our mission in Love; pray for our mission in Regina; pray for our mission in Blaine Lake" and others. He asked what it meant.

I explained that our church had made a commitment. If God ever shows us where someone desires a Bible study or a church, we will respond. He asked, "You mean to say that if I were to ask you to come and help us start a church in our town, you would respond?" I told him that we would, and he started to cry. He was a construction worker in Leroy, seventy-five miles east of us. He said that he had been pleading with people to start a Baptist church in

Leroy for twenty-four years. Nobody had wanted to help. He asked if we would come.

We established a church in Leroy. We bought two lots on the main street. This man was so excited he bought a school building and moved it to the site. Then he began functioning as a lay pastor in a work beyond Leroy. Both of his sons have now responded to the call to the gospel ministry.

As a church, we were already conditioned to seeing things that only God can do. When He let us see where He was working, we immediately saw that as our invitation to join Him. Frequently, the reason we do not join Him is we are not committed to join Him. We are wanting God to bless us, not to work through us.

Do not look for how God is going to bless your church. Look for how God is going to reveal Himself to accomplish His purposes. The working of God in you will bring a blessing. The blessing is a by-product of your obedience and experience of God at work in your midst.

Who can tell what a solitary visit by a stranger can mean in your church? Ask some questions about what God is doing where that person is. Then you will know how to adjust your life to be an instrument of God so that God can do what He wants to do. When you begin to see God moving, adjust your life and respond. Two more factors are important in responding to God's invitation.

WHEN GOD SPEAKS . . .

When God reveals to you what He is doing, that is when you need to respond. *He speaks when He is about to accomplish His purposes.* That is true throughout Scripture. Now, keep in mind, the final completion may be a long time off. Abram's son was born twenty-five years after the promise from God.

The time God comes to you, however, is the time for your response. You need to begin adjusting your life to Him. You may need to make some preparations for what He is going to do through you.

WHAT GOD INITIATES . . .

When God said through Isaiah, "Indeed I have spoken it; I will also bring it to pass. I have purposed it; I will also do it" (Isa. 46:11), he confirmed that *what God initiates, He completes*. Earlier he warned God's people, saying, "The Lord of hosts has sworn, saying, 'Surely, as I have thought, so it shall come to pass, and as I have purposed, so it shall stand . . .' For the LORD of hosts has purposed, and who will annul it? His hand is stretched out, and who will turn it back?" (Isa. 14:24, 27). God says that if He ever lets His people know what He is about to do, it is as good as done—He Himself will bring it to pass. (See also 1 Kings 8:56 and Phil. 1:6.)

What God speaks, He guarantees will come to pass. This holds enormous implications for individual believers and churches. When we come to God to know what He is about to do where we are, we also come with the assurance that what God indicates He is about to do is certain to come to pass.

You may have trouble agreeing with this statement. Be sure you always base your understanding of God on Scripture, not on personal opinion nor experience alone. Throughout history, people have said they have a word from the Lord and then it does not come to pass. You cannot look to these kinds of experiences to determine your understanding of God. According to the Scriptures, God accomplishes what He purposes to do.

WHAT AM I LOOKING FOR?

When God speaks to me, what does that indicate about God's timing?

SUMMARY

God takes the initiative to involve His people with Him in His work. He does this on His timetable, not on ours. He is the One who is already at work in our world. When He opens your spiritual eyes to see where He is at work, that revelation is your invitation to join Him. You will know where He is working when you see Him doing things that only God can do. When God reveals His work to you, that is the time He wants you to begin adjusting to Him and His activity. What God purposes He Himself guarantees to complete.

The third reality on God's invitation is very closely related to the fourth on God's speaking. In fact, they are inseparable. They occur together. The next several chapters will describe more fully how to know when God is speaking to you. As you read them, allow God time to teach you to recognize His voice.

EXPERIENCING GOD TODAY

Think about the things that only God can do. Spend some time with the Lord reviewing your past. Are there times when God showed you His activity and you missed it? Is there something that God has been trying to get you involved in and you have been refusing to join Him? Has He spoken to you during this chapter regarding His activity around you? Ask the Lord how He wants you to respond to what He reveals.

MY SURRENDER TO GOD'S INVITATION

God, when You invite me to join You in Your work. I will respond immediately. I will adjust my life to You. Show me how to respond to what You lovingly reveal to me. It is an awesome privilege to be in a love relationship with You and have You trust me to join in Your work. I am ready to join You. Show me Your timing. Make clear to me what You are doing. I praise You that You have promised to complete whatever You start. I surrender to Your invitation. Lead me to where I should begin.

He who belongs to God hears what God says. The reason you do not hear is that you do not belong to God.

JOHN 8:47 (NIV)

10

GOD SPEAKS TO HIS PEOPLE

If anything is clear from a reading of the Bible, this fact is clear: God speaks to His people. He spoke to Adam and Eve in the Garden of Eden in Genesis. He spoke to Abraham and the other patriarchs. God spoke to the judges, kings, and prophets. God was in Christ Jesus speaking to the disciples. God spoke to the early church, and God spoke to John on the

Isle of Patmos in Revelation. God does speak to His people, and you can anticipate that He will be speaking to you also.

Years ago I spoke to a group of young pastors. When I finished the first session, a pastor took me aside and said, "I vowed to God I would never, ever again listen to a man like you. You talk as though God is personal and real and talks to you. I just despise that."

I asked him, "Are you having difficulty having God speak to you?" He and I took time to talk. Before long, we were on our knees. He was weeping and thanking God that God had spoken to him. Oh, don't let anyone intimidate you about hearing from God.

One critical point to understanding and experiencing God is knowing clearly when God is speaking. If the Christian does not know when God is speaking, he is in trouble at the heart of his Christian life! In the following chapters we will focus our attention on how God speaks by the Holy Spirit to reveal Himself, His purposes, and His ways. We will examine ways God speaks through the Bible, prayer, circumstances, and the church or other believers. Read some of what the Bible says about God speaking to His people.

> God, who at various times and in various ways spoke in time past to the fathers by the prophets, has in these last days spoken to us by His Son. (Heb. 1:1)
>
> "But the Helper, the Holy Spirit, whom the Father will send in My name, He will teach you all things, and bring to your remembrance all things that I said to you." (John 14:26)
>
> "However, when He, the Spirit of truth, has come, He will guide you into all truth; for He will not speak on His own authority, but whatever He hears He will speak; and He will tell you things to come." (John 16:13–14)
>
> "He who is of God hears God's words; therefore you do not hear, because you are not of God." (John 8:47)

GOD SPEAKS TO ME

Why is important for me to know when God is speaking to me? Am I in trouble at the heart of my Christian life? In what ways does God speak to me?

GOD SPOKE IN THE OLD TESTAMENT

In the Old Testament God spoke at many times and in a variety of ways. He spoke through:

- angels (Gen. 16)
- visions (Gen. 15)
- dreams (Gen. 28:10–19)
- the use of the Urim and Thummim (Exod. 28:30)
- symbolic actions (Jer. 18:1–10)
- a gentle whisper (1 Kings 19:12)
- miraculous signs (Exod. 8:20–25)
- and others

That God spoke to people is far more important than how He spoke. When He spoke, the person knew God was speaking; and he knew what God was saying. I see four important factors each time God spoke in the Old Testament. The burning bush experience of Moses in Exodus 3 is an example.

When God spoke, it was usually unique to that individual. For instance, Moses had no precedent for a burning bush experience. He could not say, "Oh, this is my burning bush experience. My fathers, Abraham, Isaac, and Jacob, had theirs, and this is mine." There were no other experiences of God speaking this way. It was unique. God wants our experience with Him, and His voice, to be personal to us. He wants us to look to Him in a relationship rather than depend on some method or technique. The key is not *how* God spoke, but *that* He spoke. That has not changed. He will speak to His people today, and how He speaks will not be nearly as important as the fact that He does speak.

When God spoke, the person was sure God was speaking. Because God spoke to Moses in a unique way, Moses had to be certain it was God. The Scripture testifies that Moses had no question that his encounter was with God—The "I AM WHO I AM" (Exod. 3:14). He trusted God, obeyed Him, and experienced God responding just as He said He would. Could Moses logically prove to someone else that he had heard from God through a burning bush? No, all Moses could do was testify to his encounter with God. Only God could cause His people to know that the word He gave Moses was a word from the God of their fathers.

When someone like Gideon lacked assurance, God was very gracious to reveal Himself even more clearly. When Gideon first asked for a sign, he prepared a sacrifice. "Then the Angel of the LORD put out the end of the staff that was in His hand and touched the meat and the unleavened bread; and fire rose out of the rock and consumed the meat and the unleavened bread. And the Angel of the LORD departed out of his sight. Now Gideon perceived that He was the Angel of the LORD. So Gideon said, 'Alas, O Lord GOD! For I have seen the Angel of the LORD face to face!'" (Judg. 6:21–22). Gideon was sure that God had spoken.

When God spoke, the person knew what God said. Moses knew what God was telling him to do. He knew how God wanted to work through him. That is why Moses raised so many objections. He knew exactly what God was expecting. This was true for Moses; and it was true for Noah, Abraham, Joseph, David, Daniel, and others. God did not use riddles. He made His message clear.

When God spoke, that was the encounter with God. Moses would have been foolish to say, "This has been a wonderful experience with this burning bush. I hope this leads me to an encounter with God!"

That *was* the encounter with God! When God reveals truth to you, by whatever means, that *is* an encounter with God. That is an experience of His presence and work in your life. God is the only One who can cause you to experience His presence or hear His voice.

This pattern of God's speaking is found throughout the Old Testament. The *method* He used to speak differed from person to person. What is important is:

- God uniquely spoke to His people.
- They knew it was God.
- They knew what He said.

When God speaks to you by the Holy Spirit through the Bible, prayer, circumstances, and the church, you will know it is God; and you will know what He is saying. When God speaks to you, that is an encounter with God.

GOD SPOKE IN THE GOSPELS

In the Gospels God spoke through His Son, Jesus. The Gospel of John begins: "In the beginning was the Word, and the Word was with God, and the Word was God. . . . The Word became flesh and dwelt among us" (John 1:1, 14). God became flesh in the Person of Jesus Christ. (See also 1 John 1:1–4.)

The disciples would have been foolish to say, "It's wonderful knowing You, Jesus; but we really would like to know the Father."

Philip even said, "Lord, show us the Father, and it is sufficient for us" (John 14:8).

Jesus responded, "Have I been with you so long, and yet you have not known Me, Philip? He who has seen Me has seen the Father; so how can you say, 'Show us the Father'? Do you not believe that I am in the Father, and the Father in Me? The words that I speak to you I do not speak on My own authority; but the

Father who dwells in Me does the works" (John 14:9–10). When Jesus spoke, the Father was speaking through Him. When Jesus did a miracle, the Father was doing His work through Jesus.

Just as surely as Moses was face-to-face with God at the burning bush, the disciples were face-to-face with God in a personal relationship with Jesus. Their encounter with Jesus was an encounter with God. To hear from Jesus *was* to hear from God.

In the Gospel accounts, God was in Christ Jesus. God spoke by Jesus. When the disciples heard Jesus, they heard God. When Jesus spoke, that was an encounter with God.

GOD SPOKE IN ACTS TO THE PRESENT

When we move from the Gospels to Acts and to the present, we quite often change our whole mind-set. We live as if God quit speaking personally to His people. We fail to realize that an encounter with the Holy Spirit *is* an encounter with God. God clearly spoke to His people in Acts. He clearly speaks to us today. From Acts to the present, God has been speaking to His people by the Holy Spirit.

The Holy Spirit takes up residence in the life of a believer. "You are the temple of God and . . . the Spirit of God dwells in you?" (1 Cor. 3:16). "Your body is the temple of the Holy Spirit who is in you, whom you have from God" (1 Cor. 6:19). Because He is always present in a believer, He can speak to you clearly at any time and in any way He chooses.

God speaks through the Holy Spirit. The Holy Spirit will teach you all things, will call to your memory the things Jesus said, will guide you into all truth, will speak what He hears from the Father, will tell you what is yet to come, and will glorify Christ as He reveals Christ to you.

Does God really speak to His people in our day? Yes! Will He reveal to you where He is working when He wants to use you?

Yes! God has not changed. He still speaks to His people. If you have trouble hearing God speak, you are in trouble at the very heart of your Christian experience.

LEARNING FROM THE BIBLE

In the Old Testament, how did God speak? What is more important than how God spoke? Does God speak to me in the same way He speaks to everybody else? When do I know I have had an encounter with God? How can I know that God speaks clearly to me today?

HOW DO I KNOW WHEN GOD SPEAKS?

Sin has so affected us (Rom. 3:10–11) that you and I cannot understand the truth of God unless the Holy Spirit of God reveals it. He is our Teacher. When He teaches you the Word of God, sit before Him and respond to Him. As you pray, watch to see how He uses the Word of God to confirm in your heart a word from God. Watch what He is doing around you in circumstances. The God who is speaking to you as you pray and the God who is speaking to you in the Scriptures is the God who is working around you.

God speaks by the Holy Spirit through the Bible, prayer, circumstances, and the church to reveal Himself, His purposes, and His ways. In future chapters we will study these ways God speaks. I cannot give you a formula, however, and say this is how you can know when God is speaking to you. I will share with you what the Scriptures say.

The evidence of the Scriptures can encourage you at this point. When God chose to speak to an individual in the Bible, the person had no doubt that it was God; and he knew what God was saying. When God speaks to you, you will be able to know He is the One speaking; and you will know clearly what He is saying to you. In John 10:2–4 and 14 Jesus said: "He who enters by the door is the shepherd of the sheep. . . . The sheep follow him, for they know his voice. . . . I am the good shepherd; and I know My sheep, and am known by My own."

The key to knowing God's voice is not a formula. It is not a method you can follow. Knowing God's voice comes from an intimate love relationship with God. That is why those who do not have the relationship ("do not belong to God") do not hear what God is saying (John 8:47). You are going to have to watch to see how God uniquely communicates with you. You will not have any other crutch. You will have to depend on God alone. Your relationship to Him is of utmost importance.

RECOGNIZING GOD'S WORD TO ME

What prevents me from understanding God's truth? Who causes me to understand God's truth? What does the Spirit use to confirm in my heart a word from God to me? To recognize God's voice, what do I have to depend on?

THE KEY TO KNOWING GOD'S VOICE: A LOVE RELATIONSHIP

An intimate love relationship with God is the key to knowing God's voice, to hearing when God speaks. You come to know His voice as you experience Him in a love relationship. As God speaks and you respond, you will come to the point that you recognize His voice more and more clearly. Some people try to bypass the love relationship. Some look for a miraculous sign or try to depend on a "formula" or a set of steps to discover God's will. No substitute, however, exists for the intimate relationship with God.

Not a miraculous sign. Sometimes in Scripture God gave a miraculous sign to assure the person that the word was from Him. Gideon is one example (Judg. 6). Asking God for a sign, however, is often an indication of unbelief. In Gideon's case God had already sent fire from stones to consume a sacrifice and even the stones it was on. Yet, in his unbelief, Gideon asked for another sign. "Putting out a fleece" like Gideon is often a sign of your unbelief or an unwillingness on your part to trust God for an answer.

When the scribes and Pharisees asked Jesus for a miraculous sign, Jesus condemned them as "an evil and adulterous generation" (Matt. 12:38–39). They were so self-centered and sinful that they could not even recognize that God was there in their midst. (See Luke 19:41–44.) Don't be like that wicked and adulterous generation by seeking for miraculous signs to validate a word from God.

Not a formula. A "correct formula" is not the way to hear God's voice either. Moses heard God speak through the burning bush. If Moses had been around today, he would have been tempted to write a book about *How to Know God's Voice in Burning Bushes.* Then people all over our land would be out trying to find *their* burning bush.

But wait. How many other burning bushes like Moses experienced were there? None. God does not want you to become an expert at using a formula. He wants an intimate love relationship with you. He wants you to depend on Him alone. Hearing God does not depend on a method or formula but a relationship.

Not a name-it-and-claim-it method. Some people have a tendency to open their Bible, pick out a verse that they want to use, and claim that they have a word from God for their circumstance. This is a very human-centered (or self-centered) approach. You may ask, "Can't I get a word from God from the Bible?" Yes, you can! But only the Holy Spirit of God can reveal to you which truth of Scripture is a word from God in a particular circumstance. Even if the circumstance is similar to yours, only God can reveal His word for your circumstance.

You also need to be very careful about claiming you have a word from God. Claiming to have a word from God is serious business. If you have been given a word from God, you must continue in that direction until it comes to pass (even twenty-five years, like Abram). If you have not been given a word from God yet you say you have, you stand in judgment as a false prophet: "And if you say in your heart, 'How shall we know the word which the LORD has not spoken?'—when a prophet speaks in the name of the LORD, if the thing does not happen or come to pass, that is the thing which the LORD has not spoken; the prophet has spoken it presumptuously; you shall not be afraid of him" (Deut. 18:21–22).

In the Old Testament law the penalty for a false prophet was death (Deut. 18:20). That certainly is a very serious charge. Do not take a word from God lightly.

Not open and closed doors. Some people try to hear God's voice and know His will only through circumstances. I hear many people say something like this: "Lord, I really want to know Your will. Stop me if I am wrong and bless me if I am right." Another version of this is: "Lord, I will proceed in this direction. Close the door if it is not Your will." The only problem is I don't see this as a pattern anywhere in the Scripture. God does use circumstances to speak to us. But we will often be led astray if that is our *only* means of determining God's directions.

We do see the case in Acts 16 where Paul sought to go into Asia and Bithynia and the Holy Spirit would not permit him to go. This, however, is not just a simple case of looking for open and closed doors. Paul depended on prayer and the shared counsel of those traveling with him. As they sought the Lord's directions, the Holy Spirit kept telling them not to go but to wait. Then when the vision of the Macedonian man came, the Holy Spirit gave affirmation that that was God's directions for their missionary work.

The Word of God is our guide. The pattern I see in Scripture is that God always gives a direction on the front end. He may not tell you all you want to know at the beginning, but He will tell you what you need to know to make necessary adjustments and to take the first step of obedience. Your task is to wait until the Master gives you instructions. If you start "doing" before you have a direction from God, more than likely you will be wrong.

You cannot allow yourself to be guided by experience alone. You cannot allow yourself to be guided by tradition, a method, or a formula. Often people trust in these ways because they are easy. People do as they please and put the whole burden of responsibility on God. If they are wrong, He must intervene and stop them. If they make a mistake, they blame Him. If you want to know the will and voice of God, you must give the time and effort to cultivate a love relationship with Him. That is what He wants!

God loves you. He wants to have an intimate relationship with you. He wants you to depend only on Him when you are seeking a word from Him. He wants you to learn to hear His voice and know His will. Your relationship to Him is the key to hearing when God speaks to you. If you do not already have that kind of relationship with God, consider praying the following prayer: "God, I pray that I will come to such a relationship with You that when You speak, I will hear and respond."

MY KEY TO KNOWING GOD'S VOICE

What is the key to knowing God's voice? How can I know which truth of Scripture is a Word of God in a particular circumstance? What is my task in finding God's Word for my circumstance? What is likely to happen if I start "doing" before I have a direction from God? What wrong ways am I tempted to follow rather than waiting for God's Word?

THE HOLY SPIRIT'S ASSIGNMENT

Because of sin, "There is none who understands; there is none who seeks after God. They have all turned aside; they have together become unprofitable; there is none who does good, no, not one" (Rom. 3:11–12). We cannot know and understand spiritual truth apart from the activity of God in our lives. Spiritual truths can be revealed only by God:

> "Eye has not seen, nor ear heard, nor have entered into the heart of man the things which God has prepared for those who love Him." But God has revealed them to us through His Spirit. For the Spirit searches all things, yes, the deep things of God . . . no one knows the things of God except the Spirit of God. Now we have received, not the spirit of the world, but the Spirit who is from God, that we might know the things that have been freely given us. (1 Cor. 2:9–12)

The Holy Spirit has the assignment of revealing spiritual truth to believers. The Holy Spirit is called the "Spirit of truth" (John 14:17; 15:26; 16:13). Jesus said the Holy Spirit would "teach you all things, and bring to your remembrance all things that I said to you" (John 14:26). "He will guide you into all truth; for He will not speak on His own authority, but whatever He hears He will speak; and He will tell you things to come. He will glorify Me, for He will take of what is Mine and declare it to you" (John 16:13–14).

ENCOUNTERING GOD

When God spoke to Moses and others in the Old Testament, those events *were* encounters with God. An encounter with Jesus was an encounter with God for the disciples. In the same way an encounter with the Holy Spirit is an encounter with God for you.

Now that the Holy Spirit is given, He is the One who guides you into all truth and teaches you all things. You understand spiritual truth because the Holy Spirit is working in your life. You cannot understand the Word of God unless the Spirit of God teaches you. When you come to the Word of God, the Author Himself is present to instruct you. You never discover truth; truth is revealed. When the Holy Spirit reveals truth to you, He is not leading you to an encounter with God. That *is* an encounter with God!

IMMEDIATELY RESPOND

When God spoke to Moses, what Moses did next was crucial. After Jesus spoke to the disciples, what they did next was crucial. What you do next after the Spirit of God speaks to you through His Word is crucial. Our problem is that when the Spirit of God speaks to us, we go into a long discussion with Him questioning the rightness of His directions.

Moses went into a long discussion with God (Exod. 3:11–4:13), and it limited him for the rest of his life. Because of his objections, God gave Aaron to be a spokesman for Moses. Moses had to speak to the people through his brother Aaron (Exod. 4:14–16). Aaron was the one who made the golden calf for the rebellious people. Aaron, together with Miriam, led a challenge to Moses' leadership. Moses paid a high price for arguing with God.

I challenge you to review what you sense God has been saying to you on a regular basis. If God speaks and you hear but do not respond, a time could come when you will not hear His voice. Disobedience can lead to a "famine . . . of hearing the words of the LORD" (Amos 8:11–12).

When Samuel was a young boy, God began to speak to him. The Scriptures say, "Samuel grew, and the LORD was with him and let none of his words fall to the ground" (1 Sam. 3:19). Be like Samuel. Don't let a single word from the Lord fail to bring adjustments in your life. Then God will do in you and through you everything He says to you.

Luke 8:5–15 records Jesus' parable of the sower and the seeds. The seed that fell on the good soil represented those who heard the word of God, retained it, and produced fruit. Jesus said, "Therefore take heed how you hear. For whoever has, to him more will be given; and whoever does not have, even what he seems to have will be taken from him" (Luke 8:18). If you hear the Word of God and do not apply it to produce fruit in your life, even what you think you have will be taken away. Be careful how you listen to God! Make up your mind now that when the Spirit of God speaks to you, you are going to do what He says.

GOD SPEAKS WITH A PURPOSE

We usually want God to speak to us so He can give us a devotional thought to make us feel good all day. If you want the God of the universe to speak to you, you need to be ready for Him to reveal to you what He is doing where you are. In the Scripture, God is not often seen coming and speaking to people just for conversation's sake. He is always up to something. When God speaks to you through the Bible, prayer, circumstances, the church, or in some other way, He has a purpose in mind for your life.

When God spoke to Abram (Gen. 12), what was God about to do? He was about to begin to build a nation. Notice the timing of God. Why did God speak to Abram when He did? Because it was then that God wanted to start to build a nation. The moment Abram knew what God was about to do, he had to make an adjustment in his life to God. He had to follow immediately what God said.

GOD SPEAKS AT THE RIGHT TIME

The moment God speaks to you is the very moment God wants you to respond. Some of us assume that we have the next few months to think about it and to try to decide whether this is really God's timing. The moment God speaks to you is His timing. That is why He chooses to speak when He does. He speaks to His servant when He is ready to move. Otherwise He wouldn't speak. As God comes into the mainstream of your life, the timing of your response is crucial. When God speaks to you, you need to believe and trust God.

How long was it from the time that He spoke to Abram (later named Abraham) that Isaac, the child of promise, was born? Twenty-five years. Why did God wait twenty-five years? Because it took God twenty-five years to make a father suitable for Isaac. God was concerned, not so much about Abram, but about a nation. The quality of the father will affect the quality of all the generations that follow. As goes the father, so goes the next several generations. God took time to build Abram into a man of character. Abram had to begin to adjust his life to God's ways immediately. He could not wait until Isaac was born and then try to become the father God wanted him to be.

God speaks when He has a purpose in mind for your life. We are so oriented to quick response that we abandon the word from God before He has a chance to develop our character. When God speaks, He has a purpose in mind for your life. The time He speaks is the time you need to begin responding to Him. When God speaks to you, you must respond immediately by adjusting your life to Him, His purposes, and His ways. The moment God speaks is God's timing.

MY ENCOUNTER WITH GOD

Why is it important for me to respond when God speaks to me?

What does His speaking tell me about His timing?

GOD DEVELOPS CHARACTER TO MATCH THE ASSIGNMENT

When God speaks with the purpose of revealing an assignment to you, you need to trust what God is doing. He knows exactly what He is doing in and through your life. Don't rule things out that God may be saying because they don't match what you want to hear.

When God called Abram, He said, "I will bless you and make your name great" (Gen. 12:2). That means: "I will develop your character to match your assignment." Nothing is more pathetic than having a small character in a big assignment. Many of us don't want to give attention to our character; we just want the big assignment from God.

Suppose a pastor is waiting for a big church to call him to be pastor. Then a small church calls and says, "Will you come and be bivocational and help us out here on the west side of Wyoming?"

"Well, no," the prospective pastor responds. He thinks, *I am here waiting for God to give me an assignment. I have done so much training, I can't waste my life by working a secular job when I can serve a church full-time. I think that I deserve something much more significant than that. I've paid my dues.*

Do you see how self-centered that viewpoint is? Human reasoning will not give you God's perspective. If you can't be faithful in a little, God will not give you the larger assignment. He may want to adjust your life and character in smaller assignments in order to prepare you for the larger ones. That is where God starts to work. When you make the adjustments and start to obey Him, you come to know Him by experience. This is the goal of God's activity in your life—that you come to *know* Him.

Do you want to experience God mightily working in your life and through your life? Then adjust your life to God in the kind of relationship where you follow Him wherever He leads you—even if the assignment seems to be small or insignificant. Wouldn't you rather hear: "Well done, good and faithful servant; you were faithful over a few things, I will make you ruler over many things. Enter into the joy of your lord" (Matt. 25:21)?

Now, you may ask, "Do I automatically assume that a request like the pastor received to the west side of Wyoming is from God because it is a small assignment?" No. Whether the assignment is large or small in your eyes, you will still have to find out whether it is from God or not. However, you always need to let God tell you that. Do not rule out an assignment, large or small, on the basis of your own preconceived ideas. Remember—you will know through the relationship with God. Don't try to bypass the relationship.

I have known people who wouldn't interrupt a fishing trip or a football game for anything. They say they want to serve God, but they keep eliminating from their lives anything that might interfere with their own plans. They are so self-centered that they do not recognize the times when God comes to them.

If you are God-centered, you will adjust your circumstances to what God wants to do. God has a right to interrupt your life. He is Lord. When you surrendered to Him as Lord, you gave Him the right to help Himself to your life anytime He wants.

Suppose that five times out of ten when the Master had something for the servant to do the servant said, "I am sorry. That is not on my schedule." What do you suppose the Master would do? The Master would discipline the servant. If the servant did not respond to the discipline, sooner or later that servant would find that the Master no longer came to him with assignments.

You may be saying, "Oh, I wish I could experience God working through me the way that John (or Sue) does." But every time God comes to John, John adjusts his life to God and is obedient. When John has been faithful in little assignments, God has given him more important assignments.

If you are not willing to be faithful in a little, God cannot give you a larger assignment. The smaller assignments of God are always used of God to develop character. God always develops character to match His assignment. If God has a great assignment for you, He has to develop a great character to match that assignment before He can give you the assignment.

When God gives direction, you accept it and understand it clearly, then give God all the time He needs to make you the kind of person that He can trust with that assignment. Do not assume that the moment He calls, you are ready for the assignment. Consider the example of these two Bible characters:

David. How long was it after God (through Samuel) anointed David king that David mounted the throne? Maybe ten or twelve years. What was God doing in the meantime? He was building David's relationship with Himself. As goes the king, so goes the nation. You cannot bypass character.

Paul. How long was it after the living Lord called the apostle Paul on the Damascus Road that Paul went on his first missionary journey? Maybe ten or eleven years. The focus is not on Paul; the focus is on God. God wanted to redeem a lost world, and He wanted to begin to redeem the Gentiles through Paul. God needed that much time to prepare Paul for the assignment.

Is it for your sake that God takes time to prepare you? No, not for you alone, but also for the sake of those He wants to reach through you. For their sake, give yourself to the kind of relationship to God we are discussing. Then, when He puts you in an assignment, He will achieve everything He wants in the lives of those you touch.

GOD DEVELOPING MY CHARACTER

When God reveals an assignment to me, what do I need to do?

What should I do if what God says to me does not match what I want to hear? What should I do if God's assignment seems small and insignificant to me? What keeps God from giving me a large assignment? How much time must I give God to make me the kind of person He can trust with His assignment?

GOD GIVES SPECIFIC DIRECTIONS

A popular teaching says God does not give you clear directives. It says He just sets your life in motion. Then you try to figure out the directions using your God-given mind. This implies that a Christian always thinks correctly and according to God's will. This does not take into account that the old nature is constantly battling with the spiritual nature (see Rom. 7). Our ways are not God's ways (see Isa. 55:8). Only God can give you the kind of specific directions to accomplish His purposes in His ways.

After God spoke to Noah about building an ark, Noah knew the size, the type of materials, and how to put it together. When God spoke to Moses about building the tabernacle, He was very specific about the details. When God became flesh in the Person of Jesus Christ, He gave specific directions to His disciples—where to go, what to do, how to respond.

What about when God called Abraham (Abram) and said, "Get out of your country, from your family and from your father's house, to a land that I will show you" (Gen. 12:1)? That was not very specific. That required faith. But God did say, "I will show you." God always will give you enough specific directions to do *now* what He wants you to do. When you need more directions, He gives you more in His timing. In Abraham's case, God later told him about the son to be born to him, the number of his descendants, the territory they would inhabit, and that they would go into bondage and be brought out.

The Holy Spirit gives clear directives today. God is personal. He wants to be intimately involved in your life. He will give you clear guidance for living. You may say, "That has not been my experience." You need to bring your experience up to the Word of God and not lower God's ways to match your experience.

If you do not have clear instructions from God in a matter, pray and wait. Learn patience. Depend on God's timing. His timing is always right and best. Don't get in a hurry. He may be withholding directions to cause you to seek Him more intently. Don't try to skip over the relationship to get on with *doing*. God is more interested in a love relationship with you than He is in what you can do for Him.

Frequently I am asked, "How can I know whether the word I receive is from God, my own selfish desires, or Satan?" Some people go to much trouble studying Satan's ways so they can identify when something appears to be a deception of Satan. I don't do that. I am determined not to focus on Satan. He is defeated. The One who is guiding me, the One who is presently implementing His will through me, is the Victor. The only way Satan can affect God's work through me is when I believe Satan and disbelieve God. Satan always will try to deceive you. Satan cannot ultimately thwart what God purposes to do.

Royal Canadian Mounted Police, the Mounties, train men in anti-counterfeiting work. They never let a trainee see a counterfeit bill. They know only one genuine type of ten-dollar bill exists. They so thoroughly study the genuine bill that anything that does not measure up to that is counterfeit.

You can't imagine all the ways people can counterfeit money. But Mounties don't study how people counterfeit money. They just study the real thing. Anything that doesn't measure up to that is fake.

When you are faced with a sense of direction, you may ask yourself, "Is this God, me, or Satan?" How can you prepare yourself to know clearly a word from God? I suggest that you know the ways of God so thoroughly that if something doesn't measure up to God's ways, turn away from it. That's what Jesus did in the temptations. In essence Jesus just quietly said, "I understand what you are saying, Satan; but that is not the last word I had from My Father. The Scriptures say . . ." (see Matt. 4:1–11). Jesus never discussed it with Satan. He never analyzed it. He just kept doing the last thing His Father told Him to do until His Father told Him what to do next.

As with Jesus' encounter with Satan, your spiritual warfare may involve being encouraged to do something that sounds good but is not God's best or God's way. Jesus knew clearly what His mission was and how the Father intended for Him to accomplish it. When Satan tried to get Jesus to go a different route for "instant success," Jesus recalled the assignment His Father had given and rejected the false counsel.

SUMMARY

God has always been speaking to His people. Today, He speaks by the Holy Spirit. The Holy Spirit will use the Bible, prayer, circumstances, and other believers to speak to you. The method, however, is not the key to knowing God's voice. You learn to know the voice of God through an intimate love relationship that He has initiated. God may choose to speak to you in a way that is unique to you. You can be assured, though, that He will be able to convince you that you have heard a word from Him.

When God speaks to you, He will do so with purpose. When He speaks is God's timing for you to begin adjusting your life and your thinking to Him. He will be working in you to develop your character for the assignment He has for you. Let God take all the time He needs to prepare you.

EXPERIENCING GOD TODAY

Take some time with God in prayer and think about the times you clearly knew God was speaking to you. Ask God to give you insight into knowing His voice. If you do not currently keep a spiritual journal, you may want to begin recording the things God has said to you in the past and the things He is now saying to you.

MY SURRENDER TO GOD'S SPEAKING

God, You continue to speak to me. Give me ears to hear, a heart to trust, and hands to act. Take away the temptation to carry out my plans and leave Yours until later. Help me get on with Your assignment the minute You give it. You know who I am better than I do myself. You know the adjustments I must make to You to carry out Your assignment. Work in my life through Your Holy Spirit. Create the image of Christ in me so that I have the character to fulfill Your assignment. I want to hear Your voice and obey Your will.

My thoughts are not your thoughts,
nor are your ways My ways.

ISAIAH 55:8

Come, let us go up to the mountain
of the Lord . . . He will teach us His ways,
and we shall walk in His paths.

MICAH 4:2

11

GOD REVEALS HIMSELF, HIS PURPOSES, AND HIS WAYS

God speaks to His people. When He speaks, what does He reveal? Throughout the Scriptures when God spoke, it was to reveal something about Himself, His purposes, or His ways. God's revelations are designed to bring you into a love relationship with Him.

GOD REVEALS HIMSELF

When God speaks by the Holy Spirit to you, He is often revealing to you something about Himself. He is revealing His name. He is revealing His nature and character. Notice in the following Scriptures what God revealed about Himself.

> When Abram was ninety-nine years old, the LORD appeared to Abram and said to him, "I am Almighty God." (Gen. 17:1)
>
> The LORD spoke to Moses saying, "Speak to all the congregation of the children of Israel, and say to them: 'You shall be holy, for I the LORD your God am holy.'" (Lev. 19:1–2)
>
> "For I am the LORD, I do not change. . . . Yet from the days of your fathers you have gone away from My ordinances and have not kept them. Return to Me, and I will return to you," says the LORD of hosts. (Mal. 3:6–7)
>
> [Jesus said to the Jews,] "I am the living bread which came down from heaven. If anyone eats of this bread, he will live forever." (John 6:51)

God speaks when He wants to involve a person in His work. He reveals Himself in order to help the person respond in faith. The person can better respond to God's instructions when he believes God is who He says He is and when he believes God can do what He says He will do.

God revealed Himself to Abram by His name—God Almighty. Ninety-nine-year-old Abram needed to know God was almighty (all-powerful—able to do anything) so he could *believe* that God could give him a son in his old age.

To Moses, God revealed His holy nature. Then through Moses, God said He was holy. His people had to believe He was holy so they would respond by being holy themselves. Their lives depended on it.

God spoke through Malachi to Israel and revealed that He is unchanging and forgiving. God revealed His forgiving nature so the people could believe that they would be forgiven if they would return to God.

Jesus revealed Himself as "living bread" and the source of eternal life. Jesus revealed that He was the source of eternal life so the Jews could believe and respond to Him and receive life.

God reveals Himself to increase faith that leads to action. You will need to listen attentively to what God reveals to you about Himself. This will be critical when you come to the crisis of belief.

- You will have to *believe* God is who He says He is.
- You will have to *believe* God can do what He says He will do.
- You will have to *adjust* your thinking in light of this belief.
- Trusting that God will demonstrate Himself to be who He says He is, you then *obey* Him.
- When you *obey*, God does His work through you and demonstrates that He is who He says He is.
- Then you will *know* God by experience.
- You will *know* He is who He says He is.

For example, when did Abram know God was almighty? Well, he knew it in his mind as soon as God said it. But he came to know God by experience as God Almighty when God did something in his life that only God could do. When God gave Abraham (one hundred years old) and Sarah (ninety years old) a son, Abraham *knew* God was God Almighty.

GOD REVEALS HIMSELF TO ME

What are some things God reveals to me about Himself? What does God seek to increase when He reveals Himself to me?

GOD REVEALS HIS PURPOSES

God reveals His purposes so you will know what *He* plans to do. If you are to join Him, you need to know what God is about to do or what He is already doing. What you plan to do for God is not important. What He plans to do where you are is very important. God speaks with a purpose in mind.

Noah. When God came to Noah, He did not ask, "What do you want to do for me?" He came to reveal what He was about to do. It was far more important to know what God was about to do. It really did not matter what Noah had planned to do for God. God was about to destroy the world. He wanted to work through Noah to accomplish *His* purposes of saving a remnant of people and animals to repopulate the earth.

Abram. Similarly, God came to Abram and spoke to him because He had a purpose in mind. He was preparing to build a nation for Himself. God was about to accomplish *His* purposes through Abram.

When God prepared to destroy Sodom and Gomorrah, He did not ask Abraham what he wanted or what he was planning to do for Him. It was crucial for Abraham to know what *God* was about to do. God revealed His purpose.

This sequence is seen throughout the entire Bible: the judges, David, the prophets, the disciples, and Paul. When God was about to do something, *He* took the initiative to come to His servants: "Surely the Lord GOD does nothing, unless He reveals His secret to His servants" (Amos 3:7). He spoke to reveal *His* purposes and plans. Then He could involve them and accomplish *His* purposes through them.

God's Purposes Versus Our Plans. We often set about dreaming our dreams of what *we* want to do for God. Then we make plans based on *our* priorities. What is important is what God plans to do where we are and how He wants to accomplish it through us. Look what the Scriptures say about our plans and purposes: "The LORD brings the counsel of the nations to nothing; He makes the plans of the peoples of no effect. The counsel of the LORD stands forever, the plans of His heart to all generations" (Ps. 33:10–11). "There are many plans in a man's heart, nevertheless the LORD's counsel—that will stand" (Prov. 19:21).

Your plans and purposes must be God's plans and purposes or you will not experience God working through you. God reveals His purposes so you will know what He plans to do. Then you can join Him. His plans and purposes will stand. They will be accomplished. The Lord foils and thwarts the plans of the nations and the purposes of the peoples.

Planning is a valuable tool, but it never can become a substitute for God. Your relationship with God is far more important to Him than any planning you can do. Our biggest problem with planning is that we plan and carry out things in our own wisdom that only God has a right to determine. We cannot know the when, or where, or how of God's will until He tells us.

God wants us to follow Him, not just some plan. If we try to spell out all the details of His will in a planning session, we have a tendency to think: *Now that we know where we are going and how to get there, we can get the job done.* Then we forget the need for a daily, intimate relationship with God. We may accomplish our plans but forget the relationship. God created us for an eternal love relationship. Life is our opportunity to experience Him at work.

Planning is not all wrong. Just be very careful not to plan more than God intends for you to plan. Let God interrupt or redirect your plans anytime He wants. Remain in a close relationship with Him so you can always hear His voice when He wants to speak to you. I have found that the best planning meetings are prayer meetings where we spend time with our Father finding out what He is up to around us.

GOD REVEALS HIS PURPOSES TO ME

Why does God reveal His purposes to me? Has planning become a substitute for God in my life? If so, how can I prevent it from doing so? What is our biggest problem with planning? What does God want us to follow rather than our plan?

GOD REVEALS HIS WAYS

Even the casual or uninformed reader of the Bible can see that God's ways and plans are different from man's. God uses kingdom principles to accomplish kingdom purposes. God reveals His ways to us because they are the only way to accomplish *His* purposes.

His goal always is to reveal Himself to people to draw them into a love relationship with Himself. His ways are redemptive. He acts in such a way to reveal Himself and His love. He does not simply wait around in order to help us achieve our goals for Him! He comes to accomplish His own goals through us—and in His own way.

God said, "For My thoughts are not your thoughts, nor are your ways My ways" (Isa. 55:8). We will not accomplish God's work in our own ways. This is one of the basic sin problems people face: "All we like sheep have gone astray; we have turned, every one, to his own way" (Isa. 53:6).

Our ways may seem good to us. We may even enjoy some moderate successes. But when we do the work of God in our own ways, we will never see the power of God in what we do. God reveals His ways because that is the only way to accomplish His purposes. When God accomplishes His purposes in His ways through us, people will come to know God. They will recognize that what has happened can only be explained by God. He will get glory to Himself!

Using kingdom ways is seen in the life of the disciples. Jesus asked them to feed the multitudes. Their response was, "Send them home!" But Jesus, using *kingdom* principles, sat them down, fed them, and had baskets full of leftovers. They saw the Father work a miracle. What a contrast! The disciples would have sent the people home empty and hungry. God displayed to a watching world His love, His nature, and His power. This kind of display would draw people to Himself through His Son Jesus. This kind of mighty display happened many times in the lives of the disciples. They had to learn to function according to kingdom principles to do kingdom work.

God's purposes accomplished in His ways bring Him glory. We must do kingdom work in kingdom ways. "Let us go up to the mountain of the Lord . . . . He will teach us His ways, and we shall walk in His paths" (Mic. 4:2).

When I was first learning how to walk with God, I depended too much on other people. I would run to other people and say, "Do you think this is really God? Here is what I think. What do you think?" I would unconsciously, or consciously, depend on them rather than on the relationship I had with God.

Finally I had to say, "I am going to go to the Lord and clarify what I am absolutely convinced He is saying to me. Then, I am going to proceed and watch to see how God affirms it." I began that process over a period of time in many areas of my life. My love relationship with God became all-important. I began to discover a clear personal way in which God was making known His ways. God revealed His ways through His Word. In the next chapter we will look at how God speaks through His Word. In future chapters we will look at how God speaks through prayer, circumstances, and the church to confirm His will to us.

GOD REVEALS HIS WAYS TO ME

Why does God reveal His ways to me? What will I never see if I do God's work in my own ways? What will happen when God accomplishes His purposes through me?

SUMMARY

God wants us to come to know Him and follow Him. As He speaks to us, He reveals Himself so we can have faith to trust Him in the assignment He calls us to. He reveals His purposes so we will be involved in His work and not just things we dreamed up to do for God. God reveals His ways so that He can accomplish His work through us in a way that He gets all the glory.

EXPERIENCING GOD TODAY

Turn to the appendix in the back of this book. Prayerfully begin to read through the list of names by which God has already revealed Himself in Scripture. Circle or underline ones by which you have come to know Him by personal experience. See if God's revealing of Himself has increased your faith to trust Him in other areas of your life. Reflect on some of the ways and purposes God may have revealed to you through the years.

MY SURRENDER TO GOD'S SELF-REVELATION

God, You have spoken to me through the years of my love relationship with You. I pause now to reflect on some of Your ways and purposes that I have learned from You through the years. I want to live according to those ways and purposes, not my own. Give me the faith and courage to do so. Implant Your Holy Spirit within me. Create the image of Your Son in me so I can live out Your ways and purposes. Thank You, O Father, that You have patience with me and the confidence in me to take time to show personal interest in me and to reveal Yourself to me. I can only respond in obedience and in worship. I commit myself anew today to hearing Your word to me and to responding to that word immediately in obedience. As I wait for You to speak, I bow in worship and adoration before You. You alone are God—the God above all creation, the Sovereign Lord who rules the universe. All power, all glory, all honor, all praise, and all worship belong to You and You alone. I love You, Lord.

All Scripture is given by inspiration of God and is profitable for doctrine, for reproof, for correction, for instruction in righteousness, that the man of God may be complete, thoroughly equipped for every good work.

2 TIMOTHY 3:16–17

12

GOD SPEAKS THROUGH THE BIBLE

God speaks to you by the Holy Spirit to reveal Himself, His purposes, and His ways. Perhaps the questions people ask most about God's speaking are:

- How does God speak to me?
- How can I know when God is speaking?

- How can God be more real and personal to me?

God speaks to individuals, and He can do it in any way He pleases. As you walk in an intimate love relationship with God, you will come to recognize His voice. You will know when God is speaking to you. He will see to it.

KNOWING GOD'S VOICE

Jesus compared the relationship He has with His followers to the relationship a shepherd has with his sheep. He said, "He who enters by the door is the shepherd of the sheep. . . . The sheep hear his voice. . . . The sheep follow him, for they know his voice" (John 10:2–4). In just this way, when God speaks to you, you will recognize His voice and follow Him.

God is sovereign. He can do whatever He chooses to do. With the Scripture as our guide, we know God can speak in unique ways to individuals. His people will hear and recognize His voice.

In our time, God primarily speaks by the Holy Spirit through the Bible, prayer, circumstances, and the church. These four means are difficult to separate. God uses prayer and the Bible together. Often circumstances and the church, or other believers, will help confirm what God is saying to you. Frequently, God uses circumstances and the church to help you know His timing. We will talk more about that in the next chapters. Now, I want us to look at how God speaks through the Bible.

GOD LETS ME KNOW HIS VOICE

How does the quality of my relationship with God affect my knowing His voice?

THE BIBLE IS GOD'S WORD

The Bible describes God's complete revelation of Himself to humanity. It is a record of God's dealings with humanity and His words to them. God speaks to you through the Bible. Have you ever been reading the Bible when suddenly you are gripped by a fresh new understanding of the passage? That was God speaking!

A person cannot understand spiritual truth unless the Spirit of God reveals it. In fact, the Holy Spirit is "the Spirit of truth" (John 14:17). When you come to understand the spiritual meaning and application of a Scripture passage, God's Spirit has been at work. This does not *lead* you to an encounter with God; that *is* the encounter with God. When God speaks to you through the Bible, He is relating to you in a personal and real way.

When the Holy Spirit reveals a spiritual truth from the Word of God, He is personally relating to your life. That is an encounter with God. The sequence is this:

1. You read the Word of God—the Bible.
2. The Spirit of truth takes the Word of God and reveals truth.
3. You adjust your life to the truth of God.
4. You obey Him.
5. God works in and through you to accomplish His purposes.

The Spirit uses the Word of God (the sword of the Spirit—Eph. 6:17) to reveal God and His purposes. The Spirit uses the Word of God to instruct us in the ways of God. On our own we cannot understand the truths of God: "The natural man does not receive the things of the Spirit of God, for they are foolishness to him; nor can he know them, because they are spiritually discerned. But he who is spiritual judges all things" (1 Cor. 2:14–15).

Unaided by the Spirit of God, the ways and things of God will be foolishness to us (1 Cor. 2:14). Aided by the Spirit, we can understand all things (1 Cor. 2:15).

Understanding spiritual truth does not lead you *to* an encounter with God; it *is* the encounter with God. You cannot understand the purposes and ways of God unless the Spirit of God teaches you. If God has revealed spiritual truth to you through this passage of Scripture, you have encountered God Himself working in you!

GOD'S WORD FOR ME

What passage of Scripture has God used recently to grip me and give me fresh understanding? Who has been at work in my life when I understand the spiritual meaning and application of a Scripture passage? What are the five steps of the sequence God uses to relate Himself personally to me. How do I see the ways and purposes of God apart from the Spirit of God? When do I encounter God?

RESPONDING TO TRUTH

Reading the Scripture is an exciting time of anticipation for me. The Spirit of God knows the mind of God. He knows what God is ready to do in my life. The Spirit of God then begins to open my understanding about God and His purposes and His ways. I take that very seriously. Here is how I respond when God reveals truth to me in His Word.

I write down the passage of Scripture. Then I meditate on it. I try to immerse myself in the meaning of that verse or passage. I adjust my life to the truth and, thus, to God. I agree with God and take any actions necessary to allow God to work in the way He has revealed. Then I alert myself to watch for ways God may use that truth in my life during the day.

You may want to follow this same process as God reveals truth to you. When God leads you to a fresh understanding of Himself or His ways through Scripture:

- Write down the verse(s) in a notebook, spiritual journal, or diary.
- Meditate on the verse.
- Study it to immerse yourself in the meaning of the verse. What is God revealing about Himself, His purpose, or His ways?
- Identify the adjustments you need to make in your personal life, your family, your church, and your work so God can work that way with you.
- Write a prayer response to God.
- Make the necessary adjustments to God.
- Watch to see how God may use that truth in your life during the day.

Claude told me about an experience he had with God in His Word. One morning he was reading his daily Bible reading from Psalm 37. He had read this psalm many times before, but on this particular morning the Holy Spirit called his attention to verse 21: "The wicked borrows and does not repay." He was "drawn" back to that verse, and he read it again. At that very moment he remembered borrowing $500 from his parents with a promise to repay them when he got his next paycheck. Now, months later, he had almost forgotten about the debt. God used Psalm 37:21 to remind him of the unpaid debt. More importantly, God alerted Claude that wicked are the ones who borrow and don't repay. Claude said, "I prayed and asked the Lord to forgive me, and then I wrote a check for $500 and delivered it to my parents."

The Holy Spirit had spoken to him through that verse. He encountered truth. Now he understood that those who borrow and do not repay are wicked in God's sight. The Holy Spirit had called his attention to a specific instance where this verse applied to him. This was the Holy Spirit convicting him of sin. The Holy Spirit is the One who does that. Claude responded to the Lord in a prayer of confession. Then he adjusted to the truth, paid the debt, and was reconciled to his parents and to the Lord.

MY RESPONSE TO GOD'S TRUTH

What are some ways I can respond when God's Spirit reveals His truth to me from Scripture? What experience with God's Word has revealed God, His ways, or His purposes to me? What did I do in response?

ADJUST, OBEY, AND EXPERIENCE

God speaks by the working of the Holy Spirit and through His Word. God wants you to have no hindrances to a love relationship with Him in your life. Once God has spoken to you through His Word, how you respond is crucial. You must adjust your life to the truth. In Claude's case the adjustment was this:

- He agreed with the truth—those who borrow and do not repay are wicked in God's sight.
- He agreed that the truth applied to him in the particular instance brought to his memory.

This agreement with God is confession of sin. Confession means you agree with God about your sin. To agree with God, you must change your understanding to agree with His. This requires an adjustment. Is that all you must do? No! Agreeing with God is not enough.

In Claude's case he knew he would continue to be wicked in God's sight until he repaid the debt. This is where obedience is required. To obey what God had said to him through the Bible, Claude had to repay the debt.

Adjusting your mind to the truth God has revealed to you is one step short of completion. You must also respond to the truth in obedience. Then you are free to experience a more complete relationship with God. Always tie a revealed truth to your understanding of God and your relationship with Him.

Robert Sanders was a dentist in Rusk, Texas. He began to sense that God was calling him into some kind of special ministry related to missions and perhaps to be a pastor. For over a year the sense of God's call grew stronger and stronger for him. His wife Gail didn't sense God's call to be a pastor's wife, so they continued to pray and seek God's directions.

During this time, their pastor James Goforth accepted a call to New York state to work with pastors in the Adirondack Association. The people in New York asked James to lead a men's prayer retreat. When he couldn't go, he enlisted Robert and two other men to go. During the retreat several people came to Robert and said things like: "We don't have a dentist in our town. Why don't you move up here and become our dentist?" And "We don't have a pastor. Why don't you move up here and become our pastor?" Robert assumed they just wanted all three of these trained church leaders to move to New York.

Shortly after their pastor announced his plans to move, the church in Rusk held an "Experiencing God Weekend" where the whole church studied the Seven Realities of Experiencing God. On Saturday morning at 2:30 A.M. Gail woke up. The Scripture reference Luke 4 kept running through her mind. She didn't know what Luke 4 was about, but she promised the Lord she would read it when she got up. Unable to sleep, she decided she had better read Luke 4 at that moment instead of waiting.

That morning the Lord spoke to Gail through the Bible. She realized that even Jesus had to leave His hometown in order to "preach the good news of the kingdom of God to the other towns." She sensed the Holy Spirit saying that she would have to leave the comforts and security of home to go with her husband as they served the Lord together. Later that morning, in the Experiencing God Seminar, she gave her testimony of what God had said.

The leader asked: "Why did God speak to you today instead of six months ago or six months from now? Since God speaks when it is His timing, is it possible that God wants you two involved in missions in New York with your pastor?"

During the morning break, Robert asked the two other men who led the prayer retreat with him, "When we were in New York, did anyone ask you to move up there and work or pastor a church?" When both men responded, "No," Robert and Gail began to sense God's leadership more and more clearly. Then a small church in Chataguay, New York, called Robert to be their part-time pastor.

Robert and Gail sold their new home at a loss and moved a long way from their hometown in Texas. When Robert arrived in New York, the association of churches was praying about starting a ministry to thousands of Native Americans on a nearby reservation. Guess who became the dentist on the reservation? Robert! And God has continued to unfold His plans and purposes to reach the people of the Adirondacks for Himself.

Can you see how Robert and Gail learned by experience the Seven Realities of Experiencing God? They had a love relationship with the Lord. God took the initiative to invite them to join Him in His work. He spoke clearly through the Bible, prayer, circumstances, and other believers. Robert and Gail faced a crisis of belief, but they chose to walk with the Lord who called them by faith. They had to make major adjustments to join the Lord; but when they obeyed Him, they began to experience God working through them to touch people with the gospel of Jesus Christ. The way God spoke to Gail through the Bible was a major turning point in their knowing and doing God's will.

ADJUSTING, OBEYING, AND EXPERIENCING GOD

What is crucial once God has spoken to me through His Word? What do I do when I confess my sin to God? What can free me to experience a more complete relationship with God? Am I in a love relationship with God? How can I tell?

SUMMARY

As you spend time in a love relationship with God you will come to know His voice. But God has already given you many messages and commands in His Word, the Bible. As you read the Scriptures, the Holy Spirit will be at work to reveal truth about God, His purposes, and His ways. When He clearly speaks, you must adjust yourself to the truth revealed and obey God. When you obey Him, you will experience Him working in and through you to accomplish His work in His world.

EXPERIENCING GOD TODAY

Spend some time with God in prayer. Ask Him to bring to your memory times and ways He has already spoken to you through the Bible. If you have a spiritual journal, you may want to review some of the ways God has spoken in the past. As He brings experiences to your mind, you may want to list and describe what God has said.

MY SURRENDER TO GOD'S WORD TO ME IN THE BIBLE

God, I will read Your Word every day and to listen for Your Spirit to apply it to my life. I am ready to adjust my life to Your Word instead of trying to find an interpretation of Your Word I can adjust to fit my life. I promise to obey You. Then I know I will experience You. I gladly await the opportunity to see You at work through me to accomplish Your work in this world. Show me the patterns I need to see in the Scriptures Your Spirit continually reveals to me. You have shown me a truth in Your Word recently, O God. I have not yet been willing to adjust my life and agree with Your truth. Today I confess my sin. I agree with Your perspective. I will follow Your ways. You want an immediate response of obedience. I will give that to You right now. Help me adjust my life and obey. Thank You.

Likewise the Spirit also helps in our weaknesses. For we do not know what we should pray for as we ought, but the Spirit Himself makes intercession for us with groanings which cannot be uttered. Now He who searches the hearts knows what the mind of the Spirit is, because He makes intercession for the saints according to the will of God.

ROMANS 8:26–27

13

GOD SPEAKS THROUGH PRAYER

If you are not keeping a spiritual journal or diary, you need to. If the God of the universe tells you something, you should write it down. When God speaks to you in your quiet time, immediately write down what He said before you have time to forget. Then record your prayer response.

I write down the verse of Scripture He uses and what God has said to me about Himself from that verse. I write down the prayer response I am making; so I have in place the encounter with God, what God said, and how I responded to Him. I also write out what I need to do to adjust my life to God so I can begin to experience Him relating to me in this way.

TRUTH IS A PERSON

The Holy Spirit reveals truth. Truth is not just some concept to be studied. Truth is a Person. Jesus did not say, "I will teach you the truth." He said, "I am . . . the truth" (John 14:6).

When God gives you eternal life, He gives you Himself (John 17:3). When the Holy Spirit reveals Truth, He is not teaching you a concept to be thought about. He is leading you to a relationship with a Person. *He* is your life! When God gives you eternal life, He gives you a Person. When you became a Christian, Jesus didn't give you some *thing*; He gave you Himself.

MY RELATIONSHIP TO GOD

Here is a summary of how I have tried to live out my relationship to God:

- God creates in me the desire to participate in His mission to reconcile a lost world to Himself.
- I respond and come to God seeking to know His will.
- When God reveals a truth to me, I know He is trying to alert me to what He is doing in my life.

When God reveals truth through His Word, that doesn't *lead* to an encounter with God; it *is* the encounter with God. When He reveals truth to me, I am in the presence of a living Person. He is Author of the Scriptures. The Author is telling me through His Word what He is doing in my life.

The Spirit of God knows the mind of God. He will make the will of God known to me through the Word of God. I must then take that truth and immediately adjust my life to Him. I do not adjust my life to a concept or a philosophy but to a Person.

Have you ever read a Scripture you have read many times before, but suddenly you see something in it for the first time? That truth is not a concept for you to figure out how to work into your life. God is introducing you to Himself and alerting you that He is wanting to apply this truth to your life right now. When God is ready to do something in your life, the Spirit of God uses the Word to make that known to you. Then you can adjust your life to Him and what He has just revealed of Himself, His purposes, or His ways.

PRAYER IS A RELATIONSHIP

Prayer is two-way fellowship and communication with God. You speak to God and He speaks to you. It is not a one-way conversation. Your personal prayer life may primarily be one-way communication—you talking to God. Prayer is more than that. Prayer includes listening as well. In fact, what God says in prayer is far more important than what you say.

Prayer is a relationship, not just a religious activity. Prayer is designed more to adjust you to God than to adjust God to you. God doesn't need your prayers, but He wants you to pray. You need to pray because of what God wants to do in and through your life during your praying. God speaks to His people by the Holy Spirit through prayer.

When the Holy Spirit reveals a spiritual truth to you in prayer, He is present and working actively in your life. Genuine prayer does not lead to an encounter with God. It *is* an encounter with God. What happens as you seek God's will in prayer? The sequence is this:

1. God takes the initiative by causing you to want to pray.
2. The Holy Spirit, through the Word of God, reveals to you the will of God.
3. In the Spirit, you pray in agreement with the will of God.
4. You adjust your life to the truth (to God).
5. You look and listen for confirmation or further direction from the Bible, circumstances, and the church (other believers).
6. You obey.
7. God works in you and through you to accomplish His purposes.
8. You experience Him just as the Spirit revealed as you prayed.

I believe the Spirit of God often uses the Word of God when you pray. I find that when I pray about something, Scripture often comes to my mind. I don't see it as a distraction. I believe He is trying to guide me through the Scripture. I have found that as I pray about a particular matter, the Spirit of God takes the Word of God and applies it to my heart and my mind to reveal the truth. I immediately stop my praying and open the Word of God to the passage I believe the Spirit of God brought to my mind.

PRAYING IN THE SPIRIT

We are weak and do not know how we ought to pray. There is, however, some good news: "Likewise the Spirit also helps in our weaknesses. For we do not know what we should pray for as we ought, but the Spirit Himself makes intercession for us with groanings which cannot be uttered. Now He who searches the hearts knows what the mind of the Spirit is, because He makes intercession for the saints according to the will of God" (Rom. 8:26–27).

The Holy Spirit has an advantage over us — He already knows the will of God. When He prays for us, He is praying absolutely in agreement with the will of God. He then helps us know the will of God as we pray.

For his sixth birthday, my oldest son Richard was old enough to have a bicycle. I looked all around for a bicycle. I found a blue Schwinn™. I bought it and hid it in the garage. Then I had a task—to convince Richard that he needed a blue Schwinn bike. For the next little while, we began to work with Richard. Richard decided that what he really wanted for his birthday was a blue Schwinn bike. Do you know what Richard got? Well, the bike was already in the garage. I just had to convince him to ask for it. He asked for it, and he got it!

What happens when you pray? The Holy Spirit knows what God has "in the garage." It is already there. The Holy Spirit's task is to get you to want it—to get you to ask for it. What will happen when you ask for things God already wants to give or do? You will always receive it. Why? Because you have asked *according to the will of God*. When God answers your prayer, He gets the glory and your faith is increased.

Is it important to know when the Holy Spirit is speaking to you? Yes! How do you know what the Holy Spirit is saying? I cannot give you a formula. I can tell you that you will know His voice when He speaks (John 10:4). You must decide that you only want His will. You must dismiss any selfish or fleshly desires of your own. Then, as you start to pray, the Spirit of God starts to touch your heart and cause you to pray in the direction of God's will. "It is God who works in you both to will and to do for His good pleasure" (Phil. 2:13).

The Holy Spirit "will not speak on His own authority, but whatever He hears He will speak; and He will tell you things to come" (John 16:13). When you pray, anticipate that the Holy Spirit already knows what God has ready for your life. He does not guide you on His own initiative; He tells you only what He hears from the Father. He guides you when you pray.

I always write down what God is saying to me when I pray and as I read His Word. I write down what I sense He is leading me to pray. As I begin to see what God is telling me about Himself, His purposes, and His ways, I often see a pattern begin to develop. As I watch the direction the Spirit is leading me to pray, I begin to get a clear indication of what God is saying to me. This process calls for spiritual concentration!

You may be asking the question: "But how do I know that the directions I am praying are the Spirit's leading and not my own selfish desires?" Do you remember what George Mueller said he does first in seeking God's directions? He said he tries to reach the point where he has no will of his own.

GOD'S PRAYER RELATIONSHIP WITH ME

What is prayer? In what way is prayer an encounter with God? What eight steps are involved as I seek God's will and encounter Him in prayer? What happens when God answers my prayers?

DENYING SELF

The first thing you want to do is deny self. In all honesty with yourself and before God, come to the place where you are sure that your only desire is to know God's will alone. Then check to see what the Holy Spirit is saying in other ways. Ask yourself:

- What is He saying to me in His Word?
- What is He saying to me in prayer?
- Is He confirming it through circumstances?
- Is He confirming it through the counsel of other believers?

God never will lead you in opposition to His written Word. If what you sense in prayer runs contrary to Scriptures, it is wrong.

For instance, God will never, never lead you to commit adultery. He always is opposed to that. Watch for God to use the written Word to confirm what you are sensing in prayer. Don't play games with God, though. Don't just look for a Scripture that seems to say what you selfishly want to do, and then claim it is God's will. That is very dangerous. Don't do it.

PRAYING FOR ONE THING . . . AND GETTING ANOTHER

Have you ever prayed for one thing and gotten another? I have. Then some dear soul would say, "God is trying to get you to persist. Keep on praying until you get what you want." During one of those times I kept asking God in one direction, and I kept getting something else.

In the middle of that experience, I started reading from the second chapter of Mark in my quiet time. That is the story of the four men who brought their crippled friend to Jesus to be healed. Because of the crowd, they opened a hole in the roof and let the man down in front of Jesus. Jesus said, "Son, your sins are forgiven you" (Mark 2:5).

I started to read on, but I sensed that the Spirit of God said, "Henry, did you see that?" I went back and began to meditate on that Scripture. Under the guiding, teaching ministry of the Holy Spirit, I began to see a wonderful truth.

The four men were asking Jesus to heal the man, but Jesus forgave the man's sins. Why? They asked for one thing, and Jesus gave another! This man and his friends asked for a particular gift, but Jesus wanted to make the man a child of God so he could inherit everything!

I found myself weeping before God and saying: "Oh God, if I ever give You a request and You have more to give me than I am asking, cancel my request!"

WHAT IS HAPPENING WHEN YOU PRAY?

If I start asking God for one thing and something different happens, I always respond to what begins happening. I have found that God always has far more to give me than I can even ask or think. Paul said, "Now to Him who is able to do exceedingly abundantly above all that we ask or think, according to the power that works in us, to Him be glory in the church by Christ Jesus to all generations, forever and ever!" (Eph. 3:20–21).

You can't even think a prayer that comes close to what God wants to give you. If God wants to give you more than you are asking, would you rather have what you are asking or what God wants to give? Only the Spirit of God knows what God is doing or purposing in your life. Let God give you all that He wants to give. "For the Spirit searches all things, yes, the deep things of God. For what man knows the things of a man except the spirit of the man which is in him? Even so no one knows the things of God except the Spirit of God. Now we have received, not the spirit of the world, but the Spirit who is from God, that we might know the things that have been freely given to us by God" (1 Cor. 2:10–12).

Suppose you wanted to start a mission church in a particular area of town. You have taken a survey to identify the needs. You have made all your long-range plans. You have asked God to bless and guide your work. Then God begins to bring to your church a group of ethnic people who don't live in the target area. What would you do? You might have these options:

- I would "keep on keeping on" in my praying until God helps us start the mission church we have planned.
- I would get frustrated and quit.
- I would start asking questions to see if we should start an ethnic mission church instead of or in addition to the other one.

Do you know what I would do with that? I would immediately go before God and clarify what He is saying. If I have been working and praying in one direction and I see God working in a different direction, I adjust my life to what God is doing. In this kind of situation, you have to decide whether you are going to do what you want and ask God to bless it, or go to work where He is working.

We started a special emphasis to reach university students in Vancouver. We began with thirty students in the fall. By the end of the spring semester, we had about 250 attending. Two-thirds of these were international students. We could have said, "We didn't plan for a ministry to internationals. Please go somewhere else, and may God bless you." Of course we didn't do that. We adjusted our plans to what God began to do around us.

DENYING MYSELF BEFORE GOD IN PRAYER

What will I do when God gives me something different from what I ask Him for? Do I prefer to have what God wants to give or what I ask for? Why? Am I willing to adjust my life to what God is doing?

SPIRITUAL CONCENTRATION

Our problem is that we pray and then never relate anything that happens to our praying. After you pray, the greatest single thing you need to do is turn on your spiritual concentration. When you pray in a direction, immediately anticipate the activity of God in answer to your prayer. I find this all the way through the Scripture; when God's people prayed, He responded.

Here's what happens if you pray and then forget about what you have prayed. Things start to happen during the day that are not normal for your day. You see them all as distractions and try to get rid of them. You fail to connect them with what you have just prayed.

When I pray, I immediately begin to watch for what happens next. I prepare to make adjustments to what begins to happen in my life. When I pray, it never crosses my mind that God is not going to answer. Expect God to answer your prayers, but stick around for the answer. His timing is always right and best.

THE SILENCES OF GOD

I went through a lengthy time when God was silent. You probably have had that experience too. I had been praying over many days, and there seemed to be total silence from God. I sensed that heaven was shut up. I didn't understand what was happening. Some folk have told me that if God does not hear my prayer, I have sin in my life. They gave me a "sin checklist" to work through. I prayed through the sin checklist on this occasion. As far as I could tell, I was okay. I could not understand the silence of God.

Do you remember a biblical person who had a problem like this? Job did. His counselors told him that all his problems were because of sin. Job kept saying, "As best I know, God and I are on the right terms." Job did not know all that God was doing during that time, but his counselors were wrong. There was another reason for what God was doing.

The only thing I knew to do was go back to God. I believe that the God who is in a love relationship with me will let me know what is going on in my life when and if I need to know. So I prayed, "Heavenly Father, I don't understand this silence. You are going to have to tell me what You are doing in my life." He did—from His Word! This became one of the most meaningful experiences in my life.

I did not frantically go searching for an answer. I continued the daily reading of the Word of God. I was convinced that as I was reading the Word of God, the Spirit of God (who knew the mind of God for me) was in the process of helping me understand what God was doing in my life. God will let you know what He is doing in your life when and if you need to know.

ON GOD'S TIME

One morning I was reading the story of the death of Lazarus (John 11:1–45). Let me review the sequence of events. John reported that Jesus loved Lazarus, Mary, and Martha. Having received word that Lazarus was sick unto death, Jesus delayed going until Lazarus died. In other words, Mary and Martha asked Jesus to come help their brother, and there was silence. All the way through the final sickness and death of Lazarus, Jesus did not respond. They received no response from the One who said He loved Lazarus. Jesus even said He loved Mary and Martha. Yet there was still no response.

Lazarus died. They went through the entire funeral process. They fixed his body, put him in the grave, and covered it with a stone. Still they experienced silence from God. Then Jesus said to His disciples, "Let's go."

When Jesus arrived, Lazarus had been dead four days. Mary said to Jesus, "Lord, if You had been here, my brother would not have died" (v. 32).

Then the Spirit of God began to help me understand something. It seemed to me as if Jesus had said to Mary and Martha:

> You are exactly right. If I had come, your brother would not have died. You know that I could have healed him because you have seen Me heal many, many times. If I had come when you asked Me to, I would have healed him. But, you would have never known any more about Me than you already know. I knew that you were ready for a greater revelation of Me than you have ever known in your life. I wanted you to come to know that I am the resurrection and the life. My refusal and My silence was

> not rejection. It was an opportunity for Me to disclose to you more of Me than you have ever known.

When that began to dawn on me, I almost jumped straight out of my chair. I said, "That's what's happening in my life! That's what's happening! The silence of God means that He is ready to bring into my life a greater revelation of Himself than I have ever known." I immediately changed the attitude of my life toward God. With great anticipation, I began to watch for what God was going to teach me about Himself. I then had some things happen in my life that I might never have responded to without that kind of readiness and anticipation.

Now, when I pray and there is a silence from God, I still pray through my sin checklist. Sometimes God's silences are due to sin in my life. If there is unconfessed sin in my life, I confess it and make it right. If, after that, there is still a silence with God, I get ready for a new experience with God that I have never known before. Sometimes God is silent as He prepares to bring you into a deeper understanding of Himself. Whenever a silence comes, continue doing the last thing God told you and watch and wait for a fresh encounter with Him.

You can respond to the silence of God in two ways. One response is for you to go into depression, a sense of guilt, and self-condemnation. The other response is for you to have an expectation that God is about to bring you to a deeper knowledge of Himself. These responses are as different as night and day.

Do you know what set me free? Truth. Truth is a Person who is actively involved in my life. The moment that I understood what God might have been doing, I made an adjustment of my life. I put away the depression and guilt. I quit feeling that maybe I was of no use to God and that He wouldn't hear me anymore. I made the major adjustment in my life to an attitude of expectation, faith, and trust.

The moment I did that, God began to show me how I could respond to Him in such a way that I would know Him in a greater way.

CONCENTRATING BEFORE GOD

When I pray, am I looking for God to act? How do I respond when God is silent? What do I need to do until God breaks His silence? Are there sins in my life that could account for God's silence? How will I deal with these sins?

SUMMARY

Prayer is not just a religious activity you go through once a day or three times at meals. Prayer is a relationship to a Person. It is a two-way communication with the God of the universe. When you pray, you are present in the throne room of heaven—the nerve center of the universe. You do not have to enter prayer alone. Jesus and the Holy Spirit are intercessors with you. The Holy Spirit helps you know what to pray and how to pray. He guides your praying according to the will of God. He already knows what God wants to give or do. His job is to guide you in praying that direction.

Often the Holy Spirit will use the Scripture to reveal truth. But truth is not just a concept. Truth is a Person. When the Holy Spirit reveals truth, you adjust your life to God and obey Him. Prayer as a relationship is probably your best indication about the health of your love relationship with the Father. If your prayer life has been slack, your love relationship probably has grown cold.

EXPERIENCING GOD TODAY

Spend some time today in a prayer relationship with your heavenly Father. Begin by asking the Holy Spirit to direct your praying according to the will of the Father.

This might be a good week to take another prayer walk with your heavenly Father. The only way to cultivate the intimacy with Him that He desires and that you yearn for is to spend time with Him. When you go on your walks with God, don't take a mental agenda with you. Spend your time in worship, praise, and thanksgiving. Allow the Holy Spirit to direct your praying according to the Father's will.

MY SURRENDER TO GOD'S WORD TO ME THROUGH PRAYER

Dear Lord, You do speak to me in prayer, when I am quiet long enough to let You bring Scripture to mind and to let You show me what You are planning. Holy Spirit, direct my praying today. Pray with and through me that my prayer will be according to the will of the Father. Help me pray without ceasing by being attentive to Your answers to my prayers in the coming days. Show me the way You want to go. Show me how to adjust my ways to meet Your ways. Help me see the connections between how You have me praying and the activity I see You engaged in day by day. Do You want to move me to another place in Your service? Do not let the world tie me down to this place. Make me willing and ready to move where You are at work and want me to join in. God, at times Your silence is too hard for me to bear. Help me not go the route of despair. Show me how to read and listen to Your Word and wait for You to speak to me again in prayer. I love You. I trust You. I want to obey You.

Trust in the Lord with all your heart, and lean not on your own understanding; in all your ways acknowledge Him, and He shall direct your paths.

PROVERBS 3:5–6

14

GOD SPEAKS THROUGH CIRCUMSTANCES

At times as I'm leading a seminar, someone will get upset with me and say, "Well, I don't care what you say; I've experienced this."

I respond as kindly as I know how by saying, "I do not deny your experience. I do question your interpretation of what you experienced because it is contrary to what I see in the Word of God."

Our experiences alone cannot be our guide. Every experience must be controlled and understood by the Scriptures. The God revealed in Scripture does not change. Throughout your life, you will have times when you want to respond based on your experiences or your wisdom. Seeking to know God's will based on circumstances alone can be misleading. This should be your guideline: Always go back to the Bible for truth (or for the Holy Spirit to reveal truth).

When you study the Scriptures, look to see how God works *throughout* the Scriptures. Don't rely on one isolated case. When you learn how God has worked throughout history, you can depend on His working in a similar way with you. Your experience is valid only as it is confirmed in the Scriptures. I never deny any experience that a person has had, but I always reserve the right to interpret it according to what I understand in the Scripture.

THE BIBLE IS YOUR GUIDE

I use the Word of God as a guide to what we should be doing. Some people say, "Henry, that is not practical." They want to move me away from the Bible and rely on the world's ways or on personal experience. As a Christian disciple, I cannot abandon the guidance I find in the Bible. The Bible is my guide for faith and practice.

How do you let the Word of God become your guide? When I seek God's direction, I insist on following the directives that I see in the Word of God. The Holy Spirit uses the Bible, prayer, and circumstances to speak to us or show us the Father's will.

JESUS WATCHED THE FATHER'S ACTIVITY

Jesus knew the Father's will for His life and daily activity by watching the Father's activity. Jesus described the process in John 5:17, 19–20: "My Father has been working until now, and I have been working. . . . Most assuredly I say to you, the Son can do nothing of Himself, but what He sees the Father do; for whatever He does, the Son also does in like manner. For the Father loves the Son, and shows Him all things that He Himself does."

Jesus said that He did not take the initiative in what to do for the Father (v. 19). Only the Father has that right. The Father had been working up until Jesus' earthly time, and was still working (v. 17). The Father would let the Son know what He was doing (v. 20). When the Son saw the Father's activity, that was the invitation for the Son to join Him. God used circumstances to reveal to Jesus what He was to do. The circumstances were the things Jesus saw the Father doing. There are some things that only the Father can do.

Jesus always looked for where the Father was at work and then joined Him. The Father loved the Son and showed Him everything He was doing. Jesus did not have to guess what to do. Jesus did not have to dream up what He could do for the Father. He watched to see what the Father was doing around His life, and Jesus put His life there. The Father could then accomplish His purposes through Jesus.

This is exactly what Jesus wants us to do with His lordship in our lives. We see what He is doing and adjust our lives, our plans, and our goals to Him. We are to place our lives at His disposal—where He is working—so He can accomplish His purposes through us.

The example of Jesus is a positive way God speaks through circumstances. Sometimes circumstances appear to be "bad." Maybe you have found yourself in the middle of a "bad" circumstance and you wanted to ask God, "Why is this happening to me?" You are not alone.

GOD'S GUIDE FOR MY LIFE

When did I last interpret my experience in the wrong way and draw a wrong conclusion about God? How did Jesus know the will of God for His life and for His daily activity? Can I use the same ways He used? Why or why not?

GOD'S PERSPECTIVE IS VITAL

Job had a similar experience. He did not understand why everything he owned was destroyed, why his children were killed, and why he developed sores all over his body (Job 1–2). Job wrestled with understanding his circumstances. He did not know what was happening from God's perspective (Job 1:6–12; 2:1–7). Neither did he know the last chapter (Job 42:12–17) where God would restore his property, his family, and his health.

Job's friends thought they had God's perspective and told Job to confess his sin. Job could not find any unrighteousness in his life to confess. If you didn't have that last chapter and didn't know God's perspective, whose side do you think you would be on? God's or Job's? You probably would be with Job, saying, "I want to ask God what is going on. Why is He allowing this to happen?" Without God's perspective, you would think God was being cruel to Job.

When you face difficult or confusing circumstances, they can overwhelm you. If you put yourself in the middle of the circumstances and try to look at God, you will always have a distorted understanding of God.

For instance you might say, "God doesn't love me" or "God is not fair." Both of those statements about God are false. Have you ever been in the middle of a tragic or confusing circumstance where, in your prayers, you began to accuse God of some things that you know are not really true? Perhaps you began to question God's love or His wisdom. Maybe you were afraid to say that He was wrong, but you sort of said, "God, you deceived me in letting me believe that this was the right thing to do. Why didn't you stop me?" A whole lot of wrong conclusions can result if you try to look at God from the middle of a painful circumstance.

What do you do? First, go to God and ask Him to show you His perspective on your circumstance. Look back at your circumstances from the heart of God. When you face difficult or confusing circumstances, the Spirit of God again will take the Word of God and help you understand your circumstances from God's perspective. He will reveal to you the truth of the circumstance. Then you can adjust yourself and your thinking to God's perspective.

OUR DAUGHTER'S CANCER

Earlier I told you about our daughter Carrie's bout with cancer. That was a difficult circumstance for our whole family. The doctors prepared us for six or eight months of chemotherapy plus radiation. We knew God loved us. We prayed, "What are you purposing to do in this experience that we need to adjust ourselves to?"

As we prayed, a Scripture promise came that we believed was from God. Not only did we receive the promise, but we received letters and calls from many people who quoted this same Scripture. The verse reads, "This sickness is not unto death, but for the glory of God, that the Son of God may be glorified through it" (John 11:4).

Our sense that God was speaking to us grew stronger as the Bible, prayer, and the testimony of other believers began to line up and say the same thing. We then adjusted our lives to the truth and began to watch for ways God would use this situation for His glory.

During this time, people from many places in Canada, Europe, and the United States began praying for Carrie. Individuals, college student groups, and churches called to tell us of their prayers. Many said something like this: "Our prayer life (prayer ministry) has become so dry and cold. We haven't seen any special answers to prayer in a long time. But when we heard about Carrie, we put her on our prayer list."

After *three* months of treatments, the doctors ran more tests. They said, "We don't understand this, but all the tests are negative. We cannot find any trace of the cancer." I immediately began to contact those who had committed to pray for Carrie, and shared with them this demonstration of prayer being answered. In instance after instance, people said that seeing God answer prayer totally renewed their prayer life. Church prayer ministries were revitalized. Student prayer groups found new life.

FOR GOD'S GLORY

Then I began to see what God had in mind for this circumstance. Through this experience God was glorified in the eyes of His people. Many, many people sensed a fresh call to prayer. They personally began to experience anew the presence of Truth—and Truth as a Person. Some of Carrie's closest friends began to pray fervently at this time. Some students even came to know the Lord after observing what God had done in and through Carrie. God did bring glory to Himself through this sickness.

Do you see what happened? We faced a trying situation. We could have looked back at God from the middle of that and gotten a very distorted understanding of God. Instead we went to Him. We sought His perspective.

The Holy Spirit took the Word of God and revealed to us God's perspective on the end result of that circumstance. We believed God and adjusted our lives to Him and to what He was doing. We then went through the circumstance looking for ways His purposes would be accomplished in ways that would bring Him glory. So when the answer to prayer came, I knew immediately my job was to "declare the wonderful works of the Lord" to His people. In the process we came to know God in a new way because of the compassion He showed us by revealing His perspective on our situation.

Let me summarize how you can respond when circumstances are difficult or confusing:

- Settle in your own mind that God has forever demonstrated His absolute love for you on the cross. That love will never change.
- Do not try to understand what God is like from the middle of your circumstances.
- Go to God and ask Him to help you see His perspective on your situation.
- Wait on the Holy Spirit. He may take the Word of God and help you understand your circumstances.
- Adjust your life to God and what you see Him doing in your circumstances.
- Do all He tells you to do.
- Experience God working in and through you to accomplish His purposes.

Remember that God is sovereign. You may face a situation like Job experienced where God does not tell you what He is doing. In those instances acknowledge God's love and sovereignty and depend on His sustaining grace to see you through the situation.

SEEKING GOD'S PERSPECTIVE ON MY CIRCUMSTANCE

When can I turn to other people to find God's perspective on my circumstances? How can circumstances give me a distorted picture of God? How do I find God's perspective in the middle of "bad" circumstances?

THE TRUTH OF YOUR CIRCUMSTANCE

You cannot know the truth of your circumstance until you have heard from God. In Exodus 5–6 Moses did as he was told and asked Pharaoh to let Israel go. Pharaoh refused and multiplied the hardship on the Israelites. The Israelites turned on Moses and criticized him for causing so much trouble. What would you have done if you had been in Moses' place?

The human tendency would be to assume you missed God's will. You might get mad at Israel for treating your good intentions so harshly, or you might have gotten mad at God.

Moses' story really encourages me. He blamed God and accused Him of failing to do what He promised. I guess many of us would have responded in a similar way. Moses said, "Lord, why have You brought trouble on this people? Why is it You have sent me? For since I came to Pharaoh to speak in Your name, he has done evil to this people; neither have You delivered Your people at all" (Exod. 5:22–23). Moses was so discouraged he was ready to quit (Exod. 6:12).

I'm glad God is patient with us, too! God took time to explain to Moses His perspective. God explained that He *wanted* Pharaoh to resist so the people could see God's mighty hand of deliverance. He wanted the people to come to know Him (by experience) as the great "I AM."

Learn from Moses' example. When you face confusing circumstances, don't start blaming God. Don't just give up following Him. Go to God. Ask Him to reveal the truth of your circumstances. Ask Him to show you His perspective. Then wait on the Lord.

You need to have your life radically oriented to God. The most difficult thing you will ever have to do is deny self, take up the will of God, and follow after Him. The most difficult part of your relationship to God is being God-centered. If you were to record a whole day in your life you might find that your prayers, your attitudes, your thoughts, everything about that day is radically self-centered. You may not be seeing things from God's perspective. You may try to explain to God what your perspective is. When He becomes the Lord of your life, He alone has the right to be:

- the Focus in your life;
- the Initiator in your life;
- the Director of your life.

That is what it means for Him to be Lord.

HEARING FROM TRUTH

When the Holy Spirit talks to you, He is going to reveal Truth to you. He is going to talk to you about a Person. He is going to talk to you about Jesus. Truth is a Person! Jesus said, "I am . . . the truth" (John 14:6).

Truth in a Storm. The disciples were in a boat in a storm. Jesus was asleep in the back of the boat. If you had gone to those disciples in the middle of that storm and said to them, "What is the truth of this situation?" what would they have said? "We perish!" Was that the truth? No, Truth was asleep at the back of the boat. Truth is a Person. In just a moment Truth Himself would stand up, and He would still the storm. Then they knew the Truth of their circumstance. Truth is a Person who is always present in your life. You cannot know the truth of your circumstance until you have heard from God. He is the Truth! And the Truth is present and active in your life!

Truth at a Funeral. Notice the difference Truth made in the following circumstance.

> [Jesus] went into a city called Nain; and many of His disciples with Him and a large crowd. As He came near the gate of the city, behold, a dead man was being carried out, the only son of his mother; and she was a widow. And a large crowd from the city was with her. When the Lord saw her, He had compassion for her and said to her, "Do not weep." Then He came and touched the open

> coffin, and those who carried him stood still. And He said, "Young man, I say to you, arise." So he who was dead sat up and began to speak. And He presented him to his mother.
>
> Then fear came upon all, and they glorified God, saying, "A great prophet has risen up among us"; and, "God has visited His people." And this report about Him went throughout all Judea and all the surrounding region. (Luke 7:11–17)

If you had asked the widow who was in the funeral procession of her only son, "What's the truth of this situation?" she might have replied, "My husband died at a young age. I had one son, and I had anticipated that we would spend wonderful days together. He would care for me, and we would have fellowship together. Now my son is dead, and I must live the rest of my life alone." Was that the truth?

No, Truth was standing there! When Truth reached out and touched her son and restored him, all was changed. You never know the truth of any situation until you have heard from Jesus.

When Jesus was allowed to reveal Himself in this circumstance, the people "glorified God, saying, 'A great prophet has risen among us'; and 'God has visited His people.' And this report about Him went throughout Judea and all the surrounding region" (Luke 7:16–17). Never, ever determine the truth of a situation by looking at the circumstances. Don't evaluate your situation until you have heard from Jesus. He is the Truth of all your circumstances.

Truth with Hungry People. In John 6:1–15 Jesus was surrounded by five thousand hungry people. He wanted to feed them. In a test of Philip's faith, Jesus asked him where they could buy bread to feed the multitude. If you had asked the disciples at that moment about the truth of the situation, they might have said, "We can't do it. Lord, the truth of the situation is that it is impossible." Was that true? No. We know the other half of the story. Wouldn't we be better off if we trusted God with the other half of the story in our lives? Truth Himself fed five thousand men plus their families and had twelve baskets full of leftovers!

I wonder if God ever tests our faith as He did Philip's. Does He say, "Feed the multitudes" and the church responds, "We don't have that much money in our budget"? Truth stands in the middle of the church, and the Head of the church says, "Believe Me. I will never give you an order that I will not release the power to enable it to happen. Trust Me, obey Me, and it *will* happen."

YES, LORD

In making a decision, the greatest difficulty may not be in choosing between good and bad, but in choosing between good and best. You may have several options that all appear to be good. The place to start is to say with all of your heart: "Lord, whatever I know to be Your will, I will do. Regardless of the cost and regardless of the adjustment, I commit myself to follow Your will. Lord, no matter what that will looks like, I will do it!"

You need to say that *before* you begin to seek God's will. Otherwise you do not mean, "Thy will be done." Instead, you are saying, "Thy will be done as long as it does not conflict with my will." Two words in the Christian's language cannot go together: No, Lord. If you say, "No," He is not Lord. If He really is your Lord, your answer must always be "Yes." In decision making, always begin here. Do not proceed until you can honestly say, "Whatever you want of me, Lord, I will do it."

PHYSICAL MARKERS OF SPIRITUAL ENCOUNTERS

When Israel crossed the Jordan River into the Promised Land, God gave Joshua the following instructions: "Take for yourselves twelve men from the people, one man from every tribe, and command them, saying, 'Take for yourselves twelve stones from here, out of the midst of the Jordan, from the place where the priest's feet stood firm. You shall carry them over with you and leave them in the lodging place where you lodge tonight'" (Josh. 4:2–3).

These stones were to serve as a sign to the Israelites. Joshua explained: "that this may be a sign among you when your children ask in time to come, saying, 'What do these stones mean to you?' Then you shall answer them that the waters of the Jordan were cut off before the ark of the LORD; when it crossed over the Jordan, the waters of the Jordan were cut off. And these stones shall be for a memorial to the children of Israel forever" (Josh. 4:6–7).

The stones were to be a reminder of a mighty act of God in behalf of His people. On many other occasions men built altars or set up stones as a reminder of a significant encounter with God (Noah: Gen. 6–8; Abram: Gen. 12:1–8 and 13:1–18; Isaac: Gen. 26:17–25; Jacob: Gen. 28:10–22 and 35:1–7; Moses: Exod. 17:8–16 and 24:1–11; Joshua: Josh. 3:5–4:9; Gideon: Judg. 6:11–24; and Samuel: 1 Sam. 7:1–13).

Often men in the Old Testament set up a stone marker or altar as a reminder of their encounters with God. Places like Bethel ("house of God") and Rehoboth ("room") became reminders of God's great activity in the midst of His people. Moses named an altar "The Lord is my Banner"; and Samuel named a stone "Ebenezer" saying, "Thus far the LORD has helped us" (1 Sam. 7:12). These altars and stones became physical markers of great spiritual encounters with God. They provided an opportunity for people to teach their children about the activity of God in behalf of His people.

MY RESPONSE TO THE TRUTH

How does God respond when I express my anger and frustration to Him? What do I need to do with my life when I face confusing circumstances? What work have I seen God accomplish in my life recently? What kind of marker have I established to remind myself and my family of God's work in and through us?

A SPIRITUAL INVENTORY

I have found it helpful to identify "spiritual markers" in my life. Each time I encounter God's call or directions, I mentally build a spiritual marker at that point. A spiritual marker identifies a time of transition, decision, or direction when I clearly know that God has guided me. Over time I can look back at these spiritual markers and see how God has faithfully directed my life according to His divine purpose. When I review my spiritual markers, I can see more clearly the directions in which God has been moving my life and ministry.

At times I may face several options where I could serve God. I need to know which of these good things is what God desires of me. When I face a decision about God's direction, I review my spiritual markers. I don't take the next step without the context of the full activity of God in my life. This helps me see God's perspective for my past and present. Then I look at the options that are before me. I look to see which one of the options seems to be most consistent with what God has been doing in my life. Often one of these directions will be most consistent with what God already has been doing. If none of the directions seems consistent, I continue to pray and wait on the Lord's guidance. When circumstances do not align with what God is saying in the Bible and in prayer, I assume that the timing may be wrong. I then wait for God to reveal His timing.

When I was approached about coming to the Home Mission Board to direct the emphasis on prayer and spiritual awakening, I had never had such a job in my life. Only God could reveal whether this was part of His divine purpose. I recalled the spiritual markers in my life to see this decision from God's perspective.

My heritage goes back to England, where a number of my family were graduates of Spurgeon's College when Spurgeon was trying to win England to Christ. I grew up in a town in Canada where there was no evangelical witness to Christ. My father served as a lay pastor to help start a mission in that town.

Way back in my teen years I began to sense a deep burden for communities all across Canada that did not have an evangelical church. In 1958, when I was in seminary, God assured me that He loved my nation enough to want to bring a great movement of His Spirit across our land. When I accepted God's call to go to Saskatoon as a pastor, God used the prospect of a spiritual awakening there to affirm my call. A revival and spiritual awakening did start there and spread across many parts of Canada in the early 1970s.

In 1988, Bob Hamblin from the Home Mission Board called me. He said, "Henry, we have prayed much about filling a position in prayer for spiritual awakening. We have been seeking a person for over two years to fill this position. Would you consider coming and directing Southern Baptists in the area of spiritual awakening?"

As I reviewed God's activity in my life (my spiritual markers), I saw that an emphasis on spiritual awakening was an important element throughout my ministry. I said to Bob, "You could have asked me to do anything in the world, and I would not have even prayed about leaving Canada—except spiritual awakening. That has been a deep current that has run through my life since the time I was an older teenager and more particularly since 1958." After much prayer and confirmation in the Word and by other believers, I accepted the position at the Home Mission Board. God didn't shift me; He focused me in something He had already been doing down the course of my life.

MY SPIRITUAL MARKERS

What events can I list recalling times when I clearly know that God has guided me? What direction has God been moving my life and ministry? How can I use my spiritual markers to determine God's consistent pattern for my life? What has been the consistent theme or purpose running through my life with God?

SUMMARY

God used circumstances to reveal to Jesus what He was to do. Jesus watched circumstances to know where the Father wanted to involve Him in His work. God may use circumstances to reveal His directions to you also. However, you must check these directions against what God may be saying through the Scriptures and prayer. Reviewing your spiritual markers is one way God may give you a sense of direction using circumstances. When God gets ready for you to take a new step or direction in His activity, it will be in sequence with what He has already been doing in your life.

Sometimes you may find yourself in difficult or confusing circumstances. To understand bad or difficult circumstances, God's perspective is vital. Never, ever determine the truth of a situation by looking at the circumstances. You cannot know the truth of any circumstance until you have heard from God.

EXPERIENCING GOD TODAY

Spend some time with God in prayer. Ask Him to assist you in identifying your own spiritual markers. These may begin with your heritage, your salvation experience, times you made significant decisions regarding your future, and so forth. What are some of the times of transition, decision, or direction in your life when you knew clearly that God guided you? Start developing a list of your own spiritual markers, but don't feel like you have to have a comprehensive list. Add to it as you reflect and pray about God's activity in your life.

MY SURRENDER TO GOD'S WORD TO ME THROUGH CIRCUMSTANCES

Dear God, You have consistently led me through life's circumstances ever since I first came into a love relationship with You. I have learned to trust You to know what is best for my life. Sometimes my circumstances seem so dark and hopeless. I am so tempted to let my situation in life turn me away from You or make me have wrong ideas about who You are and how You work in my life. I now dedicate myself to Your will. I say yes, Lord, I will carry out Your will as You reveal it to me. I make no conditions. Whatever Your will is, I will do it. I will make whatever adjustments You show me are necessary to line my life up with Your will. I want all my life to be God-centered and not self-centered. Guide me through these circumstances to find Your perspective and Your purpose in them. Thank You for loving me and guiding me.

But, speaking the truth in love, [we] may grow up in all things into Him who is the head—Christ—from whom the whole body, joined and knit together by what every joint supplies, according to the effective working by which every part does its share, causes growth of the body for the edifying of itself in love.

EPHESIANS 4:15–16

15

GOD SPEAKS THROUGH THE CHURCH

In Vancouver I served as interim pastor of a small church. A Laotian refugee family had joined the church the week before I came. I knew that God never adds members to the body of Christ by accident. Those added to the church are my ministry. My responsibility as pastor was to see what God was doing when He added them to our church. I needed to see what God wanted to do in their lives through our church. I needed to see what God wanted to do through them in the life of our church. I (and others) had opportunity to see God's activity in the Laotians' lives. As we prayed and shared together, the church helped Thomas, the father, better understand God's plan for his life.

Thomas had been saved in a refugee camp in Thailand. His life was so gloriously transformed that he wanted his Laotian people to know Jesus. He went all through the community trying to lead his Laotian brothers to Christ. The first week Thomas led fifteen adults to the Lord. The next week he led eleven to the Lord, and he wept because he felt he was so unfaithful to the Lord.

In our next church business meeting I said, "I sense we need to start a Laotian mission church." I shared all I knew of what God was doing. "I believe God is leading those people to the Lord so we can start a Laotian mission," I explained. Then I asked the church to decide how they sensed God wanted us to respond. They voted to start a Laotian mission church.

Then I said, "I believe we ought to call Thomas as the pastor." I told them what God was doing in Thomas's life. God had given him a pastor's heart. He had a burden for evangelism. He had just enrolled in a local Baptist theological college to get training to do anything God wanted to do through him. They voted to call Thomas as pastor of the new mission, and Thomas accepted.

Two months later Thomas was invited to a meeting for ethnic pastors in St. Louis. Thomas asked if he could go. I said, "Sure."

Then he asked, "Can I take some friends with me?" I didn't know what that meant until he said he wanted to take eighteen friends with him. Then he said, "Henry, would you mind if I came back through all the major cities of Canada? My brothers are in all these cities. God wants me to go and lead some of them to the Lord. If God will help me, I'll find a pastor for them. Then they can have a church in every major city of Canada." Then I knew that God was doing something special.

I said, "Oh Thomas, please go!" He did. Later that year, at Christmas, Laotian people from all across Canada came to celebrate the new life in Christ they had found.

Some time later I went back to Vancouver to visit. I asked about Thomas. The Laotian government had granted permission to start churches. Thomas returned to Laos and preached the gospel, and 133 members of his family came to know the Lord. He started four mission churches. He linked the church in Vancouver with the Laotian churches with the heart's desire of seeing all the Laotian people come to know the Lord.

Initially all we saw was one Laotian refugee. What did God see? He saw a people and a whole nation being drawn to Himself. When God honors your church by placing a new member in the body, ask God to show you what He is up to. Then share what you are sensing of God's activity. God speaks through the members of the body to help others know and understand God's assignment for their lives.

THE PARABLE OF THE TRAIN TRACKS

Suppose the eye could say to the body, "Let us walk down these train tracks. The way is clear. Not a train is in sight." So the body starts down the tracks.

Then the ear says, "I hear a whistle coming from the other direction."

The eye argues, "But nothing is on the track as far as I can see. Let's keep on walking." The body listens only to the eye and keeps on walking.

Soon the ear says, "That whistle is getting louder and closer!" Then the feet say, "I feel the rumbling motion of a train coming. We better get our body off these tracks!" If this were your body, what would you do?

- Would you try to ignore the conflict and hope it passed away?
- Would you take a vote of all your body members and let the majority rule?
- Would you trust your eye and keep on walking since your eyes have never let you down before?

No. You would get off the train tracks as soon as possible. Those may seem like silly questions to ask. God gave our bodies many different senses and parts. When each part does its job, the whole body works the way it should. In our physical bodies we do not take votes based on majority rule, ignore conflicting senses, nor choose to listen only to one sense and ignore the others. To live that way would be very dangerous.

Because a church is the body of Christ, it functions best when all members are able to share what they sense God wants the church to be and do. Members of a church cannot fully know God's will for their lives in the body apart from the body. A church also needs to hear the whole counsel of God through its members. Then it can proceed in confidence and in unity to do God's will.

GOD'S WORD TO ME THROUGH MY CHURCH

What unusual member(s) has God added to my church recently? Have I asked God to show me His purpose in this? How has my church helped me find God's assignment for my life? How does my church encourage all members to share what they have learned of God's purposes and activities in our midst?

THE BODY OF CHRIST

One of the problems many evangelical churches face today is that they have so emphasized the doctrine of the priesthood of believers that they have lost their sense of corporate identity. What does that mean in simple words? Christians think they stand alone before God and that they are not accountable to anyone else, including the church.

Christians do have access to God through Christ as their one Mediator. God, however, created the church as His redemptive agent in the world. He has a purpose for the church. God places every member in a church to accomplish His redemptive purposes through that church.

A church is a body. It is the body of Christ (1 Cor. 12:27)! Jesus Christ is present as Head of a local church (Eph. 4:15), and every member is placed in the body as it pleases God (1 Cor. 12:18). The Holy Spirit manifests Himself to every person for the common good (1 Cor. 12:7). The whole body is fitted together by the Father. Members are enabled and equipped by the Holy Spirit to function where the Father has placed them in the body. The body then functions to build itself up into the Head, until *every member* comes to the measure of the stature of the fullness of Christ (Eph. 4:13). God made us mutually interdependent. We need each other. What one member lacks, others in the body can supply.

Therefore, what God is doing in and through the body is essential to my knowing how to respond to Him. Where I see Him working in the body, I adjust and put my life there. In the church, I let God use me in any way He chooses to complete His work in each member. This was Paul's goal when he said, "Him we preach, warning every man and teaching every man in all wisdom, that we may present every man perfect in Christ Jesus" (Col. 1:28). Paul was constantly requesting the believers to become vitally involved with his life and ministry. The effectiveness of Paul's ministry rested on them (Col. 4:3; 2 Thess. 3:1, 2; Eph. 6:19).

THE CHURCH HELPED ME KNOW GOD'S WILL

While I was in seminary, I was involved in a local church. The first year I taught teenage boys. I did that with a willing heart. The next year I was asked to be music and education director. I had never done anything like that before. I had sung in a choir, but had never led a bit of music. I knew nothing about directing the educational program of a church. Here is how I approached the decision.

The people of God at this church needed a leader. As they prayed they sensed that God put me there purposely to meet that need. I, too, saw the need and realized God could use me there. As a servant of Jesus Christ, I did not have an option to say no. I believed that the Head—Jesus Christ—could speak through the rest of the body to guide me to know how I should function in the body. I said I would do the best I knew to do, and for two years I served as music and education director.

Then the church voted to call me to be their pastor. I hadn't preached three sermons in my life. I had not come to the seminary because I felt called to be a pastor. I did, however, feel called of God to enter into a *relationship* with Him for *whatever* He had in mind. I sensed that I needed to put the seminary training in place so that I would have some tools for God to work with. I didn't say, "I am going into foreign missions or home missions." I didn't say music, or education, or preaching. I said, "Lord, whatever You direct me to do in relation to Your body, I will do. I am Your servant for Your purposes." So I agreed to be their pastor.

Apart from the body, you cannot know God's will for your relationship to the body. Without the eye, the hand does not know where to touch. Without the ear, the body may not know when or how to respond. Every member needs to listen to what other members say. If the members are not talking about what they sense God is doing, the whole body is in trouble. As I function in relationship to the church, I depend on others in the church to help me understand God's will.

GOD'S PURPOSE FOR MY CHURCH

To whom am I accountable as a Christian? How am I accomplishing God's redemptive mission through my church? What do I lack that my church and its other members supply for me? What adjustments in my life with God have I made because I saw Him working in my church?

DEPENDING ON GOD TO SPEAK THROUGH THE CHURCH

In the church, the need does not constitute the call. The need, however, is not to be ignored. Don't ever be afraid to let the body of believers assist you in knowing God's will. Sometimes God may speak through one person, but His Spirit convinces you that the message is from Him. Keep in mind, however, that one individual is not the church. In the final analysis, you are going to have to take all the counsel of people and go to God for the clear direction. What you will find is that a number of things begin to line up. What you are hearing from the Bible and prayer and circumstances and the church will begin to say the same thing. Then you can proceed with confidence.

You may say to me, "Henry, you don't know my church. I can't depend on them to help me know God's will." Be careful. When you say that, you have said more about what you believe about God than what you believe about your church. You are saying, "Henry, not even God can work through these people. He just is not powerful enough." You don't believe that in your mind, I don't think. But what you do says more about what you believe about God than what you say.

Trust God to provide you counsel through other believers. Turn to them for counsel on major decisions. Listen attentively to anything the church has to say to you. Then let God confirm what His message is for you.

SHARING IN THE BODY

In Saskatoon, as God moved and expressed His will to church members, I guided them to share with the other members of the body. We could not adjust our lives to God if we did not know what He was saying. When the Head spoke to any member, all of us had to listen and hear what He said to our church. All were given an opportunity and encouraged to share. Each was encouraged to respond as God guided him or her. This happened not only in worship (usually at the close of a service), but also in prayer meetings, committee meetings, business meetings, Sunday School classes, home Bible studies, and personal conversations. Many called the church office and shared what God was saying to them in their quiet times. Still others shared what they experienced at work or at school. The entire church became experientially and practically aware of Christ's presence in our midst.

Often sharing what God is doing in your life may help someone else encounter God in a meaningful way. For instance, when someone was led to make a significant commitment to the Lord in one of our services, I gave that person an opportunity to share with the body. Sometimes that testimony prompted others to respond in a similar way. In this way God spoke through the church to other believers.

TRUSTING GOD AND OTHER BELIEVERS

What might recognition of a need indicate to me about God's will? What person or persons in the church should I depend upon to help me understand God's will? When can I proceed with confidence that I know and am doing God's will? What am I really saying when I claim I cannot depend on my church to help me know God's will? How should I proceed when I need to make a major decision? Do I automatically take the word I hear from the church as God's will in the decision I am making? How can my church give members opportunities to share what God is saying to each of us? What will happen when we do?

SUMMARY

God speaks to His people by the Holy Spirit. He can speak in any way He chooses; but the most common ways through which God speaks today include the Bible, prayer, circumstances, and the church. He speaks to reveal Himself, His purposes, and His ways. When what God says through the Bible, prayer, circumstances, and the church begin to line up to say the same thing, you can proceed with confidence to follow God's directions.

Because each believer is added by God to the body of Christ, he or she is interdependent on other believers to function correctly in that body. You cannot know God's will for your involvement in the body of Christ apart from the counsel God provides through other members. All the members of the body belong to each other, and they need each other. You can and should depend on God to speak through other believers and the church to help you know what assignment you are to carry out in the ministry of the kingdom.

EXPERIENCING GOD TODAY

Pray for your church and the way God is working in and through her members to help believers understand God's call. Reflect on times and ways God has spoken to you through other believers and thank God for using them to speak to you. Sometime soon, get together with two or three other believers from your church to pray for each other.

MY SURRENDER TO GOD'S WORD TO ME THROUGH HIS CHURCH

Lord of the church, You have made me a part of Your body, the church. Forgive me when I try to perform the functions of all the parts of Your body instead of being satisfied with the part You have made me. Teach me to operate within the body, letting each member minister and share with me as I try to minister and share with each of them. You know the decision and problems I face right now. Speak through the church to show me Your will in these matters. Teach me to trust Your body. Confirm Your word through the body by showing me the same word in my circumstances and in Your Holy Word. Make our church a house of prayer. Lead us to reach out to Your harvest and bring new members into Your body. Show each of our members Your place of ministry and Your word for them. Thank You for my church. Bless us and use us to accomplish Your will in Your world in our day.

But without faith it is impossible to please Him, for he who comes to God must believe that He is, and that He is a rewarder of those who diligently seek Him.

HEBREWS 11:6

16

GOD'S INVITATION LEADS TO A CRISIS OF BELIEF

This chapter focuses on a turning point in your following God's will. When God invites you to join Him in His work, He presents a God-sized assignment for you to accomplish. You will realize that you cannot accomplish it on your own. If God doesn't help you, you will fail. This is the crisis point where many decide not to follow what they sense God is leading them to do. Then they wonder why they do not experience God's presence, power, and activity the way other Christians do.

The word *crisis* comes from a word that means "decision." The same Greek word is often translated judgment. We are not talking about a crisis in your life like an accident or death. The *crisis of belief* is a turning point or a fork in the road that demands that you make a decision. You must decide what you *believe* about God. How you respond when you reach this turning point will determine whether you go on to be involved with God in something God-sized that only He can do or whether you will continue to go your own way and miss what God has purposed for your life. This is not a one-time experience. It is a daily experience. How you live your life is a testimony of what you believe about God.

A GOD-SIZED TASK FOR ME

Have I ever been called to a God-sized assignment where I had to trust God to work through me or provide for me? How did I respond?

A FAITH BUDGET FOR OUR CHURCH

One year the people on our finance committee said, "Pastor, you have taught us to walk by faith in every area of the life of our church except in the budget." I asked them to explain. They said, "Well, when we set the budget, we set the budget on the basis of what we believe we can do. It does not reflect that we expect God to do anything."

"Hmmm," I said. "Then how do you feel we ought to set the budget?"

They said, "First, we should determine all that God wants to do through us. Second, we need to estimate what the cost will be.

Finally, we need to divide the budget goal into three categories: (1) what we plan to accomplish through our tithes, (2) what others have promised to do, and (3) what we must depend on God to do."

As a church we prayed and decided that God did want us to use this approach to budgeting. We did not try to dream our own dreams for God. We had to be absolutely sure God was leading us to do the things we put in the budget. Then we listed what that would cost. We listed what we thought our people would give and what others (denominational board, partnership churches, and individuals) had said they would give. The difference between what we could reasonably expect to receive and the total was what we would ask God to provide.

The big question was: What is our operating budget? Well, by faith we adopted the grand total as our operating budget. At this point we reached a crisis of belief. Did we really believe that the God who led us to do these things also would provide the resources to bring them to pass? Anytime God leads you to do something that has God-sized dimensions, you will face a crisis of belief. When you face a crisis of belief, what you do next reveals what you really believe about God.

The budget of our church normally would have been $74,000. The budget we set was $164,000. We pledged to pray daily that God would meet our needs. Any money that came in that we did not anticipate we credited to God. At the end of that year we had received $172,000. God taught our church a lesson in faith that radically changed us all.

The greatest crisis came when we decided to operate on the grand total rather than what we knew we could do. Operating on the $74,000 amount would not take much faith. We were sure we could do that much. Operating on a budget of $164,000 required faith. We could not see any way to get that much money unless God provided it.

Do you see the turning point—the crisis of belief? We could have decided on the lesser budget and never known anything more about God. People in the community watching our church would have only seen what people can do. They would never have seen God and what He can do.

THE CRISIS OF BELIEF

An encounter with God requires faith.
Encounters with God are God-sized.
What you do in response to God's revelation (invitation) reveals what you believe about God.
True faith requires action.

ENCOUNTERS WITH GOD REQUIRE FAITH

When God speaks, your response requires faith. All through Scripture when God revealed Himself, His purposes, and His ways, the response to Him required faith. God is interested in your walking with Him by faith. Read the following Scriptures to see what God has to say about faith.

> Now faith is the substance of things hoped for, the evidence of things not seen. (Heb. 11:1)
>
> For we walk by faith, not by sight. (2 Cor. 5:7)
>
> [Jesus said,] "He who believes in Me, the works that I do he will do also; and greater works than these he will do, because I go to My Father." (John 14:12)
>
> "For assuredly, I say to you, if you have faith as a mustard seed, you will say to this mountain, 'Move from here to there,' and it will move; and nothing will be impossible for you." (Matt. 17:20)

> [Paul said,] "My speech and my preaching were not with persuasive words of human wisdom, but in demonstration of the Spirit and of power, that your faith should not be in the wisdom of men but in the power of God." (1 Cor. 2: 4–5)
>
> If you will not believe, surely you shall not be established. (Isa. 7:9)

Faith is confidence that what God has promised or said will come to pass. Sight is an opposite of faith. If you can see clearly how something can be accomplished, more than likely faith is not required. Remember the illustration about our church budget? If we had chosen to operate on what we knew we could do, faith would not have been necessary.

Your faith does not rest in a concept or an idea. Faith must be in a Person—God Himself. If you or someone else decides something would be nice to have happen and then leads people to "believe" or "have faith," you are in a dangerous position. Faith is only valid in God and what He says He is purposing to do. If the thing you expect to happen is from you and not God, then you must depend on what you can do. Before you call yourself, your family, or your church to exercise faith, be sure you have heard a word from God.

With only mustard-seed (very small) sized faith in God, nothing is impossible. Jesus said His followers would do even greater things than He had done. Our faith, however, must be based on God's power and not human wisdom. Without a firm faith, you will stumble and fall.

MY FAITH RESPONSE

What does God's Word teach me about faith? What is my faith based on?

SOMETHING ONLY GOD CAN DO

Moses could never have delivered the children of Israel from Pharaoh's army, crossed the Red Sea on dry land, provided water from a rock, or furnished to his people bread and meat. Moses had to have faith that the God who called him would do the things He said He would do. Joshua could not take the Israelites across the Jordan River on dry land, bring down walled cities, defeat enemies, or make the sun stand still. Only God could have done these things. Joshua had to have faith in God.

In the New Testament this also was true for the disciples. On their own, they could not feed the multitudes, heal the sick, still a storm, or raise the dead. Only God could do these things. But God called servants to let Him do these things through them.

When God lets you know what He wants to do through you, it will be something only God can do. What you believe about Him will determine what you do. If you have faith in the God who called you, you will obey Him; and He will bring to pass what He has purposed to do. If you lack faith, you will not do what He wants. That is disobedience.

Jesus questioned those around Him, "Why do you call me, 'Lord, Lord,' and not do the things which I say?" (Luke 6:46). Jesus frequently rebuked His disciples for their lack of faith and unbelief. Their unbelief revealed that they really had not come to know who He was. Thus, they did not know what He could do.

OBEDIENCE SHOWS FAITH

Faith was required of Moses and the disciples. When God calls a person to join Him in a God-sized task, faith is always required. Obedience indicates faith in God. Disobedience often indicates a lack of faith. Without faith, a person cannot please God. Without faith, a church cannot please God.

We face the same crisis Bible characters faced. When God speaks, what He asks of us requires faith. Our major problem, however, is our self-centeredness. We think we have to accomplish the assignment on our own power and with our current resources. We think, "I can't do that. That is not possible."

We forget that when God speaks He always reveals what He is going to do—not what He wants us to do for Him. We join Him so He can do His work through us. We don't have to be able to accomplish the task within our limited ability or resources. With faith, we can proceed confidently because we know that *He* is going to bring to pass what *He* purposes. "Jesus looked at them and said, 'With men it is impossible, but not with God; for with God all things are possible'" (Mark 10:27). The Scriptures bear witness that this is true.

LEARNING FROM THE BIBLE

What power did Moses have to deliver Israel from Egypt and lead them through the wilderness? What power did Joshua have to cross the Jordan and conquer Canaan? How did Jesus' disciples perform miracles? What does Jesus expect from me if I am to accomplish the God-sized tasks He gives me? What is the major problem that causes me not to exercise faith?

LEN KOSTER AND MISSION CHURCHES

In the Saskatoon church we sensed that we needed to be of use to God in reaching people for Christ throughout Saskatchewan. The province contained over two hundred cities, towns, and villages. This meant we would have to start new (mission) churches. To do that, we felt God was leading us to call Len Koster to become a minister of mission outreach. He would equip the church to start churches.

For fourteen years Len and Ruth had pastored small churches. Len was so committed to the Lord that he worked as a service station attendant for fourteen years in order to pastor bivocationally. Without a part-time pastor these churches would have had no pastor at all. In that time Len and Ruth had saved seven thousand dollars, hoping that one day they would have enough money to buy their own home. When Len felt absolutely convinced that he ought to come help us start churches, I said, "Len, we have no money to move you and no money to pay you."

He said, "Henry, the God who has called me will help me. We will take the money from our savings, and we will move." Later, Len came into my office and said, "Henry, my wife and I prayed and talked all night. I have worked bivocationally for fourteen years, and I have no problem of working to provide for my family. But the need here is so great, and the direction of God is such that I feel I need to be full time. My wife and I realized last night that the money we have in the bank is God's, and He wants us to use that to live off. When we have finished that, He will show us how to live. So," he said, "Henry, don't worry about my support."

When Len went out of that room, I fell on my face. I wept and wept before the Father. I said, "Father, I don't understand why such a faithful couple should have to make this kind of a sacrifice." I saw in Len and Ruth a great faith that was demonstrated by their actions.

Two days later I received a letter from a Presbyterian layman in Kamloops, British Columbia. It was a very short letter that simply said, "I understand a man by the name of Len Koster has come to work with you. God has laid it on my heart that I am to help support his ministry. Enclosed find a check for seven thousand dollars to be used for his support." When I opened that letter, I went back on my knees and wept before the Father. This time, I asked Him to forgive me for not trusting Him when He told me I could.

I called Len and said, "Len, you have placed your life savings on the altar of sacrifice, but God has something else in the bushes. The God who says, 'I am your Provider' has just provided!" Then I told him. Do you know what that did in Len's life? Do you know what it did in our church's life? We all grew in our faith to believe God. After that, we stepped out in faith to do things time and time again. We watched God do wonderful things. We never could have come to experience God that way had we not stepped out in faith to call Len. That experience helped us learn how to trust God.

In a similar way, an encounter with God will bring a crisis of belief. Faith will be required to meet that crisis. Without that faith you will not be able to please God.

ENCOUNTERS WITH GOD ARE GOD-SIZED

God is interested in the world's coming to know Him. The only way people will know what God is like is when they see Him at work. They know His nature when they see His nature expressed in His activity. Whenever God involves you in His activity, the assignment will have God-like dimensions to it.

Some people say, "God will never ask me to do something I can't do." I have come to the place in my life that, if the assignment I sense God is giving me is something that I know I can handle, I know it probably is *not* from God. The kind of assignments God gives in the Bible are always God-sized. They are always beyond what people can do because He wants to demonstrate His nature, His strength, His provision, and His kindness to His people and to a watching world. That is the only way the world will come to know Him.

You could name many God-sized assignments in Scripture. He told Abraham to father a nation when Abraham had no son and Sarah was past the age to bear children. He told Moses to deliver the children of Israel, to cross the Red Sea, and to provide water from a rock.

He told Gideon to defeat a Midianite army of 120,000 with 300 men. Jesus told the disciples to feed the multitudes and to make disciples of all the nations. None of these things were humanly possible. When God's people and the world see something happen that only God can do, they come to know God.

PEOPLE COME TO KNOW GOD

God wants people to come to know Him. That is why He chooses to work through us. People know us. They know what we can do. When they see things happen that can only be explained by God's involvement, they will come to know Him.

Moses and the Red Sea. God had Moses lead the Israelites to camp beside the Red Sea. God knew He was going to deliver them by dividing the sea and letting them cross on dry ground. God said, "I will gain honor over Pharaoh and over all his army, that the Egyptians may know that I am the LORD" (Exod. 14:4). What was the result? "Thus Israel saw the great work which the LORD had done in Egypt; so the people feared the LORD, and believed the LORD and His servant Moses" (Exod. 14:31).

Joshua and the Jordan River. God commanded Joshua to lead the Israelites across the Jordan River at flood stage. Why? "That all the peoples of the earth may know the hand of the LORD, that it is mighty, that you [Israel] may fear the LORD your God forever" (Josh. 4:24).

King Jehoshaphat and Israel against a Vast Army. A vast army came to make war against Israel. King Jehoshaphat proclaimed a fast and led the people to seek God's counsel. He prayed, "O our God . . . we have no power against this great multitude that is coming against us; nor do we know what to do, but our eyes are upon You" (2 Chron. 20:12).

God responded, "Do not be afraid nor dismayed because of this great multitude, for the battle is not yours, but God's. . . . You will not need to fight in this battle. Position yourselves, stand still and see the salvation of the LORD, who is with you" (2 Chron. 20:15, 17). Jehoshaphat sent a choir in front of the army singing praise to God for His enduring love. God destroyed the invading army before Jehoshaphat and Israel got to the battlefield. Then: "The fear of God was on all the kingdoms of those countries when they heard that the LORD had fought against the enemies of Israel" (2 Chron. 20:29).

Shadrach, Meshach, and Abed-nego. Shadrach, Meshach, and Abed-nego chose to obey God rather than the pagan King Nebuchadnezzar. Before being thrown into a blazing furnace, they said, "Our God whom we serve is able to deliver us from the burning fiery furnace, and He will deliver us from your hand" (Dan. 3:17). The bystanding soldiers died, but God delivered these three faithful men.

King Nebuchadnezzar said, "Blessed be the God of Shadrach, Meshach and Abed-nego, who sent His Angel and delivered His servants. . . . Therefore I make a decree that any people, nation, or language which speaks anything amiss against the God of Shadrach, Meshach and Abed-nego shall be cut in pieces, and their houses shall be made an ash heap; because there is no other God who can deliver like this" (Dan. 3:28–29). This king then wrote to announce to the whole nation, "I thought it good to declare the signs and wonders that the Most High God has worked for me. How great are His signs, and how mighty His wonders!" (Dan. 4:2–3).

The Early Church. Christians in the early church followed the directions of the Holy Spirit. Here is the testimony of the impact God had on their world:

- The disciples were filled with the Holy Spirit and spoke in foreign languages they had not learned. Then Peter preached and "those who gladly received his word were baptized; and that day about three thousand souls were added to them." (Acts 2:41)

- God used Peter and John to heal a crippled beggar in the name of Jesus. They preached, and "many of those who heard the word believed; and the number of men came to be about five thousand." (Acts 4:4)
- God used Peter to raise Dorcas from the dead. "And it became known throughout all Joppa, and many believed on the Lord." (Acts 9:42)

What our world often sees are devoted, committed Christians serving God. But they are not seeing God. They comment, "Well, there's a wonderful, dedicated, committed group of people serving God." They, however, do not see anything happening that can only be explained in terms of the activity of God. Why? Because we are not attempting anything that only God can do.

THE WORLD COMES TO KNOW GOD

Our world is not attracted to the Christ we serve because they cannot see Him at work. They do not hesitate to attack the Christian position on morality because they have no fear of the God we serve. They see us doing good things for God and say, "That is wonderful, but that is not my thing." The world is passing us by because they do not want to get involved in what they see. They are not having an opportunity to see God.

Let the world see God at work, and He will attract people to Himself. Let Christ be lifted up—not in words, but in life. Let them see the difference that a living Christ makes in a life, a family, or a church; that will make a difference in how they respond. When the world sees things happening through God's people that cannot be explained except that God Himself has done them, then the world will be drawn to the God they see. Let world leaders see the miraculous signs of an all-powerful God, and they, like Nebuchadnezzar, will declare that He is the one true God.

The world comes to know God when they see God's nature expressed through His activity. When God starts to work, He accomplishes something that only He can do. When God does that, both God's people and the world come to know Him in ways they have never known Him before. That is why God gives God-sized assignments to His people.

The reason much of the world is not being attracted to Christ and His church is that God's people lack the faith to attempt those things that only God can do. If you or your church are not responding to God and attempting things that only He can accomplish, then you are not exercising faith. "Without faith it is impossible to please Him" (Heb. 11:6). If people in your community are not responding to the gospel as they did in the New Testament, one possible reason is that they are not seeing God in what you are doing as a church.

God is far more interested in your having an experience with Him than He is interested in getting a job done. You can complete a job, and never experience God at all. He is not interested just in getting a job done. He can get the job done anytime He wants. What is He interested in? You and the world, knowing Him and experiencing Him. So God will come to you and give you a God-sized assignment. When you start to do what He tells you to do, He brings to pass what He has purposed. Then you and all the people with you will rejoice that you have experienced Him. You and the people around you will know more of Him than you have ever known before.

SEEING GOD AT WORK THROUGH ME

Why are God's assignments always God-sized? What leads the world to ignore God's moral standards when I try to talk about them? When does the world come to know God in new ways? Why is God not interested in just getting a job done?

JOINING GOD REQUIRES FAITH AND ACTION

Our church in Saskatoon was growing and needed more space. We sensed God leading us to start a building program, even though we had only $749 in the building fund. The building was going to cost $220,000. We didn't have the foggiest notion how to do it.

We did much of the work to save on labor costs. Still, halfway through that building program, we were $100,000 short. Those dear, dear people looked to their pastor to see if I believed that God would do what He had called us to do. God put a confidence in my heart that the God who was leading us would show us how to do it.

God began providing the necessary funds. We were about $60,000 short toward the end. We had been expecting some money from a Texas foundation. Delay after delay came that we could not understand. One day, for two hours the currency exchange rate for the Canadian dollar hit the lowest point ever in its history. That was exactly the time the Texas foundation wired the money to Canada. You know what that did? It gave us $60,000 more than we would have gotten otherwise. Then the dollar went back up.

Does the heavenly Father look after the economy in order to help His children? Nobody in the world would believe that God did that for one single church, but I can show you a church that believes God did it! When that happened, I magnified what the Lord had done in the eyes of the people. I made sure we gave the credit to Him. God revealed Himself to us, and we came to know Him in a new way through that experience.

WHAT YOU DO TELLS WHAT YOU BELIEVE

When God speaks to a person, revealing His plans and purposes, it will always cause a crisis of belief. What you believe about God will determine what you do and how you live.

What you do reveals what you believe about God, regardless of what you say. When God reveals what He has purposed to do, you face a crisis—a decision time. God and the world can tell from your response what you really believe about God.

DAVID'S FAITH DEMONSTRATED

In 1 Samuel 16:12–13 God chose David and had Samuel anoint him to become the next king over Israel. In 1 Samuel 17 God brought David into the middle of His activity. While Saul was still king, the Israelites were at war with the Philistines. Still a young boy, David was sent by his father to visit his brothers in the army. When David arrived, Goliath (a giant soldier nine feet tall) challenged Israel to send one man to fight him. The losing nation would become the slaves of the winner. Israel's army was terrified. David asked in amazement, "Who is this uncircumcised Philistine, that he should defy the armies of the living God?" (v. 26). David faced a crisis of belief. He may have realized that God had brought him to the battlefield and had prepared him for this assignment.

David said he would fight this giant. He stated his belief, "The LORD, who delivered me from the paw of the lion and from the paw of the bear, He will deliver me from the hand of this Philistine" (v. 37). David refused to take the normal weapons of war. Instead he took a sling and five smooth stones. He said to Goliath, "You come to me with a sword, with a spear, and with a javelin. But I come to you in the name of the LORD of hosts, the God of the armies of Israel, whom you have defied. This day the LORD will deliver you into my hand . . . that all the earth may know that there is a God in Israel. Then all this assembly shall know that the LORD does not save with sword and spear; for the battle is the LORD's, and He will give you into our hands" (vv. 45–47). David killed Goliath, and Israel went on to victory.

David's statements indicate that he believed God was the living God and that He was Deliverer. He said that God was Almighty and that God would defend Israel's armies. David's actions verify that he really did believe these things about God. Many thought David was a foolish young boy, and even Goliath laughed at him. God delivered the Israelites, however. He gave a mighty victory through David so that the whole world would know there was a God in Israel!

SARAI'S LACK OF FAITH

God called Abram and promised to make his offspring as numerous as the stars. Abram questioned God about this promise since he remained childless into his old age. God reaffirmed, "One who will come from your own body shall be your heir. . . . And he believed in the LORD, and He accounted it to him for righteousness" (Gen. 15:4, 6).

Abram's wife Sarai was in her mid-seventies at this time. She knew she was past childbearing years, so she decided she would have to "build a family" in a different way. She gave her maid to Abram as a wife and asked for a child through her. Abram consented, and Ishmael was born to Hagar a year later. Sarai's actions indicated what she believed about God. Though Abram was commended for his faith, in this experience he joined with Sarai in trying to achieve God's purpose in man's ways.

Do you see how Sarai's actions told what she really believed about God? She did not have the faith to believe that God could do the impossible and give her a child at seventy-seven. Her belief about God was limited by her own human reason. This act of unbelief was very costly. Ishmael caused Abram and Sarai much grief in their old age. Ishmael and his Arab descendants have lived in hostility toward Isaac and the Jews from that time until today. What you do in response to God's invitation really does indicate what you believe about God.

ACTIONS SPEAK

When God invites you to join Him and you face a crisis of belief, what you do next tells what you believe about God. Your actions really do speak louder than words.

When the two blind men demonstrated that they believed Jesus was merciful and that He was the Messiah (Son of David), Jesus healed them according to their faith (Matt. 9:27–31). A woman who had been sick for years believed that just a touch of Jesus' garment would allow His healing power to flow to her. She was willing to risk public ridicule in order to experience His healing power. She acted in faith, and Jesus healed her (Matt. 9:20–22).

The disciples were caught in the middle of a storm on the sea. Jesus rebuked them, not for their human tendency to fear, but for their failure to recognize His presence, protection, and power (Matt. 8:23–27). In this case their actions revealed their unbelief rather than their faith. When the storms of life overtake us as this storm overtook the disciples, we often respond as if God does not exist or does not care.

When a centurion sought Jesus' help to heal his servant, he said, "Only speak a word, and my servant will be healed" (Matt. 8:8). Jesus commended the centurion's faith in His authority and power, and He healed the servant because of the faith of his master (Matt. 8:5–13).

In each of these biblical examples, what the people did indicated to Jesus what kind of faith they had or did not have. What you do, rather than what you say you believe, reveals what you really believe about God.

TRUE FAITH REQUIRES ACTION

When you face a crisis of belief, what you do demonstrates what you believe. "For as the body without the spirit is dead, so faith without works is dead also" (James 2:26). Faith without action is dead!

Hebrews 11 is sometimes called "The Roll Call of Faith." The individuals listed took action that demonstrated their faith. While studying Hebrews 11, however, you may notice that a faithful life does not always bring the same results in human terms.

Verses 33–35a describe the victory and deliverance some people of faith experienced. Verses 35b–38 describe the torture, mockery, and death other people of faith experienced. Were some more faithful than the others? No. They "obtained a good testimony through faith" (Heb. 11:39). They decided a "Well done!" from their Master was more important than life itself. Verse 40 explains that God has planned something far better for people of faith than the world has to offer. Therefore:

> Since we are surrounded by so great a cloud of witnesses, let us lay aside every weight, and the sin which so easily ensnares us, and let us run with endurance the race that is set before us, looking unto Jesus, the author and finisher of our faith, who for the joy that was set before Him endured the cross, despising the shame, and has sat down at the right hand of the throne of God. For consider Him who endured such hostility from sinners against Himself, lest you become weary and discouraged in your souls. (Heb. 12:1–3)

The outward appearance of success does not always indicate faith, and the outward appearance of failure does not always indicate that faith is lacking. A faithful servant is one who does what his Master tells him, whatever the outcome may be. As our example, we need only to consider Jesus who endured the cross; but now He is seated near the very throne of God! What a reward for His faithfulness! Do not grow weary in being faithful. A reward is awaiting faithful servants.

I pray that you are trying to please God by earnestly seeking Him (Heb. 11:6). In the next chapters we will look more carefully at the cost factors in following God's will. Part of the action required to demonstrate your faith will be the adjustment you must make to God. Following God's will always requires adjustments that are costly to you and even to those around you.

EXERCISING YOUR FAITH IN ACTION

What happens to me when I come to know God in a new way? What is more important to God: what I say I believe or what I do? How do I know if I am a faithful servant of God?

SUMMARY

When God invites you to be involved with Him, He is wanting to reveal Himself to you and to a watching world. Therefore, He will ask you to be involved with Him in a God-sized assignment. When you are confronted with such a great assignment, you will face a crisis of belief. You will have to decide what you really believe about the God who called you. How you respond to God will reveal what you believe regardless of what you say. Following God will require faith and action. Without faith you will not be able to please God. When you act in faith, God is pleased.

EXPERIENCING GOD TODAY

Turn to "The Roll Call of Faith" in Hebrews 11. Read this chapter and pray as you read. Ask the Lord to increase your faith to believe Him in all things. Pray that He will enable you to walk by faith even if the outcome of your faith matches the last half of the chapter rather than the first half.

Ask the Lord to identify times in your past experience where you did walk by faith and times when He may have given you an assignment when you did not respond with faith. Agree with Him regarding your faithfulness or lack of it. Renew your commitment to Him to be a faithful servant. Say, "Lord, whatever you desire from me, my answer is yes!"

MY SURRENDER AMIDST A CRISIS OF BELIEF

Dear Jesus,

Each day brings another crisis of belief. I must make decisions that show whether I trust myself or whether I depend absolutely on You. I must act on Your purposes that You have revealed to me. You have provided the chance for me to participate in God-sized tasks. Keep me from the temptation of looking for me-sized tasks. God, I want the world to see You at work in Your world, in Your church, in my life. The only way this will happen is for me to trust You, follow You, and obey You. Help me do this today. Lord, show me Your way. I will follow it today, no matter what the reaction the world has and no matter what result comes in my life.

If anyone desires to come after Me, let him deny himself, and take up his cross daily, and follow Me. For whoever desires to save his life will lose it, but whoever loses his life for My sake will save it.

LUKE 9:23–24

17

JOINING GOD REQUIRES MAJOR ADJUSTMENTS

Many of us want God to speak to us and give us an assignment. However, we are not interested in making any major adjustments in our lives. Biblically, that is impossible. Every time God spoke to people in the Scripture about something He wanted to do through them, major adjustments were necessary. They had to adjust their lives to God. Once the adjustments were made, God accomplished His purposes through those He called.

A SECOND CRITICAL TURNING POINT

The first turning point in your knowing and doing the will of God was the crisis of belief—you must believe God is who He says He is and that He will do what He says He will do. Without faith in God, you will make the wrong decision at this first turning point.

Adjusting your life to God is the second critical turning point. Making the adjustment of your life to God is also a turning point. If you choose to make the adjustment, you can go on to obedience. If you refuse to make the adjustment, you could miss what God has in store for your life.

Once you have come to believe God, you demonstrate your faith by what you *do*. Some action is required. This action is one of the major adjustments we are going to focus on in this chapter. Your obedience also will be a part of the action required. Your adjustments and obedience will be costly to you and those around you.

A need arose in one of our mission points that was forty miles away. I asked the church to pray that God would call someone to move to that community and be a lay pastor of the mission. A young couple responded. He was attending the university, and they had very little financially.

If they took up residence in the mission community, he would have to commute eighty miles a day to the university. I knew they couldn't afford to do it. I said, "No, I can't let you do that." I went through all the reasons why that would not be fair.

This young couple was deeply grateful that God had saved them. The young man looked at me and said, "Pastor, don't deny me the opportunity to sacrifice for my Lord." That statement crushed me. How could I refuse? Yet I knew that this couple would have to pay a high price because our church had been obedient to start new missions.

We had prayed for God to call out a lay pastor. I should have been open to God's answering our prayers in an unexpected way. When this couple responded with such a deep sense of commitment and personal sacrifice, the body (our church) affirmed their sense of call—and God provided for their needs!

ADJUSTING MY LIFE TO GOD

Why are major adjustments required in my life if I am to accomplish God's assignment? What happens when I make such adjustments? What should I expect from God when I pray for something according to His purposes?

YOU CAN'T STAY WHERE YOU ARE AND GO WITH GOD

When God speaks to you, revealing what He is about to do, that revelation is your invitation to adjust your life to Him. Once you have adjusted your life to Him, His purposes, and His ways, you are in a position to obey. Adjustments prepare you for obedience. You cannot continue life as usual or stay where you are, and go with God at the same time. That is true throughout Scripture.

- *Noah* could not continue life as usual and build an ark at the same time (Gen. 6).
- *Abram* could not stay in Ur or Haran and father a nation in Canaan (Gen. 12:1–8).
- *Moses* could not stay on the back side of the desert herding sheep and stand before Pharaoh at the same time (Exod. 3).
- *David* had to leave his sheep to become king (1 Sam. 16:1–13).

- *Amos* had to leave the sycamore trees in order to preach in Israel (Amos 7:14–15).
- *Jonah* had to leave his home and overcome a major prejudice in order to preach in Nineveh (Jonah 1:1–2; 3:1–2; 4:1–11).
- *Peter, Andrew, James,* and *John* had to leave their fishing businesses in order to follow Jesus (Matt. 4:18–22).
- *Matthew* had to leave his tax collector's booth to follow Jesus (Matt. 9:9).
- *Saul* (later Paul) had to completely change directions in his life in order to be used of God to preach the gospel to the Gentiles (Acts 9:1–19).

Enormous changes and adjustments had to be made! Some had to leave family and country. Others had to drop prejudices and change preferences. Others had to leave behind life goals, ideals, and desires. Everything had to be yielded to God and the entire life adjusted to Him. The moment the necessary adjustments were made, God began to accomplish His purposes through the individuals. Each one, however, learned that adjusting one's life to God is well worth the cost.

You may be thinking: *But God will not ask me to make major adjustments.* If you look to Scripture for your understanding of God, you will see that God most certainly will require adjustments of His people. He even required major adjustments of His own Son: "You know the grace of our Lord Jesus Christ, that though He was rich, yet for your sakes He became poor, that you through His poverty might become rich" (2 Cor. 8:9). Jesus emptied Himself of position and wealth in heaven in order to join the Father in providing redemption through His death on the cross—that was a major adjustment!

If you want to be a disciple—a follower—of Jesus, you have no choice. You will have to make major adjustments in your life to follow God. Following your Master requires adjustments in your life. Until you are ready to make any adjustment necessary to follow and obey what God has said, you will be of little use to God. Your greatest single difficulty in following God may come at the point of the adjustment.

Our tendency is to want to skip the adjustment and go from believing God to obedience. If you want to follow Him, you don't have that choice. His ways are so different from yours. God says, "As the heavens are higher than the earth, so are My ways higher than your ways, and My thoughts than your thoughts" (Isa. 55:9). The only way to follow Him will require an adjustment of your life to Him and His ways.

THE RICH YOUNG RULER REFUSED TO ADJUST

The rich ruler wanted eternal life, but he didn't make the necessary adjustment to Jesus (Luke 18:18–27). His money and wealth were more important. Jesus knew that he could not love God completely and love his money at the same time (Matt. 6:24). Jesus asked the young man to put away the thing that had become his god—his wealth. The young ruler refused to make the necessary adjustment, and he missed out on experiencing eternal life.

The rich young ruler's love of money and his greed made him an idolater (Eph. 5:5). He missed coming to know the true God and Jesus Christ whom God had sent. He wanted eternal life, but he refused to make the necessary adjustment of his life to the true God.

Many people may face some of the same struggle today. Prosperity and the love of the things of the world may tempt you to refuse to adjust your life to God. The love for money and things can become a substitute for a love relationship with God. Jesus said, "You cannot serve God and mammon" (Matt. 6:24). This will be a major adjustment that many must make in order to be rightly related to their true Master, the heavenly Father.

ELISHA MADE THE MAJOR ADJUSTMENTS

Elisha responded very differently (1 Kings 19:15–21). Elijah was told to select Elisha as his successor. He found Elisha in a field plowing with twelve yoke of oxen. When Elisha heard God's call through Elijah, he made major adjustments. He left his family and career (farming) in order to follow God's call. You have heard the phrase about "burning your bridges behind you." Well, Elisha burned his farm equipment and killed his twenty-four oxen. He then cooked the meat and with it fed the people of the community. He was not about to turn back!

When Elisha made the necessary adjustments, he was in a position to obey God. As a result, God worked through Elisha to perform some of the greatest signs and miracles recorded in the Old Testament (2 Kings 2–13). Elisha had to make the adjustments on the front end of his call. Not until he made the adjustments was God able to work through him to accomplish the miracles.

No one can sum up all God is able to accomplish through one solitary life, wholly yielded, adjusted, and obedient to Him! Do you want to be wholly yielded, adjusted, and obedient to God? When God invites you to join Him, the task will have such God-sized dimensions you will face a crisis of belief. Your response will first require faith. Faith will be demonstrated by action. The first action will involve the adjustment of your life to God. The second action will be obedience to what God asks you to do. You cannot go on to obedience without first making the adjustments.

LEARNING FROM THE BIBLE

What type of adjustments did people in the Bible have to make? Did Jesus have to make adjustments in His life? Why? Am I willing to make any adjustment necessary even before God shows me what the adjustments are? What do I miss if I do not make the adjustments? What must I do before I can obey God?

KINDS OF ADJUSTMENTS

What kind of adjustments are required? Trying to answer that question is like trying to list all the things God might ask you to do. The list could be endless. I can, however, point you to some examples and give you some general categories of adjustments that may be required.

Adjustments may be required in one or more of the following areas:

- In your circumstances (like job, home, finances, and others)
- In your relationships (family, friends, business associates, and others)
- In your thinking (prejudices, methods, your potential, and others)
- In your commitments (to family, church, job, plans, tradition, and others)
- In your actions (how you pray, give, serve, and others)
- In your beliefs (about God, His purposes, His ways, your relationship to Him, and others)

The list could go on and on. The major adjustment will come at the point of acting on your faith. When you face the crisis of belief, you must decide what you believe about God. That mental decision may be the easy part. The hard part is adjusting your life to God and taking an action that demonstrates your faith. You may be called upon to attempt things that only God can do, where formerly you may have attempted only that which you knew you *could* do.

Sometimes an adjustment may involve several of these areas at once. For instance, Peter was a faithful Jew. He only ate kosher food. He had no dealings with "unclean" Gentiles. One day on the housetop, God interrupted Peter with a vision. God had to convince Peter that all He had created was not to be called unclean. Peter then was told to go with some Gentiles to preach to Cornelius and his household.

Peter's experience with Cornelius probably required adjustments in Peter's thinking and beliefs about what is clean and unclean, his commitments to the traditions of the Jews, and his actions regarding fellowship with Gentiles (Acts 10:1–20). Peter made the necessary adjustments and obeyed God. When he did, God worked through him to bring Cornelius's whole household to Christ.

Being able to place a title on an adjustment is not as important as your identifying what change God wants you to make to Him, His purposes, or His ways. He will help you know what you must do. Then you must choose to make the adjustment.

ABSOLUTE SURRENDER

God frequently requires adjustments in areas you have never considered in the past. You may have heard someone say something like this: "Don't ever tell God something you will *not* do. That is what He will ask you to do." God is not looking for ways to make you "squirm." He does, however, want to be Lord of your life. Whenever you identify a place where you refuse to allow His lordship, that is a place He will go to work. He is interested in absolute surrender. God may or may not require you to do that very thing you identified, but He will keep working until you are willing for Him to be Lord of all.

Because God loves you, His will is always best! Any adjustment God expects you to make is for your good. As you follow Him, the time may come that your life and future may depend on your adjusting quickly to God's directives.

The adjusting is always to a Person. You adjust your life to God. You adjust your viewpoints to be like His viewpoints. You adjust your ways to be like His ways. After you make the necessary adjustments, He will tell you what to do next to obey Him. When you obey Him, you will experience Him doing through you something only God can do.

Some people question whether *major* adjustments are always necessary. Anytime you go from where you are to where God is working, from your way of thinking to God's way of thinking, from your ways to God's ways, or from your purposes to His purposes, a *major* adjustment will be required. Now, you may make some adjustments at a point in your life so that you will not have to make further major adjustments when God gives you the next assignment. Sooner or later you will have to make the major adjustments to join Him.

TOTAL DEPENDENCE ON GOD

Another adjustment that is a part of knowing and doing the will of God is that of coming to a total dependence on God to complete what He wants to do through you. Jesus said our relationship to Him would be like a vine and its branches. He said, "Without Me you can do nothing" (John 15:5). When you are God's servant, you must remain within that intimate relationship in order for Him to complete His work through you. You must depend on God alone.

The adjustment requires moving from doing work *for* God according to *your* abilities, *your* gifts, *your* likes and dislikes, and *your* goals to being totally dependent on *God* and *His* working and *His* resources. This is a *major* adjustment! It is never easy to make.

Read the following Scriptures and notice why you must depend on God to carry out His purposes.

> "I am the vine, you are the branches. He who abides in Me, and I in him, bears much fruit; for without Me you can do nothing." (John 15:5)
>
> By the grace of God I am what I am, and His grace toward me was not in vain; but I labored more abundantly than they all, yet not I, but the grace of God which was with me. (1 Cor. 15:10)
>
> I have been crucified with Christ; it is no longer I who live, but Christ lives in me; and the life which I now live in the flesh I live by faith in the Son of God, who loved me and gave Himself for me. (Gal. 2:20)
>
> The Lord of hosts has sworn, saying, "Surely, as I have thought, so it shall come to pass, and as I have purposed, so it shall stand." (Isa. 14:24)
>
> "Fear not, for I am with you; be not dismayed, for I am your God. I will strengthen you, yes, I will help you, I will uphold you with My righteous right hand." (Isa. 41:10)
>
> "I am God, and there is no other. . . . My counsel shall stand, and I will do all My pleasure. . . . I have spoken it; I will also bring it to pass. I have purposed it; I will also do it." (Isa. 46:9–11)

Without God at work in you, you can do nothing to bear kingdom fruit. As you are crucified with Christ, He lives through you to accomplish His purposes by His grace. When God purposes to do something, He guarantees that it will come to pass. He is the One who will accomplish what He purposes to do. If you depend on anything other than God, you will be asking for failure in kingdom terms.

WAITING ON THE LORD

Sometimes as you begin making adjustments, God will require that you wait on Him. This is not because God cannot keep up with you or that He does not know what to do next. God is interested in a love relationship with you. Your waiting on Him develops your absolute dependence on Him. Your waiting on Him assures that you will act on His timing and not your own. The Scriptures frequently commend waiting on the Lord:

> My voice you shall hear in the morning, O LORD; in the morning I will direct it to You, and I will look up. (Ps. 5:3)
>
> Our soul waits for the LORD; He is our help and our shield. (Ps. 33:20)
>
> Wait on the LORD, and keep His way, and He shall exalt you to inherit the land. (Ps. 37:34)
>
> For in You, O LORD, I hope; You will hear, O Lord my God. (Ps. 38:15)
>
> Those who wait on the LORD shall renew their strength; they shall mount up with wings like eagles, they shall run, and not be weary, and they shall walk, and not faint. (Isa. 40:31)

You may think of waiting as a passive, inactive time. Waiting on the Lord is anything but inactive. While you wait on Him, you will be praying with a passion to know Him, His purposes, and His ways. You will be watching circumstances and asking God to interpret them by revealing to you His perspective. You will be sharing with other believers to find out what God is saying to them. As you wait on the Lord, you will be very active in asking, seeking, and knocking: "Ask, and it will be given to you; seek, and you will find; knock, and it will be opened to you. For everyone who asks receives, and he who seeks finds; and to him who knocks it will be opened" (Matt. 7:7–8).

While you wait, continue doing the last thing God told you to do. In waiting, you are shifting the responsibility of the outcome to

God—where it belongs. Then when God gives you specific guidance, He will do through you more in days and weeks than you could ever accomplish in years of labor. Waiting on Him is always worth the wait. His timing and His ways are always right. You must depend on Him to guide you in His way and in His timing to accomplish His purpose.

ADJUSTMENTS I MUST MAKE

In what areas of my life is God asking me to make adjustments? What adjustments have I already made? Why have I not made other adjustments? Can I count on God to act immediately if I make adjustments to Him? What does waiting on God develop? What do I do while I wait? Who bears the responsibility for the outcome of any assignment God gives? Why is waiting on God always worth the wait?

SUMMARY

I have tried to help you understand that you cannot stay where you are and go with God in obedience to His will. Major adjustments must come first. To go from your ways, thoughts, and purposes to God's will always requires major adjustments. God may require adjustments in your circumstances, relationships, thinking, commitments, actions, and beliefs. Once you have made the necessary adjustments, you can follow God in obedience. Keep in mind—the God who calls you is also the One who will enable you to do His will.

When you are willing to surrender everything in your life to the lordship of Christ, you, like Elisha, will find that the adjustments are well worth the reward of experiencing God. If you have not come to the place in your life where you have surrendered *all* to His lordship, decide today to deny yourself, take up your cross, and follow Him (Luke 9:23).

EXPERIENCING GOD TODAY

People who have been mightily used of God have always had to make major adjustments in their lives. I want you to read the following statements by some godly servants of God. Think about the significant level of commitment that is reflected in each of the following quotes and mark one that is most meaningful to you.

David Livingstone considered his work as a medical missionary to Africa as a high honor, not a sacrifice. He said: "Forbid that we should ever consider the holding of a commission from the King of Kings a sacrifice, so long as other men esteem the service of an earthly government as an honor. I am a missionary, heart and soul. God Himself had an only Son, and He was a missionary and a physician. A poor, poor imitation I am, or wish to be, but in this service I hope to live. In it I wish to die. I still prefer poverty and missions service to riches and ease. This is my choice."[1]

Jim Elliot. Jim Elliot was a missionary to the Quichua Indians in South America. He was willing to give up earthly things for heavenly reward. Jim's famous quote is: "He is no fool who gives what he cannot keep to gain what he cannot lose."[2] Jim was killed by South American Indians as he sought to spread the gospel to those who had never heard about Jesus. Later his wife and others were able to share the gospel message with Jim's murderers and many have come to a saving knowledge of Christ.

Bob Pierce. Bob's prayer was this: "Let my heart be broken by the things that break the heart of God."[3] He allowed God to adjust his thinking so that he cared about the needy people God cared about. Bob Pierce was used by God to establish World Vision and Samaritan's Purse to minister to needy people around the world.

Oswald Smith. He so wanted God's plan for his life that he was willing to be content with any pleasure or adversity. He said, "I want Thy plan, O God, for my life. May I be happy and contented whether in the homeland or on the foreign field; whether married or alone, in happiness or sorrow, health or sickness, prosperity or adversity—I want Thy plan, O God, for my life. I want it; oh, I want it!"[4] He was a missionary statesman from Canada.

C. T. Studd said, "If Jesus Christ be God and died for me, then no sacrifice is too great for me to give for Him."[5] He served as a missionary to China, India, and Africa.

Which of these quotes was most meaningful or moving to you? If you are willing to make a similar commitment to the lordship of Christ, spend a few moments in prayer expressing to Christ your willingness to adjust your life to Him, His purposes, and His ways.

MY SURRENDER TO MAJOR ADJUSTMENTS

Lord, I know I am too comfortable with life as usual. Forgive me. God, You have an assignment for me that is God-sized. To accomplish it, I must have the faith to make the adjustments You require in my life. Show me how. I am willing, Jesus. You may change my circumstances. You may change my relationships. You may change my thinking. You may change my commitments and priorities. You may change my actions. You have my permission to change my beliefs, even those I have so proudly held on to for these many years. Change whatever is necessary for me to carry out Your assignment. I surrender to You. I depend entirely on You. I wait for Your call to action. I want to think Your thoughts, act in Your ways, and focus on Your purposes.

Make me ready to obey. I want to experience You. Thank You for caring enough about me to want to change me.

ENDNOTES

1. David & Naomi Shibley, *The Smoke of a Thousand Villages* (Nashville: Thomas Nelson Publishers, 1989), 11.
2. Elizabeth Elliot, *Shadow of the Almighty: The Life and Testament of Jim Elliot* (New York: Harper & Brothers Publishers, 1958), 247.
3. Franklin Graham with Jeanette Lockerbie, *Bob Pierce: This One Thing I Do* (Waco, Texas: Word Books, 1983), 220.
4. Shibley, 11.
5. Shibley, 98.

Jesus replied, "If anyone loves Me, he will keep My word; and My Father will love him, and We will come to him and make Our home with him."

JOHN 14:23

Whoever of you does not forsake all that he has cannot be My disciple.

LUKE 14:33

18

JOINING GOD REQUIRES OBEDIENCE

You cannot stay where you are and go with God. You cannot continue doing things your way and accomplish God's purposes in His ways. Once you have adjusted your life to God, His purposes, and His ways you are prepared to obey Him.

Earlier (chap. 7) you studied the relationship between love and obedience. You found that obedience is the outward expression of your love of God. Jesus said, "If you love Me, keep My commandments. He who does not love Me does not keep My words" (John 14:15, 24). By way of review, here are some statements from that chapter:

- Obedience is the outward expression of your love of God.
- The reward for obedience and love is that He will reveal Himself to you.
- If you have an obedience problem, you have a love problem.
- If you love Him, you will obey Him!

Jesus said, "For whoever does the will of My Father in heaven is My brother and sister and mother" (Matt. 12:50). Jesus clearly said that by obedience a person indicates his love relationship with God (John 14:15–21).

James, in his letter to the believers, went to great lengths to indicate that faith that does not obey in actions is dead, or has no life. When the disciples obeyed Jesus, they saw and experienced God's mighty power working in and around them. When they did not act in faith and do His will, they did not experience His mighty work.

WHAT IS OBEDIENCE?

Servants of God do what He directs. They obey Him. The servant does not have the option of deciding whether or not he wants to obey. Choosing not to obey is rebellion, and such disobedience will bring serious consequences.

Many people are so self-centered they want to do their own "thing." They do not stop to consider what obedience may mean in their lives. Jesus told a parable about obedience: "What do you think? A man had two sons, and he came to the first and said, 'Son, go, work today in my vineyard.' He answered and said, 'I will not,' but afterward regretted it and went. Then he came to the second and said likewise. And he answered and said, 'I go, sir,' but he did not go" (Matt. 21:28–30).

Which son did the will of his father? Was it the one who said no but later repented, or the one who said yes but never went? The first son is the one who obeyed the father. Obedience means doing what is commanded.

OBEY WHAT YOU ALREADY KNOW TO BE GOD'S WILL

Some people want God to give them an assignment. They vow to do whatever He asks. But when God observes their lives, He notices they have not obeyed in the things He already has told them to do.

God gave the Ten Commandments. Are you obeying? Jesus has told you to love your enemies. Are you able to do that? Jesus ordered the church to make disciples of all nations. Are you doing all you know to obey Him? God tells you through Scripture to live in unity with your Christian brothers and sisters. Do love and harmony characterize your fellowship?

God's commands are not given so you can pick and choose the ones you want to obey and forget the rest. He expects you to obey *all* His commands out of your love relationship with Him. When He sees you are faithful and obedient in a little, He will be able to trust you with more.

OBEDIENCE AND GOD'S ASSIGNMENTS

God has always been at work in our world. He is now at work where you are. When God is ready for you to be involved with Him in an assignment, He always will take the initiative to come to you and reveal what He is doing, or what He is about to do. When He does, this will be His invitation for you to join Him.

Joining Him will require major adjustments of your life to Him so He can accomplish His will through you. When you know what God has said, know what He is about to do, and have adjusted your life to Him, there is yet one remaining necessary response to God. *To experience Him at work in and through you, you must obey Him. When you obey Him, He will accomplish His work through you; and you will come to know Him by experience.*

This chapter brings us to a focus on the last of our seven realities: You come to know God by experience as you obey Him and He accomplishes His work through you. After God has taken the initiative to involve you in His work, you believe Him and adjust your life to Him. This entire process may happen very quickly or it may be extended over a lengthy period of time. The adjustments, however, must be made. Only then do you get to the place of obedience. You must obey Him first. Then He will accomplish His work through you. When God does a God-sized work through your life, you come to know Him intimately by experience.

MOMENT OF TRUTH

In many ways, obedience is your moment of truth. What you *do* will:

1. Reveal what you believe about Him
2. Determine whether you will experience His mighty work in you and through you
3. Determine whether you will come to know Him more intimately

When you come to a moment of truth, you must choose whether to obey God. You cannot obey Him unless you believe and trust Him. You cannot believe and trust Him unless you love Him. You cannot love Him unless you know Him.

Each "new" command or assignment will require a new knowledge and understanding of Him. The Holy Spirit will teach you about Jesus so you can trust Him and obey Him. Then you will experience Him in new ways. This is how you grow in Him. As 1 John 2:3–6 says: "We know that we know Him, if we keep His commandments. He who says, 'I know Him,' and does not keep His commandments, is a liar, and the truth is not in him. But whoever keeps His word, truly the love of God is perfected in him. By this we know that we are in Him. He who says he abides in Him ought himself also to walk just as He walked."

Jesus stated it a different way when He said:

> "Not everyone who says to Me, 'Lord, Lord,' shall enter the kingdom of heaven, but he who does the will of my Father in heaven. Many will say to Me in that day, 'Lord, Lord, have we not prophesied in Your name, cast out demons in Your name, and done many wonders in Your name?' And then I will declare to them, 'I never knew you; depart from Me, you who practice lawlessness!'" (Matt. 7:21–22)

I LEARN TO OBEY

What areas of my life now stand in disobedience or lack of obedience to God? What happens when I choose to obey God? What is the relationship between my obeying, trusting, loving, and knowing God?

THE IMPORTANCE OF OBEDIENCE

Obedience is very important. If you know that God loves you, you should never question a directive from Him. It will always be right and best. When He gives you a directive, you are not just to observe it, discuss it, or debate it. You are to obey it. Notice what the Scriptures say about obedience:

> If you diligently obey the voice of the LORD your God, to observe carefully all His commandments which I command you today, that the LORD your God will set you high above all nations of the earth. . . . The LORD will command the blessing on you in your storehouses and in all to which you set your hand. (Deut. 28:1, 8)
>
> If you do not obey the voice of the LORD your God, to observe carefully all His commandments and His statutes which I command you today . . . The LORD will send on you cursing, confusion, and rebuke in all that you set your hand to do, until you are destroyed and until you perish quickly, because of the wickedness of your doings in which you have forsaken Me. (Deut. 28:15, 20)
>
> "Obey My voice, and I will be your God, and you shall be My people. And walk in all the ways that I have commanded you, that it may be well with you." (Jer. 7:23)
>
> "Why do you call Me, 'Lord, Lord,' and not do the things which I say? Whoever comes to Me, and hears My sayings and does them, I will show you whom he is like: He is like a man building a house, who dug deep and laid the foundation on the rock. And when the flood arose, the stream beat vehemently against that house, and could not shake it, for it was founded on the rock. But he who heard and did nothing is like a man who built a house on the earth without a foundation, against which the stream beat vehemently; and immediately it fell. And the ruin of that house was great." (Luke 6:46–49)

> Jesus answered them and said, "My doctrine is not Mine, but His who sent Me. If anyone wills to do His will, he shall know concerning the doctrine, whether it is from God or whether I speak on My own authority." (John 7:16–17)

God blesses those who are obedient to Him (Deut. 28:1–14). The benefits of obedience are beyond our imagination; but they include being God's people (Jer. 7:23), having a solid foundation when the storms of life come against you (Luke 6:46–49), and knowing spiritual truth (John 7:16–17).

Rebellion against God is the opposite of obedience. Disobedience is a serious rejection of God's will. Deuteronomy 28:15–68 speaks of some of the costs of disobedience. (For further study on the results of obedience and disobedience, see Deut. 30 and 32.)

LEARNING FROM THE BIBLE

Why should I never question a direction God gives me? What one thing should I do when God gives me a directive? What are the benefits of obedience? What are the costs of disobedience?

THE COST OF OBEDIENCE

Obedience, however, is costly to you and to those around you. You cannot know and do the will of God without paying the price of adjustment and obedience. Willingness to pay the price of following His will is one of the major adjustments you will have to make. At this very point "many of His disciples went back and walked with Him no more" (John 6:66). This also is a point where churches will not know and experience the fulfilling of God's purposes and will through them because they are not willing to pay the price of obedience. Those who are willing to pay the price and follow in obedience will experience the power and presence of God working through them.

Saul, for instance, was established in the religious power structure of Jerusalem. He had taken a lead in searching out Christians and having them imprisoned or executed. On his way to Damascus, Saul (later named Paul) had an encounter with the living Christ. The resurrected Christ told Saul that he had been chosen to preach the gospel to the Gentiles. He had to make a total about-face in direction. He went from persecuting Christians to proclaiming that Jesus was the Christ.

God will ask you to follow Him in ways that will require adjustments in your plans and directions. For Paul the adjustment was costly. It even put his life at risk with the Jews. The adjustments and obedience required of you will be costly as well.

Sometimes obedience to God's will leads to opposition and misunderstanding. Because of his obedience, Paul suffered much for the cause of Christ. The list of beatings, imprisonments, and danger sound like more than one person could bear. He concluded one letter by saying, "I bear in my body the marks of the Lord Jesus" (Gal. 6:17). Paul had not had these experiences before he began to do the will of his Lord. Obedience was costly to him. Even so, Paul still could say: "that I may know Him and the power of His resurrection, and the fellowship of His sufferings, being conformed to His death, if, by any means, I may attain to the resurrection from the dead. Not that I have already attained, or am already perfected; but I press on, that I may lay hold of that for which Christ Jesus has also laid hold of me" (Phil. 3:10–12).

The apostle Paul revealed the adjustments that he made to do the will of God when he said, "I have become all things to all men, that I might by all means save some" (1 Cor. 9:22). Your adjustments and obedience to Christ will be costly as well. The Scriptures are full of examples of costly adjustments and obedience.

Moses and the Israelites. When Moses was obedient and told Pharaoh to let Israel go, what did it cost the Israelites? When Moses obeyed God, the workload of the children of Israel was increased and the Israelite foremen were beaten. The Israelites paid a high cost for Moses to do the will of God (Exod. 5:1–21).

Jesus and Mary. When Jesus obeyed and went to the cross, what was the cost to His mother as she stood there and watched Him die? When the Lord Jesus did the will of the Father and died on the cross, His mother, Mary, had to suffer the agony of watching her Son be cruelly killed (John 19:17–37). Jesus' obedience put His mother through an experience where her heart was broken. His obedience put fear and pain in the lives of every one of His disciples. For Jesus to do the will of God, others had to pay a high cost.

Paul and Jason. When Paul was obedient in preaching the gospel to the Gentiles at Thessalonica, what did it cost Jason? When Paul followed God's will in preaching the gospel, others were led to respond to God's work in their own lives. Jason and some others were arrested by a rioting mob and accused of treason because of their association with Paul. Frequently Paul's obedience to God's will endangered the lives of those who were with Him (Acts 17:1–9).

You must not overlook this very real element in knowing and doing the will of God. God will reveal His plans and purposes to you, but your obedience will cost you and others around you. When, for instance, a pastor surrenders his life to missions, it may cost those around him (his family, his church) more than what it will cost him. If he leads his church to become directly involved in doing missions, it may cost some in the church more than it will cost the pastor.

COST TO MY FAMILY FOR ME TO DO GOD'S WILL

When Marilynn and I committed ourselves to do mission work, one of the great costs we had to face was what it would cost our children for me to be gone so much. Our oldest was eight when we went to Saskatoon. Our youngest was born a few months after the move. I was gone from home much of the time during those years the children were growing up. Marilynn also had to pay a high price by rearing all five children with me gone so much.

I have heard many people of God say, "I really think God is calling me; but my children need me. I can't put my family through that." Your children do need your care. But do you suppose that if you were to respond obediently to the activity of God, He would have a way to take care of your children? We did!

We believed God would honor our obedience to Him. We believed the God who called us would show us how to rear our children. We came to believe that the heavenly Father, who loves His servants, could take better care of our children than we ever could. We believed that God would show us how to relate to our children in a way that would make up for the lost time with them. Now, I could not let that become an excuse for neglecting my family. But when I was obeying the Father, I could trust Him to care for my family.

We baptized three persons the first year we were in Saskatoon. After two and a half years of hard, hard labor, we were running thirty in Sunday School. Marilynn said to me, "Henry, Richard came to me today and said he really feels sorry for you. He said, 'Dad preaches such good sermons. He gives an invitation week after week, and nobody comes.'"

I went to Richard and said, "Richard, don't ever be sorry for your father. Even if God lets me labor for ten years and see very little results, I will hardly be able to wait for the day when He brings the harvest." I had to help Richard understand what was taking place. I explained God's promise: "He who continually goes forth weeping, bearing seeds for sowing, shall doubtless come again with rejoicing, bringing his sheaves with him" (Ps. 126:6). God worked through me at that moment to teach my son a deeply meaningful spiritual truth.

GOD TOOK CARE OF MARILYNN

I remember a time when Marilynn hit a low point. She had gotten discouraged. The next Sunday, after I preached, Richard came down the aisle to make a decision. He said, "I feel called to the ministry."

Right behind him came our neighbor, also named Richard. Marilynn had spent hundreds of hours taking care of this young lad from a troubled home. He came saying, "I also feel that God has called me to the ministry." Then he turned and said, "And a lot of the credit goes to Mom Blackaby."

Another boy named Ron stood up in that same service and said, "I want you to know that God is calling me to the ministry also. And I want you to know that it is due largely to Mother Blackaby." At a crisis time in his life, our family had ministered to him and encouraged him to seek God's will for his life. Marilynn had done much to show love to Ron. At this very critical time for Marilynn, God took care of her.

Now, all five of our children sense God's call to vocational ministry or mission work. Richard is now serving as president of the Canadian Baptist Theological Seminary. Only God could have done such a beautiful work with our children. I want you to know that you can trust God with your family! I would rather entrust my family to God's care than to anyone else in the whole world.

THE PRICE I WILL PAY

Who else besides me must pay the cost for my obedience? What will I experience if I am willing to pay the price of obedience? Are there types of suffering I will not endure to obey Jesus? Are there limits to the costs I am willing to make my spouse and children pay for my obeying God?

ADJUSTMENTS IN PRAYER AND THE COST

When our church encountered a directive from God, I often experienced a crisis in my prayer life. I learn more about prayer at those times than almost any other time. There were some things that only prayer could bring about. Often God waits until we ask. The crisis was this: Was I willing to pray until God brought it about? Mark 11:24 has been a prayer promise that has been challenging to me regarding the relationship of faith and prayer: "Whatever things you ask when you pray, believe that you receive them, and you will have them" (Mark 11:24).

This verse is sometimes used to teach a "name-it-and-claim-it" theology. *You* decide what *you* want. *You* name that in *your* request, claim it, and it's *yours*. That is a self-centered theology. Remember that only God takes the initiative. He gives you the desire to do His will (Phil. 2:13). His Holy Spirit guides you to pray according to God's will (Rom. 8:26–28). The God-centered approach would be to let God lead you to pray according to His will (in the name and character of Jesus). Believe that what He has led you to pray, He Himself will bring to pass. Then continue praying in faith and watching for it to come to pass.

When God encounters you, you face a crisis of belief that may require major adjustments in your life. You need to learn how to pray. Prayer will be exceedingly costly to you. You may need to let God wake you up in the middle of the night to pray. You may need to spend much time in prayer. Times may come when you pray into the night or even all night. Becoming a person of prayer will require a major adjustment of your life to God. Prayer will always be a part of the obedience. It is in a prayer relationship that God gives further direction.

Another cost will come as you try to guide the people around you to pray. Most of our churches have not learned how to pray together. The greatest untapped resource that I know of is the united prayer of God's people. Jesus, quoting from Isaiah 56:7, said, "My house is a house of prayer" (Luke 19:46). Helping your church become a praying church will be a rewarding experience. Every church needs to be a praying church!

SECOND CHANCES

Frequently people will ask me the question, "When a person disobeys God's will, does God give him or her a second chance?" The answer is yes, sometimes. He does not always give second chances, and He is not obligated to.

I am comforted to know that God often gives a second chance. When God had a plan to call Nineveh to repentance, He asked Jonah to join Him in His work. Jonah disobeyed because he was prejudiced against these "pagan enemies." Jonah would have rather seen God carry out the destruction of the city. Disobedience to God is very serious. Jonah went through the trauma of being thrown into a raging sea and spending three days in the belly of a big fish. Jonah confessed and repented of his disobedience. Then God gave him a second chance to obey.

The second time Jonah did obey (though reluctantly). On his first day Jonah preached a one-sentence message, and God used the message to call 120,000 people to repentance. Jonah said, "I know that You are a gracious and merciful God, slow to anger and abundant in lovingkindness, One who relents from doing harm" (Jonah 4:2). God's response to Jonah and Nineveh taught Jonah much about how deeply God cares for all peoples and wants them to come to repentance.

Some of the great people of God were broken by sin and disobedience, yet God did not give up on them. If God allowed people only one mistake, Moses would never have come to be the person he was. He made several mistakes (for example, Exod. 2:11–15). Abraham started out with a great walk of faith, but He went into Egypt and blew it—more than once (for example, Gen. 12:10–20). David muffed it (for example, 2 Sam. 11), and so did Peter (for example, Matt. 26:69–75). Saul (Paul) even began his "service for God" by persecuting Christians (Acts 9:1–2).

DISOBEDIENCE IS COSTLY

Disobedience, however, is never taken lightly by God. Jonah's disobedience almost cost him his life. Moses' murder of the Egyptian cost him forty years in the wilderness. David's sin with Bathsheba cost the life of his son. Paul's early ministry was greatly hindered because of his disobedience. Many people were afraid to get near him because of his reputation as a persecutor of Christians.

God is interested in developing your character. At times He lets you proceed in your disobedience, but He will never let you go too far without discipline to bring you back. In your relationship with God, He may let you make a wrong decision. Then the Spirit of God causes you to recognize that it is not God's will. He guides you back to the right path. He will clarify what He wants. He may even take the circumstance of your disobedience and work that together for good (Rom. 8:28) as He corrects you and teaches you His ways.

Even though God forgives and often gives second chances, you must not take disobedience lightly. Sometimes He does not give a second chance. Aaron's two sons, Nadab and Abihu, were disobedient in offering unholy incense to the Lord; and God struck them dead (Lev. 10).

Moses stole God's glory in front of all Israel and struck the rock saying, "Hear now, you rebels! Must we bring water for you out of this rock?" (Num. 20:10). Notice the word "we." God was the One who would bring water from the rock. Moses took God's glory, and God refused to take away the consequences of that disobedience. He refused to allow Moses to go with Israel into the Promised Land. With that experience God gave no second chance to get it right.

THE PRAYER PRICE I PAY

When do I learn most about prayer? What costly sacrifices in time and energy and forfeiting other priorities have I made so I can pray as God wants me to pray? What has God done or what is He doing to develop my character through my prayer life? Do I take my disobedience seriously enough?

OBEDIENCE PROVIDES FUTURE BLESSING

Although obedience is costly, it is always worth the cost. In fact whenever you are tempted to consider the cost too high, you need to consider what it will cost you not to do the will of God. That cost is even greater.

When we were still a very small church with a Sunday School attendance of forty-five, we had three mission churches we were trying to staff and support. We were asked to sponsor another mission in Winnipeg, Manitoba. It was 510 miles from Saskatoon. Someone would have to drive this 1,020-mile round-trip in order to provide them a pastor. At first glance, this sounded like an impossible and unreasonable task for our little group.

I shared with our congregation how a faithful group of people had been meeting for more than two years. They wanted to start a Southern Baptist church. We were the closest possible sponsoring church. We had to determine whether this was God's work and whether He was revealing His work to us. Was this our invitation to join Him in what He was doing? The church agreed this was God's doing. We knew we had to obey Him. We agreed to sponsor the new mission. Then we asked God to show us how and to give us the strength and resources to do it.

I drove a number of times to Winnipeg to preach and minister to the people. Sooner than for any of our other mission churches, God provided a pastor and a salary! The story of our obedience did not end there, however. Friendship Baptist Church has become the mother church to nine other mission churches and started an entire association of churches.

When our oldest son, Richard, finished seminary, this church in Winnipeg called him to be their pastor. This was his first pastorate! Our second son, Tom, was called to be on the staff of this church to guide music, education, and youth. Little did I know that this one act of obedience—that at first appeared impossible—held such potential for future blessing for the kingdom and for my family as well. How grateful I am that we chose to obey God in starting a church in Winnipeg!

WHY I OBEY

How has God made obedience worth the cost for me? What story can I tell of God bringing unexpected future blessings from an act of obedience on my part?

SUMMARY

Both major adjustments and costly obedience come before the experience of God's presence and power working through you. Many Christians and churches come to this moment of truth and decide the cost is too great. What they often do not do is consider what it may cost them not to obey. When God calls you to an assignment, the obedience will be costly to you and to those around you. Whatever the cost, however, obedience to God is not an option. It is required of every servant. When you obey, God will accomplish what He purposed, and you will be overwhelmed with the experience of God's power and presence. You and those around you will come to a greater knowledge of God through the experience.

EXPERIENCING GOD TODAY

Has God ever invited you or your church to join Him and you refused because the cost was too high? Ask God to reveal to you any act of disobedience or lack of obedience in your past. If God brings something to mind, agree with Him by confessing your sin. Surrender your life afresh to His lordship and agree that you will obey no matter what the cost.

Whenever you sense that obedience is too costly, it indicates that you have misunderstood who you are and what you have. As a disciple of Christ, you have been bought with a price and you are not your own. Everything you have belongs to God as well; you are just a steward of God's resources. Since you and everything you have belongs to Him, renew your dedication to Him for His purposes. Pray and agree with God that anything He asks is reasonable. Commit yourself to pay any cost to obey His will. Begin watching now for the first opportunity when God will test the sincerity of your commitment, and don't let God down.

MY SURRENDER TO OBEDIENCE

My Lord,

You paid such a price for my sin. How can I refuse to pay any price You ask in obedience to You? I surrender myself now to total obedience to whatever You ask of me. Show me where You are at work. Give me faith to trust that what You have shown me is true. Teach me to pray every situation through until You accomplish what You have shown me You would accomplish in the situation. Teach me to trust my family to Your loving care. I know You in a personal love relationship. Thus I love You from the deepest part of my heart. I believe every word You give me and trust You to bring each work You show me to completion. I will obey You and join You in that work. In so doing, I will encounter and experience You. Give me faith and courage to pay the cost in every area of my life to obey You fully.

He who does the truth comes to the light, that his deeds may be clearly seen, that they have been done in God.

JOHN 3:21

My counsel shall stand, and I will do all My pleasure. . . . Indeed I have spoken it; I will also bring it to pass. I have purposed it; I will also do it.

ISAIAH 46:10–11

19

GOD ACCOMPLISHES HIS WORK

When we experience God's invitation to join Him, we often insist upon seeing some kind of sign. It is as if we are saying: "Lord, prove to me this is You, and then I will obey." When Moses stood before the burning bush and received his invitation to join God, God told him that he would receive a sign that God sent him. God told Moses, "This shall be a sign to you that

I have sent you: When you have brought the people out of Egypt, you shall serve God on this mountain" (Exod. 3:12). In other words: "Moses, you obey Me. I will deliver Israel through you. You will come to know Me as your Deliverer, and you will stand on this mountain and worship Me."

God's affirmation that He had sent Moses was going to come *after* Moses obeyed, not before. This is most frequently the case in Scripture. The affirmation comes after the obedience.

God is love. Trust Him and believe Him. Because you love Him, obey Him. Then you will so fellowship with Him that you will come to know Him intimately. He will work through you to accomplish God-sized assignments that will affirm His presence and work in your life. That affirmation will be a joyous time for you!

WHAT IF THE "DOOR" CLOSES?

Suppose you sense the call of God to a task or to a place or to an assignment. You set about to do it and everything goes wrong. Often people will say, "Well, I guess that just was not God's will."

God calls you into a relationship with Himself. Be very careful how you interpret circumstances. Many times we jump to a conclusion too quickly. God is moving us in one direction to tell us what He is about to do. We immediately jump to our own conclusion about what He is doing and when He is going to do it because our conclusion sounds so logical. We start following the logic of our own reasoning, but then nothing seems to work out. We have a tendency to leave the relationship and take things into our own hands. Don't do that.

Most of the time when God calls you or gives a direction, His call is not what He wants you to do for Him. He is telling you what He is about to do where you are. As an example of this, examine this record of the apostle Paul's ministry:

> When they had gone through Phrygia and the region of Galatia, they were forbidden by the Holy Spirit to preach the word in Asia. After they had come to Mysia, they tried to go into Bithynia, but the Spirit did not permit them. So passing by Mysia, they came down to Troas. And a vision appeared to Paul in the night. A man of Macedonia stood and pleaded with him, saying, "Come over to Macedonia and help us." Now after he had seen the vision, immediately we sought to go to Macedonia, concluding that the Lord had called us to preach the gospel to them. (Acts 16:6–10)

Already on the Damascus road, God had told Paul that He was going to reach the Gentiles through him. God, not Paul, was going to reach the Gentiles. Paul started to go in one direction and the Spirit stopped him (Acts 16:6–10). He started to go another direction. Again, the Spirit stopped him. What was the original plan of God? To reach the Gentiles. What was Paul's problem? He was trying to figure out what he ought to do, and the "door" of opportunity closed. Did the door close? No. God was trying to say, "Listen to me, Paul. Go and sit in Troas until I tell you where you are supposed to go."

In Troas, Paul had the vision to go over to Macedonia and help them. What was happening? God's plan was to turn the gospel to the west toward Greece and Rome. God was at work in Philippi and wanted Paul to join Him in His work there.

When you begin to follow and circumstances *seem* to close doors of opportunity, go back to the Lord and clarify what God said. Better yet, always try to make sure on the front end of a sense of call exactly what God is saying. He most often is not calling you to a task only, but to a relationship. Through that relationship He is going to do something through your life. If you start off in a direction and everything is stopped, go back and clarify what God has said. Do not deny what God has said, but clarify what God has said.

Moses had to do that constantly. He obeyed God and spoke to Pharaoh, and everything went wrong. Moses didn't quit. He went to the Lord to clarify what was happening. God began to give him directions about the plagues He was bringing on Egypt. Pharaoh seemed to be getting more and more difficult to deal with. Moses daily sought God's directions and obeyed them. Later Moses could look back and see God's handiwork in all that took place. God delivered Israel from the Egyptians in such a way that Israel, Egypt, and all the surrounding nations knew that God had done it.

A COUPLE'S CALL TO STUDENT WORK

I talked with a wonderful couple who said they were invited to go to Saskatoon to do student work. They started the process for assignment as missionaries and the mission board said, "No."

Their conclusion was: "Then we made a mistake." I advised them not to jump to that conclusion, but to go back and recall what God said when they sensed His call. They were canceling the whole plan of God because one detail did not work out as they thought it would.

I asked them to go back and clarify what God had called them to do. Was He calling them to missions? Was He calling them to student work? Was He calling them to Canada? They did sense God was calling them to Canada and student work.

Then, I said, "Keep that sense of call in place. Because one door closed, don't assume that the assignment is over. Watch to see how the God who called you is going to implement what He said. When God speaks a word of direction, He will bring it to pass. Be very careful that you do not let circumstances cancel what God said."

God may have a different city in mind for them. He may want them to have a different means of financial support. Or He may need more time to prepare them for the assignment. Let Him work out the details in His timing. In the meantime, do all you know to do, and then wait for the next word of instruction. When things seem to go wrong after you take a step of obedience:

- Clarify what God said and identify what may have been your "additions" to what He said.
- Keep in place what God has said.
- Let Him work out the details in His timing.
- Do all you know to do.
- Then wait on the Lord until He tells you what to do next.

God's greatest single task is to get His people adjusted to Himself. He needs time to shape us until we are exactly what He wants us to be. Suppose you sense that God is going to do something great because of what He has said in His Word and prayer. You sense He is going to do it because of the way circumstances are working out, and other believers (church) agree. Then six months pass and you still haven't seen anything great. Don't get negative and depressed and discouraged. *The God who initiates His work in a relationship with you is the One Himself who guarantees to complete it.* Watch to see what God is doing in you and in the people around you to prepare you for what He is going to do. The key is your relationship with God.

SLOW GOING

Does God seem to be working slowly in your life? Jesus had been with His disciples about three years when He said: "I still have many things to say to you, but you cannot bear them now. However, when He, the Spirit of truth, has come, He will guide you into all truth; for He will not speak on His own authority, but whatever He hears He will speak; and He will tell you things to come" (John 16:12–13).

Jesus had more He needed to teach the disciples, but they were not ready to receive it. Jesus knew, however, that the Holy Spirit would continue to guide these disciples into truth on God's timetable.

You may be saying, "God, hurry up and make me mature."

And God is saying, "I'm moving just as fast in your life as you will allow me. When you are ready for your next lesson, I will bring a new truth into your life." If God does not seem to be giving you a new assignment, you may want to ask yourself these questions:

- Am I responding to all God already is leading me to do?
- Have I obeyed all I already know to be His will?
- Do I really believe that He loves me and will always do what is best and right?
- Am I willing to wait patiently on His timing and obey everything I know to do in the meantime?

Grass that is here today and gone tomorrow does not require much time to mature. A big oak tree that lasts for generations requires much more time to grow and mature. God is concerned about your life through eternity. Allow Him to take all the time He needs to shape you for His purposes. Larger assignments will require longer periods of preparation.

Would you be willing for God to take all the time He needs to prepare you for the assignments He may have purposed for your life? If so, spend some time right now in prayer telling Him so.

GOD'S WORK DONE THROUGH ME

How intimately do I know God? When did I last experience joyous affirmation from God? How long has it been since God gave me a new assignment? How patient and prayerful am I in waiting for God's assignment?

GOD ACCOMPLISHES HIS WORK THROUGH YOU

When you obey God, He will accomplish through you what He has purposed to do. When God does something through your life that only He can do, you will come to know Him more intimately. If you do not obey, you will miss out on some of the most exciting experiences of your life.

When God purposes to do something through you, the assignment will have God-sized dimensions. This is because God wants to reveal Himself to you and to those around you. If you can do the work in your own strength, people will not come to know God. However, if God works through you to do what only He can do, you and those around you will come to know Him. Jesus said, "He who does the truth comes to the light, that his deeds may be clearly seen, that they have been done in God" (John 3:21).

The Holy Spirit will never misunderstand the Father's will for your life. The Father has a purpose to work out through your life. In order that you not miss it, He places His Spirit in you. The Spirit's job is to guide you according to the will of the Father. Then the Spirit enables you to do God's will. You are completely dependent on God for the knowledge *and* the ability to accomplish His purposes. That is why your relationship to Him is so important. That is why you need to wait until you have heard a word from Him about His purposes and ways.

Jesus is your example of One who never failed to know and do the will of His Father. Every solitary thing the Father purposed to do through His life, the Lord Jesus did it immediately. What was the key to His success? He was always rightly related to the Father! If you walk in a consistent relationship with God's provision for you—the Holy Spirit, and His own presence in your life—then you should never come to a time that you do not know the will of God. There should never be a time when you are not enabled to carry out the will of God.

In Jesus you have a picture of a solitary life in a love relationship with God, consistently living out that relationship. He is the perfect example. You and I will come quickly to the conclusion that we are a long way from that. True! But the Christ who lived His life in complete obedience is fully present in you to enable you to know and do His will. We need to adjust our lives to God and consistently live out that relationship with absolute dependence on Him. He will never fail to pull your life into the middle of His purpose and enable you to do it.

The God-sized dimensions of an assignment from God create the crisis of belief. You have to believe that God is who He says He is and that He can and will do what He says He will do. When you obey Him, you have to allow Him to do what He has said. He is the One who accomplishes the assignment, but He does it through you.

Moses. Only in the act of obedience did Moses begin to experience the full nature of God. What he began to know about God grew out of his obedience to God. In Moses' life we can see this pattern of God speaking, Moses obeying, and God accomplishing what He purposed to do. We see this pattern throughout Moses' life:

- God invited Moses to join Him in what He was doing to deliver Israel.
- God told Moses what he was to do.
- Moses obeyed.
- God accomplished what He purposed to do.
- Moses and those around him came to know God more clearly and intimately.

For instance, when the people stood between the Red Sea and the oncoming Egyptian army, God told Moses to hold his staff over the sea. Moses obeyed. God parted the sea and the people crossed on dry ground (Exod. 14:1–25). Then Miriam led the people in a hymn of praise describing their new understanding of God.

When the people were thirsty and had no water to drink, they complained to Moses. God told Moses to strike a rock with the staff. Moses obeyed, and God caused water to flow from the rock (Exod. 17:1–7). We see this pattern in Moses' life again and again.

Men of Faith. When Noah obeyed, God preserved his family and repopulated the earth. When Abraham obeyed, God gave him a son and built a nation. When David obeyed, God made him a king. When Elijah obeyed, God sent down fire and consumed a sacrifice. These people of faith came to know God by experience when they obeyed Him, and He accomplished His work through them.

The Disciples. Luke records a beautiful experience of Jesus' disciples that follows this same pattern. Jesus invited seventy (seventy-two, in the NIV) to join Him in the Father's work. The disciples obeyed and experienced God accomplishing through them some things they knew only God could do.

Jesus gave these followers specific directions. They obeyed Him and experienced God working through them to heal and cast out demons. Jesus told them that their own salvation ought to bring more joy than the submission of the spirits (v. 20). Jesus praised God the Father for revealing Himself to these followers (vv. 21–22). Then Jesus turned to His disciples and said, "Blessed are the eyes which see the things you see; for I tell you that many prophets and kings have desired to see what you see, and have not seen it, and to hear what you hear, and have not heard it" (Luke 10:23–24).

These disciples were blessed. They had been chosen especially by God to be involved in His work. What they saw, heard, and came to know about God was something even prophets and kings wanted to experience and did not. These disciples were blessed!

You, too, will be blessed when God does a special, God-sized work through you. You will come to know Him in a way that will bring rejoicing to your life. When other people see you experiencing God that way, they are going to want to know how they, too, can experience God that way. Be prepared to point them to God.

If you are obedient, God will work some wonderful things through you. You will need to be very careful that any testimony about what God has done only gives glory to Him. Pride may cause you to want to tell your experience because it makes you feel special. That will be a continuing tension. You will want to declare the wonderful deeds of the Lord, but you must avoid any sense of pride. Therefore: "He who glories, let him glory in the Lord" (1 Cor. 1:31).

LEARNING FROM THE BIBLE

How has obedience led me to a more intimate relationship with God? In what work have I participated with God that has clearly shown that God did the work through me? What was the key to Jesus' success in doing God's work? Am I willing to let God do what He says He will do? Give examples from Scripture of God accomplishing His work through obedient people. How am I pointing people to God by allowing God to reveal Himself through me?

YOU COME TO KNOW GOD

God reveals Himself to His people by what He does. When God works through you to accomplish His purposes, you come to know God by experience. You also come to know God when He meets a need in your life.

In Scripture when God did something through an obedient person or people, they came to know Him in new and more intimate ways. God revealed His personal name to Moses, "I AM WHO I AM" (Exod. 3:14). Jesus expressed Himself to His disciples by saying:

"I am the bread of life." (John 6:35)
"I am the light of the world." (John 8:12)
"I am the door." (John 10:9)
"I am the good shepherd." (John 10:11)
"I am the resurrection and the life." (John 11:25)
"I am the way, the truth, and the life." (John 14:6)
"I am the true vine." (John 15:1)

Jesus identified Himself with the I AM (name of God given to Moses at the burning bush) of the Old Testament. Knowing and experiencing Jesus in these ways requires that you "believe in Him" (have faith in Him). For instance, when He says to you, "I am the way," what you do next in your relationship with Him will determine if you come to experience Him as "the way" in your own life. When you believe Him, adjust your life to Him, and obey what He says next, you come to know and experience Him as "the Way." This is true about everything God reveals to you day by day. As you follow Him obediently, He works in and through you to reveal Himself to you and those around you.

MY EXPERIENCE IN KNOWING GOD

In what experiences has God revealed Himself to me so that I encountered Him? Can I trace the seven realities of experiencing God in my own experiences with God? Why or why not?

SUMMARY

God is at work in the world reconciling a lost world to Himself through His Son Jesus Christ. God takes the initiative to invite you to be involved with Him. When you obey Him, He accomplishes His work through you in such a way that you and everyone else know that God has been at work. When you experience God working in and through you, you will come to know Him more fully. That is exactly what Jesus had in mind when He said, "This is eternal life, that they may know You, the only true God, and Jesus Christ whom you have sent" (John 17:3). You come to know Him as you experience Him in your life.

EXPERIENCING GOD TODAY

God longs for you to desire Him and His ways. Do you? Read the following prayer of the psalmist and make it your own prayer today. Ask the Lord to lead and guide you in all His ways for His glory.

> Teach me, O LORD, the way of Your statutes;
> And I shall keep it to the end.
> Give me understanding, and I shall keep Your law;
> Indeed, I shall observe it with my whole heart.
> Make me walk in the path of Your commandments,
> For I delight in it. (Psalm 119:33–35)

MY SURRENDER TO ACCOMPLISHING GOD'S WORK

Dear God,

I want to experience You. I want to see You working through my life. I know that this means I will face a crisis of belief day by day. I must trust You to be who You say You are and to do what You have said You will do. I must adjust my life to You. I will obey You. Work through me to accomplish all that You desire to accomplish. Do not let me give in to unpromising circumstances when You are speaking to me. Do not let me be impatient. Show me where I have been disobedient. Help me trust that You are always doing what is best for me. Give me patience to let You prepare me for the task You have assigned me. Place the Holy Spirit in my life to direct me according to Your ways, Your purposes, and Your work. Make our love relationship even more intimate than it already is. Thank You, dear Lord, for being so close to me. I love You.

[I pray] that He would grant you, according to the riches of His glory, to be strengthened with might through His Spirit in the inner man, that Christ may dwell in your hearts through faith; that you, being rooted and grounded in love, may be able to comprehend with all the saints what is the width and length and depth and height—to know the love of Christ which passes knowledge; that you may be filled with all the fullness of God.
Now to Him who is able to do exceedingly abundantly above all that we ask or think, according to the power that works in us, to Him be glory in the church by Christ Jesus to all generations, forever and ever. Amen.

EPHESIANS 3:16–21

CLOSING REMARKS

In preparing this book, my prayer has been that you would come to know God more intimately as you experience Him at work in and through your life. Has God been speaking to you? Has He been teaching you, guiding you, or encouraging you? Has He been calling you into a love relationship with Himself? Has He invited you to be involved with Him in His work? Can you identify what God has been doing in your life? I pray that you can answer yes to these questions.

May I recommend that you spend time taking a spiritual inventory of your present walk with Him. If God has been working in your life as you read this book, He has been preparing you for more intimate fellowship with Himself and for assignments in His kingdom. I hope you have come to this time with a deep sense of God's presence and activity in your life. What God has begun in your life He Himself will bring to perfect completion: "He who has begun a good work in you will complete it until the day of Jesus Christ" (Phil. 1:6).

God has been so gracious to allow me to join Him as He has been working in your life. I thank God and praise Him for the many wonderful things He has done in our day.

APPENDIX

NAMES, TITLES, AND DESCRIPTIONS OF GOD

To assist your own research, at least one Scripture reference is given for each name or title.

abounding in goodness and truth (Exod. 34:6)
acquainted with grief (Isa. 53:3)
Adam, the last (1 Cor. 15:45)
Advocate with the Father (1 John 2:1)
all (Col. 3:11)
Almighty, the (Job 5:17; 1:8)
Alpha (Rev. 1:8; 21:6)
Amen, the (Rev. 3:14)
Ancient of Days, the (Dan. 7:22)
anointed (Ps. 2:2; Acts 4:27)
Apostle and High Priest of our confession (Heb. 3:1)
author and finisher of our faith, the (Heb. 12:2)
author of eternal salvation, the (Heb. 5:9)
banner to the people, a (Isa. 11:10)
Beginning of the creation of God, the (Rev. 3:14)
Beginning, the (Rev. 21:6)
Beloved, My (Matt. 12:18)
Branch of the LORD, the (Isa. 4:2)
Branch, a (Isa. 11:1)
Branch, a righteous (Jer. 23:5)
BRANCH, the (Zech. 6:12)
bread from heaven, true (John 6:32)
bread of life, the (John 6:35)
breath of the Almighty (Job 32:8; 33:4)
bridegroom, the (Matt. 9:15)
brightness of His glory, the (Heb. 1:3)
brother of James, Joseph, Judas, and Simon, of (Mark. 6:3)
builder and maker (Heb. 11:10)
carpenter, the (Mark 6:3)
carpenter's son, the (Matt.13:55)
chief cornerstone, elect, precious (1 Pet. 2:6)
chief cornerstone, the (Matt. 21:42; Mark 12:10; Eph. 2:20)
Child Jesus (Luke 2:27)
chosen of God, the (Luke 23:35)
Christ, the chosen of God (Luke 23:35)
Christ Jesus my Lord (Phil. 3:8)
Christ of God (Luke 9:20)
Christ, the (Matt. 16:16)

comforter (2 Cor. 1:4)
Commander of the Lord's army, the (Josh. 5:15)
confidence of all the ends of the earth and . . . (Ps. 65:5)
Consolation of Israel, the (Luke 2:25)
cornerstone, a precious (Isa. 28:16)
Counselor, Wonderful (Isa. 9:6)
covenant to the people (Isa. 42:6)
Creator of Israel, the (Isa. 43:15)
Creator of the ends of the earth (Isa. 40:28)
Creator, a faithful (1 Pet. 4:19)
Creator, your (Eccles. 12:1)
crown of glory, a (Isa 28:5; 62:3)
Dayspring, the (Luke 1:78)
defender of widows, a (Ps. 68:5)
deliverer, my (2 Sam. 22:2; Ps. 18:2)
Deliverer, the (Rom. 11:26)
Desire of All Nations (Hag. 2:7)
diadem of beauty (Isa. 28:5)
diadem, a royal (Isa. 62:3)
door of the sheep, the (John 10:7)
door, the (John 10:9)
dwelling place, our (Ps. 90:1)
dwelling, your (Ps. 91:9)
End, the (Rev. 21:6)
Excellent Glory, the (2 Pet. 1:17)
express image of His person, the (Heb. 1:3)
everlasting strength (Isa. 26:4)
Faithful and True (Rev. 19:11)
Father (Matt. 11:25)
Father of glory, the (Eph. 1:17)
Father of lights, the (James 1:17)
Father of mercies, the (2 Cor. 1:3)
Father of spirits, the (Heb. 12:9)
father to the fatherless, a (Ps. 68:5)
Father to Israel, a (Jer. 31:9)
Father who honors Me, My (said by Jesus) (John 8:54)
Father, Everlasting (Isa. 9:6)
Father, Holy (John 17:11; 20:17)
Father, My (John 8:54)
Father, our (Isa. 64:8)
Father, righteous (John 17:25)
Father, your (Deut. 32:6; John 20:17)
Fear of Isaac, the (Gen. 31:42)
fire, a consuming (Deut. 4:24)
fire, the devouring (Isa. 33:14)
first to rise from the dead (Acts 26:23)
First, the (Isa. 44:6; Rev. 22:13)
firstborn among many brothers (Rom. 8:29)
firstborn from the dead, the (Col. 1:18)
firstborn over all creation, the (Col. 1:15)
firstfruits of those who have fallen asleep, the (1 Cor. 15:20)
fortress, my (Ps. 18:2; 91:2)
foundation (1 Cor. 3:11)
foundation, a sure (Isa. 28:16)
fountain of living waters, the (Jer. 2:13)
friend of tax collectors and sinners, a (Matt. 11:19)
gift, indescribable (2 Cor. 9:15)
gift, the same (Acts 11:17)
glory, their (Ps. 106:20; Jer. 2:11)
glory, your (Isa. 60:19)
God (Gen. 1:1; John 1:1)
God of Hosts, the (El Sabaoth) (Ps. 80:7)
God of my salvation, the (Ps. 18:46)
God of your Salvation, the (Isa. 17:10)
God and Father of our Lord Jesus Christ (Eph. 1:3)
God and Savior Jesus Christ, our (2 Pet. 1:1)
God and Savior, our great (Titus 2:13)
God in heaven above and on the earth beneath (Deut. 4:39; Josh. 2:11)
God Most High (Gen. 14:18)
God my Maker (Job 35:10)
God my Rock (Ps. 42:9)
God of Abraham, the (Ps. 47:9)
God of Abraham, Isaac, and Israel (1 Kings 18:36)
God of Abraham, Isaac, and Jacob (Exod. 3:16)
God of all comfort (2 Cor. 1:3)
God of all flesh (Jer. 32:27)
God of all grace (1 Pet. 5:10)
God of all the kingdoms of the earth (2 Kings 19:15)
God of Daniel (Dan. 6:26)
God of David your father (2 Kings 20:5)
God of glory (Ps. 29:3)

God of gods (Deut. 10:17)
God of heaven (Gen. 24:3; Ps. 136:26)
God of heaven and earth (Ezra 5:11)
God of Israel (Exod. 24:10;
Matt. 15:31)
God of Jacob (Ps. 20:1)
God of Jeshurun (the upright one)
(Deut. 33:26)
God of mercy (Ps. 59:10)
God of my father Abraham (Gen 32:9)
God of my father Isaac (Gen 32:9)
God of my salvation, the
(Ps. 51:14; 88:1)
God of my strength (Ps. 43:2)
God of Nahor (Gen. 31:53)
God of our fathers (Deut. 26:7)
God of our Lord Jesus Christ
(Eph. 1:17)
God of our salvation (1 Chron. 16:35;
Ps. 85:4)
God of peace (Rom. 16:20;
1 Thess. 5:23)
God of recompense (Jer. 51:56)
God of Shadrach, Meshach, and
Abednego (Dan. 3:28)
God of the armies of Israel
(1 Sam. 17:45)
God of the earth (Gen. 24:3)
God of the Hebrews (Exod. 5:3)
God of the living (Matt. 22:32)
God of the spirits of all flesh
(Num. 16:22; 27:15)
God of the whole earth (Isa. 54.5)
God of truth (Ps. 31:5)
God of truth and without injustice
(Deut. 32:4)
God of your fathers (Deut. 1:21)
God our Father (Eph. 1:2)
God our Savior (Jude 25)
God our strength (Ps. 81:1)
God over Israel (2 Sam. 7:26)
God the Father (John 6:27)
God the King of all the earth (Ps. 47:7)
God the LORD (1 Chron. 13:6; Ps. 85:8)
God who alone is wise (1 Tim. 1:17)
God who avenges (Ps. 94:1)
God who avenges me (Ps. 18:47)
God who does wonders (Ps. 77:14)
God-Who-Forgives (Ps. 99:8)
God who delivers me from my enemies,
the (Ps. 18:47–48)
God-Who-Sees, the (Gen. 16:13)
God, a jealous (Deut. 4:24)
God, Almighty (El Shaddai)
(Gen. 17:1)
God, great and awesome (Dan. 9:4)
God, Israel's (1 Chron. 17:24)
God, living (Jer. 10:10)
God, living and true (1 Thess. 1:9)
God, merciful and gracious
(Exod. 34:6)
God, Mighty (Isa. 9:6)
God, my (Gen. 28:21; John 20:17)
God, my righteousness (Ps. 4:1)
God, O King (Ps. 145:1)
God, the Everlasting (Gen. 21:33;
Isa. 40:28)
God, the faithful (Deut. 7:9)
God, great (Deut. 10:17)
God, the great and awesome (Neh. 1:5)
God, the true (Jer. 10:10)
God, your (John 20:17)
guarantee, a (2 Cor. 1:22; 5:5)
guide, our (Ps. 48:14)
habitation of justice, the (Jer. 50:7)
He who blots out your transgressions
(Isa. 43:25)
He who built all things (Heb. 3:4)
He who calls for the waters of the sea
(Amos 5:8)
He who comes in the name of the LORD
(Ps. 118:26)
He who comforts you (Isa. 51:12)
He who declares to man what His
thought is (Amos 4:13)
He who forms the mountains, and
creates the wind (Amos 4:13)
He who makes the day dark as night
(Amos 5:8)
He who makes the morning darkness
(Amos 4:14)
He who raised Christ from the dead
(Rom. 8:11)
He who reveals secrets (Dan. 2:29)
He who sanctifies (Heb. 2:11)
He who searches the heart (Rom. 8:27)
He who searches the minds and hearts
(Rev. 2:23)

King of heaven, the (Dan. 4:37)
King of Israel, the (Zeph. 3:15; John 1:49)
KING OF KINGS (Rev. 19:16)
King of kings (1 Tim. 6:15)
King of the Jews (Rev. 15:3)
King of the Jews (Matt. 27:11; John 18:39; 19:9)
King of the nations (Jer. 10:7)
King of the saints (Rev. 15:3)
King over all the earth, great (Ps 47:2)
King who comes in the name of the Lord (Luke 19:38)
King, everlasting (Jer. 10:10)
King, great (Ps. 48:2; Matt. 5:35)
King, my (Ps. 44:4)
King, our (Isa. 33:22)
King, your (Matt. 21:5; Isa. 43:15)
Lamb of God, the (John 1:29)
lamb without blemish and without spot, a (1 Pet. 1:19)
Lamb, a (Rev. 5:6)
Lamb, the (Rev. 5:8)
Lamb who was slain (Rev. 5:12)
lamp, my (2 Sam. 22:29)
Last, the (Isa. 44:6; Rev. 22:13)
Lawgiver, one (James 4:12)
Lawgiver, our (Isa. 33:22)
leader and commander for the people, a (Isa. 55:4)
life, eternal (1 John 5:20)
life, the (John 14:6)
life, our (Col. 3:4)
light (1 John 1:5)
Light, the true (John 1:8)
light of life, the (John 8:12)
light of men, the (John 1:4)
light of the world, the (John 8:12)
light to bring revelation to the Gentiles (Luke 2:32)
light to the Gentiles (Isa. 42:6)
light, a great (Isa. 9:2)
light, an everlasting (Isa. 60:19)
Light, true (John 1:9)
lily of the valleys, the (Song of Sol. 2:1)
Lion of the tribe of Judah (Rev. 5:5)
longsuffering, the (Exod. 34:6)
Lord (Luke 2:11)
Lord (Adonai) (Ps. 54:4)
LORD (Jehovah) (Gen. 15:6)
Lord and Savior, the (2 Pet. 3:2)
Lord and Savior Jesus Christ, the (2 Pet. 2:20)
LORD God (Gen. 2:4)
Lord God Almighty (Rev. 15:3)
LORD God of Gods, the (Josh. 22:22)
LORD God of hosts (2 Sam. 5:10)
LORD God of Israel (1 Chron. 29:10)
Lord God, the only (Jude 4)
LORD-Is-My-Banner, the- (Exod. 17:15; Num. 2:2)
LORD-Is-Peace, the- (Jehovah Shalom) (Judg. 6:24)
Lord Jesus (Luke 24:3; Acts 7:59)
Lord Jesus Christ (Gal. 1:3; James 2:1)
Lord Jesus Christ, our hope (1Tim. 1:1)
LORD Most High (Ps. 7:17)
LORD my Rock (Ps. 28:1)
Lord of all the earth, the (Josh. 3:13)
Lord of both the dead and the living (Rom. 14:9)
Lord of glory, the (1 Cor. 2:8; James 2:1)
Lord of heaven and earth (Matt. 11:25)
Lord of hosts (Ps. 24:10)
Lord of kings (Dan. 2:47)
LORD of LORDS (Rev. 19:16)
Lord of lords (Deu. 10:17; 1 Tim. 6:15; Rev. 17:14)
Lord of peace, the (2 Thess. 3:16)
Lord of the harvest (Matt. 9:38)
Lord of the Sabbath (Matt. 12:8; Luke 6:5)
LORD our God, the (Josh. 24:24)
LORD our Maker, the (Ps. 95:6)
LORD OUR RIGHTEOUSNESS, THE (Jer. 23:6; 33:16)
Lord our shield (Ps. 59:11)
LORD over Israel (1 Chron. 28:5)
LORD who heals you, the (Exod. 15:26)
LORD who made heaven and earth (Ps. 115:15; 121:2)
LORD who sanctifies you, the (Exod. 31:13)
LORD-Will-Provide, the- (Gen. 22:14)
LORD your God, the (Lev. 11:44)
LORD your Maker, the (Isa. 51:13)

Lord, my (John 20:28)
love (1 John 4:8)
Maker of all things, the (Jer. 10:16)
Maker of heaven and earth, the sea, and . . . (Ps. 146:6)
Maker of the Bear, Orion, and the Pleiades . . . (Job 9:9)
majestic LORD, the (Isa. 33:21)
Majesty on high, the (Heb. 1:3)
Maker, his (Prov. 14:31)
Maker, my (Job 32:22)
Maker, our (Ps. 95:6)
Maker, your (Isa. 54:5)
Man attested by God (Acts 2:22)
Man Jesus Christ, the (1 Tim. 2:5)
Man of sorrows (Isa. 53:3)
Man, a righteous (Luke 23:47)
Man, the second (1 Cor. 15:47)
Man, that just (Matt. 27:19)
Man, the (John 19:5)
Man, this (Mark 6:2)
Master (Luke 5:5; 2 Tim. 2:21)
Master in heaven, a (Col. 4:1)
Mediator, the (1 Tim. 2:5)
Mediator of a new covenant, the (Heb. 9:15)
Messenger of the covenant, the (Mal. 3:1)
Messiah, the (John 1:41)
Mighty One of Jacob, the (Ps. 132:2,5)
Mighty God (Isa. 9:6)
Mighty God of Jacob (Gen. 49:24)
morning star (2 Pet. 1:19)
Morning Star, the Bright and (Rev. 22:16)
Most High (Ps. 18:13; 92:1)
Most High over all the earth, the (Ps. 83:18)
Most Holy, the (Dan. 9:24)
Most Upright (Isa. 26:7)
Nazarene, a (Matt. 2:23)
offering and sacrifice to God, an (Eph. 5:2)
oil of gladness (Heb. 1:9)
Omega (Rev. 1:8)
only begotten of the Father, the (John 1:14)
One greater than Jonah (Matt. 12:41)
One greater than Solomon (Matt. 12:42)
One greater than the temple (Matt. 12:6)
one Lawgiver who is able to save and to destroy (James 4:12)
One who gives salvation to kings, the (Ps. 144:10)
One who is and who was and who is to be, the (Rev. 16:5)
One who remembered us in our low state (Ps. 136:23)
One you are to dread (Isa. 8:13)
One you are to fear (Isa. 8:13)
One you should hallow, the (Isa. 8:13)
One, My Elect (Isa. 42:1)
Passover, our (1 Cor. 5:7)
peace, our (Eph. 2:14)
Physician (Luke 4:23)
portion, my (Ps. 119:57)
portion in the land of the living, my (Ps. 142:5)
Portion of Jacob, the (Jer. 10:16)
portion of my inheritance, the (Ps. 16:5)
Possessor of heaven and earth (Gen. 14:22)
possession, their (priest's) (Ezek. 44:28)
Potentate, blessed and only (1 Tim. 6:15)
potter, the (Isa. 64:8; Rom. 9:21)
power of the Highest (Luke 1:35)
power of God, the (1 Cor. 1:24)
Power, the (Matt. 26:64)
praises of Israel, the (Ps. 22:3)
praise, your (Deut. 10:21)
priest forever according to the order of Melchizedek, a (Heb. 5:6)
Prince, the (Dan. 9:25)
Prince and Savior (Acts 5:31)
Prince of life (Acts 5:31)
Prince of Peace, the (Isa. 9:6)
Prince of princes, the (Dan. 8:25)
Prince of the hosts, the (Dan. 8:11)
Promise, the Father of (Acts 1:4)
prophet from Nazareth, the (Matt. 21:11)
Prophet who is to come into the world, the (John 6:14)
Prophet, the (John 7:40)
propitiation for our sins, the (1 John 2:2)

Rabbi (John 3:2)
Rabboni (Teacher) (John 20:16)
ransom for all, a (1 Tim. 2:6)
Redeemer from everlasting, our (Isa. 63:16)
Redeemer, my (Job 19:25; Ps. 19:14)
Redeemer, our (Isa. 47:4)
Redeemer, their (Ps. 78:35; Prov. 23:11)
Redeemer, your (Isa. 41:14)
refiner and purifier, as a (Mal. 3:3)
refuge and strength, our (Ps. 46:1)
refuge for the oppressed (Ps. 9:9)
refuge from the storm, a (Isa. 25:4)
refuge in the day of affliction, my (Jer. 16:19)
refuge in the day of my trouble, my (Ps. 59:16)
refuge in times of trouble, a (Ps. 9:9)
refuge, my (2 Sam. 22:3; Ps. 142:5; Isa. 91:2)
refuge, our (Ps. 46:7)
refuge of His anointed, saving (Ps. 28:8)
resurrection and the life, the (John 11:25)
reward, your exceedingly great (Gen. 15:1)
righteousness and sanctification and redemption, our (1 Cor. 1:30)
Rock of his salvation (Deut. 32:15)
rock of my refuge, the (Ps. 94:22)
rock of my salvation, the (Ps. 89:26)
rock of my strength and my refuge, the (Ps. 62:7)
rock of offense, a (1 Pet. 2:8)
Rock of our salvation, the (Ps. 95:1)
Rock of Israel, the (2 Sam. 23:3)
rock, my (Ps. 18:2; 92:15)
Rock, spiritual (1 Cor. 10:4)
Rock, the (Deut. 32:4)
Root and the Offspring of David, the (Rev. 22:16)
Root of David (Rev. 5:5)
Root of Jesse (Isa. 11:10; Rom. 15:12)
rose of Sharon, the (Song of Sol. 2:1)
ruler over the kings of the earth, the (Rev. 1:5)
Ruler, a (governor) (Matt. 2:6)
salvation, my (Exod. 15:2; Ps. 27:1)
salvation, Your (Luke 2:30)
sanctuary, a (Isa. 8:14)
Savior in times of trouble (Israel's) (Jer. 14:8)
SavioræJesus (Acts 13:23)
Savior of all men, the (1 Tim. 4:10)
Savior of the body (Eph. 5:23)
Savior of the world, the (John 4:42)
Savior, my (2 Sam. 22:3)
Savior, the (Eph. 5:23)
Savior, their (Isa. 63:8)
Savior, your (Isa. 43:3)
Sceptre (Num. 24:17)
seal, a (Eph. 1:13)
seed, His (1 John 3:9)
seed, his (Abraham's) (Gal. 3:16)
Seed, the (Gal. 3:19)
servant to the circumcision (Rom. 15:8)
Servant, holy (Acts 4:27)
Servant, My (Matt. 12:18)
Servant, My righteous (Isa. 53:11)
seven Spirits of God (the sevenfold spirit) (Rev. 5:6)
shade at your right hand, your (Ps. 121:5)
shade from the heat, a (Isa. 25:4)
shelter for His people, a (Joel 3:16)
Shepherd and Overseer of your souls, the (1 Pet. 2:25)
Shepherd of Israel (Ps. 80:1)
Shepherd of the sheep, great (Heb. 13:20)
Shepherd, one (Eccles. 12:11)
Shepherd, the Chief (1 Pet. 5:4)
shepherd, the good (John 10:11)
shield for me, a (Ps. 3:3)
shield, my (Ps. 18:2; 28:7)
shield, our (Ps. 33:20)
Son of Abraham (Matt. 1:1)
Son of David (Matt. 1:1; Luke 20:41)
Son of God (John 1:49; 1 John 4:9)
Son of Joseph (John 6:42)
Son of Mary (Mark 6:3)
Son of Man, the (Matt. 12:40; 24:27)
Son of the Blessed One, the (Mark 14:61)
Son of the living God (Matt. 16:16)
Son of the Most High God (Mark 5:7)

Son, My beloved (Mark 1:11)
song, my (Ps. 118:14)
Spirit of adoption, the (Rom. 8:15)
spirit of burning, the (Isa. 4:4)
Spirit of Christ, the (Rom. 8:9)
Spirit of counsel and might, the (Isa. 11:2)
spirit of faith, the (2 Cor. 4:13)
Spirit of glory, the (1 Pet. 4:14)
Spirit of God, the (Gen. 1:2; Matt. 3:16)
Spirit of grace, the (Heb. 10:29)
Spirit of grace and supplication, the (Zech. 12:10)
Spirit of His Son (Gal. 4:6)
Spirit of holiness, the (Rom. 1:4)
Spirit of Jesus Christ, the (Phil. 1:19)
spirit of judgement, the (Isa. 4:4)
spirit of justice, a (Isa. 28:6)
Spirit of knowledge and of the fear of the LORD, the (Isa. 11:2)
Spirit of life, the (Rom. 8:2)
Spirit of our God, the (1 Cor. 6:11)
Spirit of the living God, the (2 Cor. 3:3)
Spirit of the LORD, the (Isa. 11:2; Luke 4:18)
Spirit of truth, the (John 14:17; 15:26)
spirit of wisdom and revelation, the (Eph. 1:17)
Spirit of wisdom and understanding, the (Isa. 11:2)
Spirit of your Father, the (Matt. 10:20)
spirit of wisdom, the (Deut. 34:9)
Spirit who bears witness, the (1 John 5:6)
Spirit who dwells in us, the (James 4:5)
spirit, a life-giving (1 Cor. 15:45)
spirit, a new (Ezek. 11:19; 18:31)
Spirit, the eternal (Heb. 9:14)
Spirit, His (Num. 11:29; Eph. 3:16)
Spirit, My (Gen. 6:3; Matt. 12:18)
Spirit, the (Num. 11:17; Acts 16:7))
Spirit, Your (Neh. 9:30)
Spirit, Your good (Neh. 9:20)
Star, a (Num. 24:17)
stone of stumbling (Isa. 8:14; 1 Pet. 2:8)
stone which the builders rejected, the (Matt. 21:42; Mark 12:10; 1 Pet. 2:7)
stone, a living (1 Pet. 2:4)
stone, a tried (Isa. 28:16)
Stone of Israel, the (Gen. 49:24)
strength of my life (Ps. 27:1)
strength to the needy in his distress, a (Isa. 25:4)
strength to the poor, a (Isa. 25:4)
Strength of Israel, the (1 Sam. 15:29)
strength of my heart, the (Ps. 73:26)
Strength, his (Ps. 59:9)
strength, my (Ps. 28:7; 118:14)
Stronghold, my (Ps. 18:2)
sun and shield, a (Ps. 84:11)
support, my (2 Sam. 22:19; Ps. 18:18)
surety of a better covenant, a (Heb. 7:22)
sword of your majesty, the (Deut. 33:29)
Teacher (Mark 9:17)
Teacher, the (Matt. 26:18)
teacher who has come from God, a (John 3:2)
tower from the enemy, a strong (Ps. 61:3)
trap and a snare, a (Isa. 8:14)
trust from my youth, my (Ps. 71:5)
truth, the (John 14:6)
vine, the (John 15:5)
vinedresser, the (John 15:1)
vine, the true (John 15:1)
voice of the Almighty, the (Shaddai) (Ezek. 1:24)
voice of the LORD (Ps. 29:3)
way, the (John 14:6)
wisdom from God (1 Cor. 1:30)
wisdom of God, the (1 Cor. 1:24)
witness to the people, a (Isa. 55:4)
Witness, Faithful and True (Rev. 3:14)
witness, my (Job 16:19)
witness, the faithful (Rev. 1:5)
Word of God (Rev. 19:13)
Word of life, the (1 John 1:1)
Word, the (logos) (John 1:1)
You who dwell in the heavens (Ps. 123:1)
You who hear prayer (Ps. 65:2)
you who judge righteously, testing . . . (Jer. 11:20)